United States Policy
Toward Latin America

United States Policy Toward Latin America

A Study in Domestic and International Politics

R. Harrison Wagner

Stanford University Press, Stanford, California, 1970

Stanford University Press
Stanford, California
© *1970 by the Board of Trustees of the*
Leland Stanford Junior University
Printed in the United States of America
ISBN 0-8047-0730-8
LC 79-107651

To my mother and father

Contents

Acknowledgments

Much of the material in this book appeared, in a quite different form, in a doctoral thesis submitted to Harvard University. I am grateful to my former adviser, Samuel Huntington, for his criticisms of that earlier manuscript. It will be apparent how much I have learned from his writings, and from the writings of Kenneth Waltz, for whose comments on the present manuscript I am also grateful.

While I was finishing this book, my thinking was greatly stimulated by an unpublished manuscript on the Cuban missile crisis by Graham Allison of Harvard University. I am grateful to him for the opportunity to read his manuscript.

For encouragement and criticism of the sort that only friends can provide, I would like to thank Roderick Bell, David Edwards, Theodore Marmor, Thad Marsh, and Joseph Nye. I am grateful to my colleagues Francis Beer and Karl Schmitt for their comments on the manuscript. And to Dr. Carleton Chapman and some of his associates I owe a debt that I can never adequately acknowledge.

Finally, I would like to thank the Department of Government of the University of Texas at Austin for providing me with such a responsive environment in which to work, and especially its chairman, William S. Livingston, whose patience and tolerance helped make it all possible.

R.H.W.

United States Policy
Toward Latin America

Introduction

The policies of the United States government toward the countries of Latin America have been the subject of political and academic controversy in the United States for a long time. The chapters that follow are the result of my attempt to answer some especially puzzling questions raised in that controversy.

First, how are the decisions of the United States government to be explained? The notion that United States policies are designed primarily to serve United States business interests is one that has refused to die, despite the number of scholarly studies of the policies of the early twentieth century which show that other interests were more important. There is, of course, some reason for the persistence of this notion: business often benefits from the government's policies, and businessmen often play a very important role in making them. The real problem, however, may not be whether business or military security or ideology or some other consideration is the dominant force behind United States policies, but rather what part each interest plays and how it is related to the others. Unfortunately it is not always easy to determine how decisions made to serve one interest, such as trade and investment, will differ from decisions made to foster another, such as military security.

Often, it is one's negative evaluation of policies that leads one to look for an explanation of them. One asks: how could the decisions have been so bad? Questions of this sort are very similar to much ordinary discourse about individuals. If a person behaves in a way that seems reasonable to observers, then the reasons he offers for his behavior are accepted as the explanation of it. It is only when he does something that seems unreasonable that we demand further explanation. If a man wants to drive from Boston to Washington, D.C., we do not ask why he sets out in the direction of New York City. If he begins to drive toward Montreal, however, then we want to know why.

But why should we apply the same expectations to governments? Perhaps it is when a government succeeds in choosing means appropriate to some end that we should be surprised and ask for an explanation. Moreover, how do we decide what is a reasonable or appropriate goal? If we decided, for example, that the decisions of the United States government regarding Latin America were reasonable attempts to achieve military security, should we be satisfied with that explanation?

These questions are made more difficult by the fact that the goal of military security is ambiguous, and its implications for action are not obvious. In what way does Latin America affect the military security of the United States? What can the United States government do about it? There are people ready with confident answers, but their answers differ, and there is no obvious way to settle the differences. One's answers are affected by one's views about the very complex relations between economic and political change. They are also affected by one's views about the nature of inter-American politics. A widespread assumption has been, and still seems to be, that the Latin American governments are passive material to be molded in whatever way the United States government desires, if it would but decide what that was. This assumption is obviously false. But what is true? How much do the interests of the member governments of the Organization of American States overlap? How much do they conflict? And what strategies are available to the parties to a conflict to determine whose interests will be served by the outcome?

It should be obvious that these puzzles in United States foreign policy toward Latin America are instances of more general questions raised by the study of international politics. These general questions can be divided into two convenient categories. First, there is the problem of how to explain the behavior of governments in international politics—in particular, how to take into account both the domestic and the international determinants of that behavior. Second, there is the problem of understanding the relatively novel forms of international politics produced by two fairly recent developments: the appearance of a bipolar world, and the emergence from colonial rule of most of the territories formerly managed by the European colonial powers.[1] In Max Beloff's words, these two developments have led to the appearance of communities "whose affairs are obviously intermingled in many different spheres and between whom at the same time some obvious element of hierarchy exists."[2] This has long characterized inter-American politics, and thus an understanding of international politics in the Western Hemisphere has become a subject of general interest.

The problem that underlies the questions raised above concerns the relationship between domestic and international politics. This is an important area of inquiry in which it is not just difficult to get answers to one's questions, but difficult even to formulate one's questions satisfactorily.[3] For this reason I have been as much concerned with posing the proper questions as I have been with answering them. In some instances I have probably come closer to the former than the latter, if I have succeeded at all. Part of the difficulty lies in having to deal with a large number of factors at the same time, all of which influence each other. Since the chapters that follow necessarily divide the problem into its component parts, it may be helpful to describe here the whole problem and the way it is distributed among them.

Foreign policy decisions are made by organizations (because they involve actions that require the cooperation of many people) in a certain international and domestic environment. The decisions these organizations make are affected by their structure, i.e., by the way cooperation is organized. And the structure is affected in turn by the nature of the international and domestic environments.

The international environment consists in part of many organizations, making similar decisions, whose interests affect and are affected by each other's decisions. An international political system, in other words, is a game, in the sense in which that word is used in the theory of games, and the main players are governments. Or rather, it is a set of games, in which the outcome of one game affects the outcome of others. The inter-American economic game, which is the subject of this book, is thus related to other regional, functional, and global games. But though the notion of a game helps one to understand international politics, it is a mistake to believe that the theory of games constitutes a ready-made descriptive or normative theory of international politics.

The domestic environment likewise consists of a set of overlapping games, in which the organization that makes foreign policy participates. But the domestic environments of most recent participants in international politics are more organizationally complex than international politics and, unlike the international environment, are characterized by a greater degree of cooperation than conflict. It is therefore from their domestic environments that most governments acquire most of the resources they employ in participating in international politics. They are, however, thereby subjected to the efforts of domestic groups to shape their foreign policy decisions. Foreign policy organizations thus must devise some satisfactory relationship among the demands of international politics, their own internal routines, and the sources of domestic support. The nature of the relationships devised will affect their behavior in international politics.

Chapters 1 and 2 are an account of the inter-American economic game as it was played before 1961, the first year of the Alliance for Progress. They examine the goals of the participants, the conflicts, the strategies employed, the bargaining, and the outcomes. The subject of Chapters 3 through 7 is the effect of domestic politics in the United States on the economic policies that the United States government has applied to Latin America. Whereas in the first two chapters the United States government is sometimes credited with purposes and strategies, in the succeeding five chapters it is not considered a unitary agent, and its internal workings are examined to see how the results summarized in the first two chapters were produced. Because critics of United States policies make many allegations about the effects of domestic politics on foreign policy, their criticisms are also discussed.

But the relationship between these two parts of the discussion may seem puzzling even with that seemingly simple distinction between them held firmly in mind. The reason for that, I believe, is the need to use purposive language in talking about organizations, coupled with the inadequacy of that language as either a description or an explanation of what organizations do.

It is common to speak of organizations as agents with purposes, because organizations are explicitly created by people in order to do something that can only be done collectively. They are thus unlike gangs or markets or families. For this reason, an organization may always be criticized for doing something inconsistent with its goals, and at least some people within an organization think of their work as involving the selection of appropriate means to organizational ends. Thus we speak of the work of the Defense Department as attempts to deter or to win a war, and we criticize its actions as if they were those of a person with those objectives. And, as we do with individuals, we accept the goals as the explanation of actions taken to reach them, and seek further explanations only when the means seem inappropriate.

But this purposive language, though it probably cannot be eliminated, is inadequate. First, the tasks organizations perform are often far too complex to be expressed in it. It is usually not true that an organization is, for example, *just* trying to win a war or to deter one. It may be trying to do a range of things far too complicated for an individual to master. An individual may sit in his study and think, "If I had been making those decisions, I would have done the opposite," forgetting that it may be impossible for any single person to make such decisions and that he might not have adequately described what the organization was trying to do. Second, not everyone in the organization takes its supposed purposes seriously—indeed, hardly anyone may take them seriously. And that is not abnormal, but should be expected. Whether organizations attempt to persuade their members to subordinate their lives to the goals of the organization, or pay them money and other inducements as compensation for the fact that in the absence of such inducements they would rather have done something else, there is normally disagreement within the organization about its goals. And the difficulty of reaching agreement is increased by the complexity of the tasks organizations perform.

Because of these two inadequacies, attempts to couch explanations of organizational behavior in purposive terms appropriate for individuals can never be satisfactory. For it is clear that an organization's alleged purposes can never be a full explanation of what it does, nor can deviation from those alleged purposes be accepted as an adequate definition of what requires a more elaborate explanation. Nevertheless, it seems to me that it would be very difficult to eliminate purposive language entirely, partly because it is often convenient shorthand, and partly because purposes are one of the things that distinguish organizations from other social phenomena, and they do help explain why organizations do one thing rather than another. Although using such language uncritically leads one to be unduly surprised by the behavior of, say, the Pentagon, to eliminate it entirely would make it very difficult to describe and explain how the behavior of the Pentagon under Robert McNamara differed from its behavior in previous years.

With these distinctions in mind, I can summarize more clearly the argument of Chapters 1 through 7. To observers of United States foreign economic policies toward Latin America who say, in effect, that certain characteristics of the American political process explain why the policies have been so bad, I say, in effect, that the policies have not been as "bad" as they suggest. I have attempted to show that they have been reasonable attempts to serve a much more complex set of purposes than the purposes implied in most critical discussions. Whether the purposes were as good as they might have been or whether there might have been somewhat better means of pursuing them are questions to which it is not possible to give a definitive answer. Those who are impressed with the difficulties of making governmental organizations serve any coherent, acceptable set of purposes at all might ask how the United States government managed to achieve the degree of success it has. One might also ask why a given choice was made when a somewhat different one might have been argued for equally compellingly and adopted. My answer to these questions is to be found in the detailed examination of the policy-making process in Chapters 4 through 6. Both these strands of discussion are brought together in Chapter 7.

The first seven chapters are thus focused primarily on the puzzling relationship between foreign policy goals and the political process in the United States. In Chapter 8 I have tried to describe international politics in such a way as to take into account the effect of the workings of domestic politics in the participating countries and to apply my conclusions to a discussion of international politics in the Western Hemisphere. I believe that much of this discussion can be used to increase our understanding of many other puzzling phenomena in international politics as well.

The main concern of this book, then, is with domestic and international politics, and not economics. I have focused on questions of economic policy not because I have anything to contribute to the study of economics, but because I have long been interested in the political process of making decisions about economic issues and the political purposes economic policies were meant to serve. Economic policies were a convenient focus because more of the political forces that interest me were brought to bear on them than on any other segment of foreign policy.

I have not been interested in specific decisions about whether a loan should be granted to this country rather than that one, or whether a particular Latin American country should be encouraged to follow this broad economic strategy rather than that one, but have focused instead on the institutional framework within which these narrow decisions were made. And I have tried to discover the forces that determined the nature of the broad framework of policy and the timing of the changes that have been made in it. In the United States such changes are quite visible because they are accompanied by the creation of new institutions to administer policy.

The last major change in the basic framework of United States economic policies toward Latin America was the Alliance for Progress. This book therefore ends with its inauguration. To those who regard the Alliance for Progress as the beginning of the United States government's interest in the problems of Latin America, this may seem strange. I hope the arguments in the chapters that follow will make it seem less so. For it is my contention that there has been much continuity in the goals of United States policy in Latin America and in the domestic and international political environments in which policies have been made. The years before the Alliance for Progress were not simply years of ignorance and neglect, nor has the Alliance for Progress so transformed Latin America or inter-American politics or United States politics as to nullify all the forces that were at work before its inauguration. As the end of the Alliance for Progress decade approaches and a new Republican administration reviews the programs of the United States government in Latin America, it may be helpful to focus attention on the forces that have determined United States policies in the past. This is what I have tried to do.

Part I. International Politics

1. United States Interests and Economic Policies in Latin America

The government of the United States has rarely required more from the countries of Latin America than it could secure through private commercial activities. But it has tried to stop the governments of those countries from developing relations with nations outside the hemisphere that might threaten its own military security. Military conflict among Latin American countries, internal political instability, and dependence on foreign markets and foreign capital have all provided actual or potential opportunities for intervention by powers unfriendly toward the United States. Hence United States policy makers have tried to limit conflict in Latin America and to prevent any country from becoming economically dependent on a nation outside the hemisphere, since from economic dependence, political or military dependence might follow. To accomplish this, the United States government has often merely accelerated what would have happened anyway—the gradual transferring of most of Latin America's economic ties to the United States, at the expense of its potential antagonists.

The Organization of American States and the many regional agreements that preceded it have been useful in the control of international conflict, especially when supplemented by the influence of the United States government. Domestic political problems and economic dependence have been more difficult to cope with. Both ideology and social science have suggested that there is a causal relation between national economic dependence and domestic political conflict. The United States government was concerned with this possible connection in Latin America long before it faced the issue elsewhere; and it supported economic development in Latin America before it extended similar support elsewhere. For this reason United States security has for a long time been implicated in controversies about economic development in Latin America.

Intervention and the Good Neighbor Policy

The United States' first important experience with these problems came in the early twentieth century, when the responsibilities assumed in Cuba under the Platt Amendment were extended to the other countries of the Caribbean by the Roosevelt corollary to the Monroe Doctrine.* The United States government feared that the political instability and chronic indebtedness of the Central American countries might offer an opportunity for a European nation, most likely Germany, to extend its military power into the area. It was not the United States' original or persistent intention to assume direct and permanent responsibility for the political and economic development of Central America, but rather to resist the attempts of foreign governments to collect their citizens' debts by force, and to discourage dissident political groups from seeking foreign support—if necessary by providing military support for the incumbent government. There seems to have been little desire to go beyond this.

Yet in pursuing its objectives the United States government found itself becoming increasingly involved in the domestic politics of the region. Any debt settlement it promoted was apt to be

---

* The Platt Amendment was an amendment to the army appropriation bill of 1901, which stated the conditions under which the United States would evacuate Cuba after the Spanish-American War. Its provisions, which gave the United States government the right to intervene in Cuba to protect the lives and property of United States citizens and to protect the independence of Cuba from foreign control, were included in the constitution of independent Cuba and in a treaty between Cuba and the United States. The Roosevelt "corollary" to the Monroe Doctrine was Theodore Roosevelt's contention that in cases of civil disorder or default on foreign loans in Central America and the Caribbean area, the United States would intervene, if necessary, to forestall intervention by European nations.

overturned when the political faction that negotiated it was replaced by another. And the frequency with which this happened in itself helped produce the indebtedness that was the main source of difficulty. In an effort to break this cycle, the United States government initiated customs receiverships managed by the United States. This was a first attempt to deal with both indebtedness and political instability (it was thought that an important motive for rebellion was the prospect of seizing customs revenues). At the same time, the government encouraged private investors from the United States to invest capital in the area to compete with European capital. Soon, however, the United States found itself actually occupying several countries with its troops, engaging in extended negotiations among political factions, providing technical assistance in holding elections, and offering military assistance to local constabularies in an attempt to settle the area's chronic problems once and for all. Woodrow Wilson's Secretary of State, William Jennings Bryan, suggested that the United States provide public loans to these countries as well, in order to relieve them of their debts and enable them to build badly needed railroads. For its efforts the United States would win "such an increased influence ... that we could prevent revolutions, promote education, and advance stable and just governments."[1] Bryan's prescient suggestion was not followed.

By the early 1920's the threat of European influence had diminished, and support within the United States for the burdens of interventionist policies began to decline. Furthermore, little progress had been made in coping with the underlying problems, while considerable hostility had been aroused in Latin America. Consequently the United States liquidated the protectorates it had established and sought a new basis for inter-American relations that explicitly committed the United States to nonintervention.

These changes, which culminated in Franklin Roosevelt's "Good Neighbor Policy," took place over approximately fifteen years. Eventually they involved not only a pledge against military intervention, but also a decision to avoid exercising any influence in Latin American domestic politics, since political interference might lead to military intervention. These decisions in turn eventually made it necessary for the United States government to dissociate itself from the interests of some private investors in Latin America.[2] These changes were still under way when the increasing likelihood of a new war in Europe made the United States government think seriously once again about the importance of Latin America to its military security.[3]

World War II and the Western Hemisphere

The heightened concern for military security reinforced the new trend in the United States government's policies toward Latin America, primarily because the United States began to require greater cooperation from the Latin American governments, and intervention would have made cooperation impossible. Furthermore, although the political instability and economic dependence of Latin America were still potentially dangerous for the United States, the nature of the danger had changed somewhat and could be met within the framework of the new policies.

There were two main reasons for the United States' interest in cooperating with the governments of Latin America. One was the possibility of an actual invasion of the Western Hemisphere. (Belief in this possibility did not persist for long once the war had begun.) The other was that the United States war effort increasingly depended on Latin American raw materials as the scale of war industries grew and other sources of raw materials were closed off.

Latin America was also politically and economically vulnerable, although in ways somewhat different from the days of United States intervention. There was the prospect that Germany, by conquering most of Europe, might acquire control over a large part of the market for Latin American exports and, by offering public and private capital as well as military assistance, might gain considerable influence in Latin America. All of Latin America, not just Central America and the Caribbean, seemed to be threatened. Thus, as the power of the Axis became more apparent, the United States government felt compelled to extend its influence throughout Latin America for the first time. The enormous geographical extension of United States influence was one of the radical changes in inter-American politics produced by the war.

To cope with the European threat, the United States government initiated a public aid program for economic development. There were several reasons for it. First, it was assumed that if Latin American governments were helped to build the new industries they wanted, they would have more enthusiasm for cooperating with the United States in other ways. Second, in many cases, common interests would be served, as when the United States helped to increase production of strategic raw materials. Third, the aid money would replace German capital. Finally, an aid program, by overcoming some economic difficulties, might forestall the political problems that could make Latin American countries more vulnerable to subversion by the Germans. Once again the United States government recognized that political instability was related to economic insecurity and dependence. This time it provided public rather than private financial and commercial assistance.

And this time it was able to avoid direct political interference. Germany was at war, and there was little doubt that the hostilities had already threatened the freedom of action of most Latin American countries and would pose an even greater threat in the future. The incentive for dissident groups to cooperate with the Germans was therefore lessened. Furthermore, German influence was concentrated in Argentina, Brazil, and Chile, where existing ties of trade, investment, military assistance, and immigration were strong, and, in the case of Argentina, where affiliation with a European country was thought necessary as a counterweight to the United States. The United States government could be content with attempting to isolate a pro-German government in the southern part of Latin America, even though it probably could not have tolerated one close to its own borders or the Panama Canal.[4] For these reasons the threat to United States security posed by the political instability and economic dependence of the Latin American countries led to a different reaction by the United States government from that of the early part of the century.

Although most of the economic measures introduced in Latin America by the Roosevelt administration were designed to cope with the exigencies of the war, some members of the government hoped that they might solve some of the chronic problems of Latin America. They also hoped that many of the programs initiated during the war might be continued after it.[5] For example, an assistant to Nelson Rockefeller wrote in January 1943:

Political stability and overall security of the Latin American republics will depend upon economic development of those countries and the establishment of strong and enduring economic relations between them and the United States. All of our work should be directed towards the development of economic unity on a hemispheric scale and economic interdependence between the United States and the Latin American republics, and between the Latin American republics and themselves. The current operational activities of the CIAA [Coordinator of Inter-American Affairs] . . . should be regarded as means to an end, and that end is the economic development of the countries concerned.[6]

Anxious to avoid arousing expectations that would be disappointed after the war, however, the State Department would not support long-range projects, and eventually these interests disappeared into the larger process of postwar economic planning,[7] which was focused on the problem of making the existing international economy work, and not on the problems of underdeveloped countries.

The fact that many of these plans for the economic development of Latin America did not survive the war has been the subject of controversy ever since, especially as postwar problems have multiplied. The attack on postwar United States policies has been led by those most closely associated with Latin America during the war, including Sumner Welles, Adolf Berle, and Nelson Rockefeller. It is therefore important to examine the problems faced by the United States in Latin America immediately after the war with some care.

Postwar Problems

As a result of the war, the United States acquired for the first time a virtual monopoly of influence in Latin America. The Latin Americans were dependent on the United States for almost all military assistance and advice, and for capital and markets. It was, as a result, more difficult to gain favor in Latin America than during the 1930's, when merely renouncing unacceptable policies strengthened the position of the United States. At the same time, many of the policies adopted in wartime were seen to be inconsistent with the principles on which the government intended to base its postwar economic diplomacy.

Moreover, the end of the war seemed to remove any incentive to compromise those principles. The magnitude of United States influence in Latin America after the war was itself a reason for not using that influence in the same way as during the war, for there no longer seemed to be any competition. And unlike the European countries that had earlier competed for influence, the Soviet Union was at a great initial disadvantage. It had never been a major source of capital for Latin America, or a market for Latin American products. It had never had close relations with the Latin American military, or with any other elements of the traditional elites. Thus it did not seem to have the resources to oppose the influence of the United States.

In the aftermath of the war, the nature of the United States' interest in the countries to the south changed radically. The United States was much less directly threatened by the loss of influence in any one country than had been the case before. Damage to the Panama Canal would be both more easily prevented—because of American military superiority—and less of a blow. Venezuelan oil was important, but not vital. Thus, although any single loss of influence in Latin America would be a matter for concern, only a whole series of such losses could present a major threat. It was precisely cumulative gains in Latin America that the Soviet Union could not support. One could have argued in 1946, then, that the Soviet Union had little incentive to exploit what advantages it had in Latin American domestic politics (in the form of Communist parties) and that there were even fewer reasons for Latin Americans to welcome Soviet advances than the earlier German ones.

Furthermore, the exigencies of the war had helped to conceal many basic economic conflicts between the United States and

Latin America. It was not clear, for example, that the conflict between debtor and creditor could be eliminated simply by transferring it from the private to the public sector. Nor would the United States government necessarily be as willing in the future to compromise on the treatment of American private investors as it had been in Mexico before the war; it had used private investment to serve foreign policy interests in the past and might need to do so again, especially in light of the general scarcity of public funds for the purpose.

During the war it had been difficult to separate United States interests in economic projects from Latin American ones. The emergency basis on which most of the programs were planned, and the lack of any comprehensive criteria by which projects might be chosen meant that the United States government was subject to the influence of the recipients in choosing projects.[8] In the more sober atmosphere of peacetime, there would obviously be considerable reason to doubt that many of these projects really served long-term interests of the United States. The creation of a regional international organization after the war encouraged many to expect the negotiation of economic agreements to supplement the political agreements that were made. But multilateral economic arrangements would have diminished the United States' control over its economic relations with Latin America (which indeed helps explain the enthusiasm of the Latin Americans for such arrangements), whereas the Truman administration was mainly interested in increasing that control. It therefore sought to separate economic cooperation from other aspects of inter-American relations, such as the newly created OAS or the Good Neighbor Policy, which it thought had greater claims to permanence.[9]

Considerations such as these, along with the overall framework of United States postwar foreign economic policy, led the government to make a number of basic decisions, which can be quickly summarized. It recognized that it had considerable responsibility as the main source of capital for Latin America, the main market for goods produced there, and the main source of supply for Latin American imports. It took initial steps to provide capital assistance through the World Bank and the Export-Import Bank and decided to continue the technical assistance programs indefinitely. But it decided early that the burdens on these two institutions could be considerably lessened if the Latin American governments would be more hospitable to foreign private investment, and that public loans should therefore be offered in a way that would not remove incentives for Latin American governments to be hospitable to private capital. It also decided that although it had a long-range interest in the economic development of Latin America, there was no immediate reason for pursuing the goal at the rapid pace desired by Latin Americans.

These decisions were reinforced by the belief that the path to development chosen by several Latin American governments was not only too costly for the United States but also unnecessarily costly for the Latin Americans. It was also likely to be ineffective. The promotion of heavy industry at the expense of agriculture, the maintenance of high-cost industries through trade restrictions, and emphasis on state-owned enterprises and trading corporations were all measures that the United States government refused to support either by stating approval of them at international conferences or by offering public funds to make them feasible.

It is sometimes suggested that transformation of United States economic policies toward Latin America was retarded because of the pressure on American resources from the Marshall Plan, the Korean War, and aid programs in other parts of the world. This assertion rests on a misunderstanding. Although other commitments made it difficult to allocate resources to Latin America within the framework of policies that were chosen, there is no reason to believe that the policies would otherwise have been very different or the actual flow of resources much greater. In the absence of these other commitments, there would probably have been a somewhat greater amount of lending from existing institutions such as the Export-Import Bank. But there were more limitations on their lending than the pressure of other commitments, as the United States government discovered when it later tried to expand such lending.

These decisions clearly conflicted with the priorities of many Latin American governments. But the United States government judged that the resulting dissatisfaction could not offer very great opportunity for the Soviet Union to extend either its economic or its military power into the Western Hemisphere. Barring any change in the capabilities of the Soviet Union, the main reason for doubting this judgment was that political changes within some Latin American country might lead to a radical reassessment of the gains available through association with the Soviet Union and that in such circumstances the Soviet Union might be induced to cooperate.

These considerations had little effect on United States policies, for two reasons. The first was that the magnitude of United States economic and military superiority over the Soviet Union in the Western Hemisphere made the possibility of increased Soviet influence seem extremely remote and not very dangerous. Dexter Perkins raised this question in a book published in 1947, using as his example a hypothetical situation that seems ironic today. "Suppose . . . a fullfledged Communist regime should some day be established in Cuba, a regime which definitely asserted its acceptance of the Communist faith, and which formed close relations with the USSR?" Perkins concluded that the situation was not apt to develop:

We can easily imagine social policies more advanced than many Americans would approve; we can easily imagine dictatorships more harsh and reactionary than any American would welcome. But so close are the ties between the states of the Caribbean and the United States, so intimate the economic bonds between these states and our own, that the adoption of policies utterly at variance with American sentiment appears extremely unlikely, if not impossible.[10]

The second reason for the United States' unworried attitude had to do with the controversial connection between economic backwardness and the management of domestic political conflict in Latin America. There are powerful reasons for believing that, in the long run, the differentiation of social structure that accompanies economic development is a necessary (if not sufficient) condition for the establishment of stable, modern political institutions.[11] For the analysis of United States interests in Latin America, however, it is necessary to place extra stress on the phrases "in the long run" and "necessary (if not sufficient)."

The political problems of Latin America seemed likely, in the short run, to provide a greater impediment to joint economic planning than to maintaining stable political or military ties with the United States. And, as the earlier United States interventions had shown, efforts to assist governments in solving their domestic political problems easily led to an unacceptable degree of involvement in their political life, with no guarantee of either economic or political success in the relevant future.[12]

Since long-range efforts at economic development were not directly relevant to immediate political problems, the United States government felt secure in allowing its priorities to prevail over those of many Latin Americans. And since these political problems tended to inhibit economic development, the government insisted on what it already called in 1949 "positive self-help" and "a genuine mobilization of effort" as prior conditions for economic cooperation.[13]

Thus while trying to avoid getting involved in domestic political disputes in Latin America, the United States government sought to contain them within countries and to prevent what Secretary of State Dean Acheson called "aggression or plotting against any nation of this hemisphere."[14] A corollary of this approach was the policy of maintaining diplomatic relations with all governments on an equal basis, while promoting the development of each country according to the priorities of the United States government. Forms of economic cooperation were required that were insulated from the effects of local politics, and that fostered economic development along the lines that United States policy makers thought desirable. Both private investment and technical assistance were thought to have these virtues, among others.

Over the next decade, two kinds of events led to a modification of these policies. First, local political disputes provided the Soviet Union an opportunity to extend its political and military influence into the Western Hemisphere, and as a result the United States became embroiled once again in Latin American domestic politics. The value the United States government placed on short-run economic performance in Latin America increased, and the argument that joint economic planning would lead to unacceptable involvement in Latin American domestic politics now seemed less relevant.

Second, the generally poor economic performance in Latin America between 1955 and 1960, especially with respect to exports, altered United States policy makers' judgment about the relative productivity of public and private capital measured in terms of both economic and political effects.

These events did not remove all the conflicts between the United States and the governments of Latin America over economic issues, although the range of issues was greatly narrowed. Much ingenuity was therefore devoted to devising new frameworks for negotiations. This task was complicated by its relation to the management of domestic political conflict in Latin America. It was necessary to find a stable base of support in Latin America for any new forms of economic cooperation, without interfering greatly in Latin American domestic political processes. (This problem had many precedents in the role that the United States played in Central America and the Caribbean from 1900 to 1930.) Moreover, some government officials hoped to devise economic programs that would themselves promote political stability in Latin America. But the solutions to this problem that were available were more solidly grounded in ideology than in social science, and they varied with the time horizons adopted. Any real solution would depend heavily on the cooperation of Latin American politicians, who could not always be counted on to cooperate. These were the problems to which the major innovations in United States policies from 1958 to 1961 were addressed.

Crisis and Change, 1954–1961

The political conflicts that allowed the Soviet Union to exercise political influence in Latin America were, of course, in Guatemala and in Cuba. In the early 1950's, as a result of political weakness and lack of direction, the government of Guatemala grew increasingly dependent upon the support of the Guatemalan Communist party, and eventually it resorted to military assistance from the Soviet bloc. Inadvertently, this led it into a conflict with the United States. It proved impossible to separate international from domestic issues, particularly because the United Fruit Company was implicated. The involvement of the United States in Latin American domestic politics was deepened by the fact that at the Caracas conference in 1954 the United States government allowed itself to be closely associated with certain Latin American governments (especially that of Venezuela) that had a very narrow base of domestic support, and the fact that it chose not to be content with trying to inhibit the growth of Soviet military influence in Guatemala, but to assist in overthrowing the government of that country.[15]

The Guatemala crisis occurred at a time when the new Eisenhower administration was reviewing its economic policies toward Latin America. Though Republican criticisms of existing policies had been prominent in the presidential campaign of 1952, policies were changed very little when the new administration took over. This fact exposed the Eisenhower administration to considerable criticism, much of which referred to the situation in Guatemala to support its case. It is therefore important to emphasize how ambiguous was the significance of the Guatemala crisis for United States foreign policy, especially foreign economic policy.

Of the two characteristics of Latin American countries that made them most vulnerable to Soviet influence, economic dependence and political instability, the latter was the more important in Guatemala. Neither dissatisfaction with economic relations between Guatemala and the United States nor any effort to alter those relations by seeking the assistance of the Soviet Union was especially significant. It was the ability of the Communist party in Guatemala to provide political support for the reformist regime in power that accounted for its influence. The Soviet Union appears to have become interested only at the instigation of local party members.[16] Only the Communist parties in Latin America had much reason to believe that the Soviet Union might offer decisive support, or much hope of persuading the Soviet Union to

provide it. The international connections of Latin American Communist parties were still not a very great asset in 1954.

The domestic assets of Latin American Communist parties were
also not impressive, but insofar as they existed they seemed to be
such that the United States government would have had difficulty
competing with them. Guatemala was the only Latin American
country at the time in which the Communist party was politically
powerful. In Guatemala, the United States would have been at a
serious disadvantage compared with the Communists, either as a
source of ideas concerning the direction radical reform should
take, or as an organizer of political support for the non-Communist
reformers in power.[17] Although it could be argued that the Guatemalan government could turn against the Communist party only
at the cost of sacrificing its most ambitious domestic objectives,
the fact that members of the local elites (mostly from the army)
were willing to cooperate in overthrowing the government indicated that the United States already had assets in Central American politics that compensated for those of the local Communist
parties.

Such considerations obviously would weaken any incentive to
manipulate Latin American politics through economic aid programs whether by persuading incumbent governments to take
measures to increase their own stability or by opening contacts
with opposition groups. It was the view of United States government officials that the economic problems of all Latin America
were caused by declining export markets and the limitations on
efficient use of resources. But in 1954 it was still possible to doubt
the severity of the problems that lay ahead for Latin American
exports, and there were many difficulties associated with attempts
to stabilize the market that the government preferred to avoid. It
was argued by many officials responsible for United States economic policies that the main barrier to the flow of public and private capital to Latin America was the inability of the Latin Americans to make productive use of it, and that any evidence of willingness to alter the conditions that were tied to public funds would
remove a major incentive for making what were presumed to be
necessary alterations.[18]

However true these assumptions may have been in 1954, United States actions then may have made them less relevant for the future. The interest of the Soviet Union in Latin America may have increased as a result of the events in Guatemala. Many of those whose efforts in Guatemala failed owing to the opposition of the United States may have concluded that domestic success in the future required some way of offsetting the influence of the United States government, and that the Soviet Union provided the sole available means of doing that.[19] And the position of neutrality in Latin American domestic politics which the Truman administration had sought to maintain had been destroyed, which would lead to greater pressures for more liberal economic policies in the future.

Throughout 1954 the United States government was under increasing pressure from Latin American governments to alter its economic priorities in favor of Latin America. It made only two minor concessions to this pressure. It announced that it would try to expand the activities of the Export-Import Bank in Latin America and that it would support the creation of the International Finance Corporation, as an affiliate of the World Bank, which would provide direct assistance to private enterprise in underdeveloped countries.[20] These concessions were presented as alternatives to a regional bank, which is what the Latin Americans demanded at the time.

In 1957 and 1958 it became clear that economic assumptions on which United States policies toward Latin America had been based were no longer relevant. Little success in fostering freer trade had been achieved. The flow of private investment to underdeveloped countries everywhere had been disappointing. The United States economy had suffered a recession, which had important repercussions for underdeveloped countries dependent on the American market. And throughout Latin America there was a recession worse than any that had occurred in some time, accompanied by large reductions in the prices of raw materials.

The economic difficulties experienced by most of Latin America at this time had two main causes: the oversupply of a number of commodities, particularly coffee and minerals, and the recession in the western industrial countries. The recession affected imports of raw materials less than had been anticipated, but it nevertheless contributed to the worsened trade situation of all Latin American countries.[21] At the same time, the prices of manufactured goods in the industrial countries remained fairly stable, and consequently there was a decline in the terms of trade of underdeveloped countries.[22]

On the more positive side, capital was flowing into Latin America in greater volume than it had immediately after World War II. A sharp decline from 1957 to 1958 was due almost entirely to a drop in the rate of private investment in the Venezuelan oil industry.[23] But although there was more capital available than ever before, it was not sufficient to cover the large deficits in Latin American international payments resulting from the export crisis, and these deficits had to be made up by heavy borrowing from the International Monetary Fund and the Export-Import Bank.[24] At the same time, the rate of economic growth in most countries had failed to maintain the impressive pace of the immediate postwar years and was barely keeping up with the rate of population growth.[25] Inflation was beginning to be a problem even in countries that had had some measure of price stability before.[26] Stabilization programs were introduced in 1957 and 1958 in Argentina and Brazil, and they had already been instituted in Chile and Bolivia.[27]

Thus the governments of many Latin American countries were placed under severe strain, as they were forced to make choices that cost them the support of one group or another.[28] Such problems could not fail to lead to difficulties for the United States, given the degree to which the countries of Latin America were dependent on it. This dependence was unfortunately accentuated by the fact that the United States government was finally compelled to institute import quotas for lead, zinc, and petroleum, thereby adding to the burden of its responsibilities in Latin America.

The difficulties of 1957 and 1958 also led to some increase in the very small volume of trade between a few Latin American countries and the Soviet bloc. The main cause of concern over these developments was not the immediate influence that the Soviet Union was acquiring by controlling the economic life of any Latin American country. (Given the level of performance of the Soviet Union, there was even considerable reason for the United States to welcome Latin Americans' increased experience in dealing with that country.) Rather the most likely source of trouble was increasing dissatisfaction with economic relations with the United States and an increasingly widespread impression that large and relatively painless economic gains might be achieved through close association with the Soviet Union. This impression was obviously most prevalent among groups that lacked political power. And clearly many of the difficulties that Latin American countries experienced with the Soviet Union arose, at least in part, because the Soviet Union did not feel that any political gains it might achieve through more careful use of its economic relations with Latin America would be worth the effort. But had there been evidence that much larger political gains were possible, the Soviet Union would probably have made the necessary effort and assumed the necessary costs.[29] Even the most careful consideration of the economic interests of the Latin American countries was no bar to a sudden and radical revision in the way some Latin American country might conceive of its basic interests.

The Eisenhower administration felt compelled to increase its loans to Latin America in order to compensate for the losses in export earnings. But this merely renewed the aggravating question of what conditions would be attached to the loans. It was increasingly difficult for Latin American leaders to find support for any position on economic issues that might be acceptable to the United States—whose reputation, darkened already by the Guatemala crisis, became even blacker when a depression in Latin America was accompanied by the overthrow of several unpopular governments with which the United States had cooperated at the Caracas conference and after. Spurred on by evidence that the Soviet Union intended to play a more active role in Latin America, the government determined to find a way of helping Latin American governments aggregate support for policies that gave some chance for long-term progress, in the hope of deflecting Latin American interest in the Soviet Union. What it required was the means to play a more purposeful role in Latin American politics, and an international consensus to support its role.

To acquire the support it needed to play such a role, the government was forced to move toward accepting some of the domestic objectives of Latin American governments that it had hitherto refused to support—under the stimulus of the Cuban Revolution, it would feel compelled to support an even greater number of Latin American objectives. But, although the range of disagreements between the United States and the governments of Latin America narrowed further, some points of conflict remained. Each government held different ideas about what the prerequisites for political institutionalization and economic development were, and about how far Latin American countries had gone toward meeting them.

Beginning in early 1958, four kinds of responses to these problems began to develop within the Eisenhower administration. These were to support an international coffee agreement, to create an inter-American bank, to use United States funds to finance welfare projects (especially public housing and land reform), and to try to identify the United States government conspicuously with the progressive governments that were beginning to supplant conservative authoritarian regimes in several countries.

The main coffee-producing countries of Latin America had established an agreement in Mexico City, in October 1957, to regulate the marketing of their surpluses. In January 1958 Latin American coffee producers met at Rio de Janeiro with representatives of African coffee-producing countries, apparently as part of an attempt promoted by Brazil to persuade the Africans to join the marketing agreement. To persuade the Africans to join, and to police the agreement, the support of the United States government was indispensable. The United States sent an observer to the meeting in Rio but refused to participate in discussions of commodity agreements.

Four months later, however, when Vice-President Nixon visited Latin America, the administration had decided to participate in the discussions. At this time the United States government seems mainly to have concentrated on helping persuade the African countries to enter into an expanded version of the 1957 coffee agreement. A Coffee Study Group was established with headquarters in Washington; it included over twenty producing and consuming countries.[30] In the summer of 1958, in order further to shore up the market while negotiations proceeded, fifteen Latin American countries signed the Latin American Coffee Agreement, which took effect in October 1958. This agreement was substantially the same as the 1957 one, but included more countries. Meanwhile further attempts were made to persuade the Africans to join, with obvious support from the United States.

By the time the next international agreement was negotiated, in the following year, most African producing countries had either joined or were prepared to join. But the agreement still failed to include many importing countries. Originally designed to last for one year, this agreement was extended annually and was finally replaced by the long-term International Coffee Agreement negotiated early in the Kennedy administration. By September 1960 the short-term agreement included 28 producing countries, which were responsible for about 90 percent of the world's coffee exports.[31]

The idea of a regional development bank in the Western Hemisphere was an old one. The United States had actually agreed to participate in such an institution at the beginning of World War II, but the proposal was allowed to die during the war, and from then on the United States opposed the idea.[32] Latin American interest in the project increased considerably after the war, however, and several Latin American governments supported it especially vigorously in 1954 and thereafter. Virtually its only appeal to the United States in 1958 was as a potential aid in persuading the Latin Americans to accept the conditions that the United States wanted to attach to its economic assistance.[33] It was hoped that by giving prominent Latin Americans a role in distributing

United States funds, some resentment at the criteria of distribution employed might be diminished.

A regional bank had several other potential uses as well. Hitherto there had been little connection between the capital assistance and the technical assistance given Latin America, and thus Latin American governments were left to develop most proposals for the use of government loans themselves. This came to be accepted as one of the main explanations for the small number of applications approved after the Export-Import Bank's criteria were liberalized, specifically for the benefit of the Latin American countries, in 1954. A much more direct connection between the development of projects and the provision of loans could be arranged by a regional development bank, which could offer assistance in planning somewhat similar to that offered by the World Bank. But in this case the planning assistance would come from Latin Americans.[34]

Dr. Milton Eisenhower, the President's brother, had reached the conclusion that some Latin American governments were having trouble finding the proper agency to approach for the sort of loan they required. Thus not only were poor projects being devised, but the complicated administrative criteria set up by each lending institution were often not met, leading to the rejection of many applications. This conclusion had prompted Dr. Eisenhower to recommend that an informal committee be created to initially screen loan applications and help route them to the proper agency. The same function, of course, could also be performed by an inter-American bank.[35]

Potentially a regional bank was also relevant to the growing interest within the Eisenhower administration in the welfare aspects of economic development, or in what came to be known as "social development." Stated simply, it was an interest in influencing to a limited extent the distribution of the gains from economic development in underdeveloped countries in order to alleviate some of the tensions development created, and thus to buy more time for development to have its presumed stabilizing effects on politics.[36] In Latin America, attention was focused on the interrelated problems of urbanization and land use—how to cope with the problems associated with the massive migration of people from rural to urban areas, and how to improve the use of agricultural land in order to expand opportunities there and perhaps slow the rate of migration to the cities. Public housing, public water supplies, and farm-to-market roads were among the projects discussed.[37]

As Raymond Mikesell has pointed out, the provision of loans for social development programs requires special arrangements for joint planning by donor and recipient, chiefly because such programs are closely related to internal administration and require a legislative and administrative framework for carrying out the purposes of the loan.

For example, a loan to finance various aspects of an agricultural reform program or a slum clearance program will be of little value in the absence of detailed legislation and administrative procedures relating to land distribution and tenure, urban zoning, the right of eminent domain, etc.[38]

In 1958 there was neither an institutional framework for joint planning nor much reason to suspect that there was a consensus between the United States and Latin America to support one. A regional development bank could perhaps be useful in providing both.[39]

This last idea, however, played no part in the United States government's decision to support the creation of a bank in August 1958. The proximate cause of that decision was President Eisenhower's decision to support a regional bank in the Middle East, which made it impossible to continue resisting Latin American proposals of the same sort.[40] In Latin America, a regional bank was expected to be useful primarily as a source of technical assistance in planning projects, as a screening mechanism by which Latin American loan applications got routed to the proper agency in the proper form, and as a device for improving the quality of the dialogue between the United States and Latin American governments on economic issues.[41] As Lynn Stambaugh of the Export-Import Bank testified: "Not only would it provide a financial forum for discussion of a number of regional matters, but it also might introduce into such discussions an increased understanding of a creditor's attitude toward regional problems."[42] The United States government did offer some so-called "soft loan" funds (loans at low rates of interest repayable in local currencies) to be used by the bank, however, some of which might be used for "social development."[43]

Thus, although the new inter-American bank was, in several ways, a more flexible lending institution than any before available to the United States government for use in Latin America, it did not imply any significant liberalization of the conditions on which loans would be granted either in the terms of repayment or in the definition of the types of projects for which loans might be used and the domestic policies to which Latin American governments were expected to adhere. Consequently no immediate large-scale increase in the quantity of funds available to Latin America could be expected.[44] Any such increase would have had to result from improvements in either the planning of projects or the process of applying for loans, or from increased willingness on the part of Latin Americans to subscribe to the conditions set by the international lending institutions (with which American policies were still closely coordinated).[45] Liberalization of the criteria for loans was prevented by the way the new bank was controlled. The consent of the United States government was required for use of the soft loan funds. And, although a system of weighted voting was employed for other decisions, with the United States government controlling less than a majority of the votes, the bank had to raise most of its capital in the same financial markets as the other international lending institutions, and thus would be constrained to show that it was using its funds conservatively.[46]

Although the interest on the part of some members of the Eisenhower administration in financing social development projects in Latin America failed to find its way into public policy in 1958, it did not disappear, and two years later it was translated into the Act of Bogotá. Probably the idea gained support as its relevance to the government's desire to associate itself with the progressive, reform-minded regimes that were appearing in several Latin American countries became apparent. Indeed, as this desire became known, the government was subjected to intense pressure—both from within the United States and from Latin America—to make further changes in its policies.[47]

The first instance of pressure being applied occurred during Vice-President Nixon's well-known trip to South America in May 1958. The occasion was the inauguration of President Frondizi in Argentina. The United States government was anxious to identify itself with what it hoped would be a progressive government and to dissociate itself from the Perón regime that had preceded it. It may also have been anxious to match the impressive delegation that the Soviet Union was sending, ostensibly as part of the trade campaign it had begun to intensify in Latin America. Colombia and Venezuela had also recently replaced rightist regimes with new governments that gave some hope of progress, with which the American government hoped to associate itself. Furthermore, the Eisenhower administration undoubtedly wanted to distract attention from its difficulties with Congress over import restrictions on Latin American commodities, and to exhibit its concern over the general economic difficulties of Latin America.[48]

There ensued, as is well known, an unpleasant incident at San Marcos University in Lima, and a reception in Caracas so violent that President Eisenhower alerted American paratroopers and announced their readiness to protect the Vice-President, if necessary. These two incidents greatly weakened public support for United States policies in Latin America, and undoubtedly contributed to the innovations already described, which closely followed the Vice-President's trip.[49]

The government of Brazil was quick to exploit the uncomfortable position of the United States government, which was having some difficulty identifying itself with progress and reform in a period of economic crisis without substantially altering its economic policies. In June 1958, President Kubitschek sent President Eisenhower a letter calling attention to the riots that accompanied Mr. Nixon's visit as evidence that inter-American relations needed reexamination, and suggesting an international conference. It was President Kubitschek's intention to propose as a solution to inter-

American problems a comprehensive development plan, known as Operation Pan America, with targets of per capita income to be reached by 1980 and joint agreement on measures that would be required to meet these targets. None of these measures was made very specific, but it seems clear that liberalization of the terms on which American loans were provided and stabilization of the export markets for primary products on bases that would "ensure a fair remuneration to producers" were among the most important.[50]

President Kubitschek's suggestions were far from anything the United States government was prepared to agree to, but they had to be taken seriously because of the economic crisis and the desire of the government to strengthen and to identify itself with the forces Kubitschek represented. Although it was during the negotiations about Operation Pan America that the Eisenhower administration introduced its proposals for the Act of Bogotá, the proposals seem not to have been part of anyone's original intentions when the negotiations began. Before the United States government decided to concern itself with social development, the productivity of the negotiations that followed from the Brazilian proposal was meager.[51]

The Cuban Revolution

Before the negotiations over Operation Pan America ended, the Cuban Revolution began. It was the second major instance of domestic conflict in the Western Hemisphere in which the Soviet Union was influential. This time the role of the Soviet Union was much more direct and purposeful. The implications of its role for the foreign economic policies of the United States seemed more obvious this time for two reasons: Soviet involvement was on a large scale and seemed likely to be permanent; and the revolution affected economic objectives that the United States was pursuing in Latin America.

The extent of Soviet involvement in Cuba gradually increased as the list of the United States government's disputes with the Castro government lengthened. In February 1960, Anastas Mikoyan visited Cuba and negotiated an agreement whereby the Soviet Union would buy fixed quantities of Cuban sugar over the next four years, would lend Cuba $100 million at two and a half percent interest, and would provide limited technical assistance.[52] In March President Eisenhower requested legislation that would empower him to alter the Cuban sugar quota, and Congress passed it, in modified form, early that summer. Meanwhile, Castro demanded that three foreign oil companies in Cuba refine oil that had been acquired from the Soviet Union. The companies refused, and their plants were expropriated in late June and early July. On July 6, President Eisenhower authorized a cut in the Cuban sugar quota that would reduce Cuba's foreign exchange by $90 million.[53] The Cuban government then expropriated all enterprises owned or partly owned by United States citizens. On July 9, Premier Khrushchev, during the course of a speech in Moscow, announced his support of the Cuban government in these disagreements—which the Eisenhower administration regarded as evidence of "the clear intention to establish Cuba in a role serving Soviet purposes in this hemisphere."[54] On July 12, Khrushchev renewed his attack on the policies of the United States, this time pronouncing the death of the Monroe Doctrine.

Four months earlier, in March 1960, President Eisenhower had approved the training and arming of Cuban guerrillas by the Central Intelligence Agency.[55] But this act did not constitute a decision to back a guerrilla invasion, and the success of any invasion was far from guaranteed. Clearly the United States government faced a more formidable challenge than it had in 1954, and it did not have as ready a solution as the Guatemalan army had provided—Fidel Castro had seen to that. There seemed to be no limit to Castro's willingness to rely on Soviet support, or to the Soviets' willingness to provide it. Therefore if the United States were to take any measures against Cuba, it wanted the support of the major countries of Latin America. The governments of those countries, however, were themselves pursuing goals similar to Castro's, and they were dependent on political groups that were much impressed by the Cuban Revolution. For its part, the revolutionary government in Cuba quickly began trying to export its revolution. Soon the United States government found itself trying to oppose Cuban revolutionary activities while at the same time attempting to avoid identifying itself with the Trujillo regime in the Dominican Republic, a prominent target of Cuban revolutionary efforts.[56]

These circumstances jeopardized the effort that the United States government was making to win some acceptance of the rules by which it wanted to govern its economic relations with Latin America. Economic failure in Latin America would greatly extend the opportunities for Soviet influence; and whatever the deficiencies of United States policies might be, they clearly had no prospect of success if support for them could not be sustained within Latin America. During this period the United States was endeavoring to impose orthodox financial constraints on governments that were mainly interested in rapid industrialization. These governments and their constituents wanted to achieve independence from external economic forces, most of which were identified with the United States. It looked to them as if the United States government's failure to liberalize its economic policies was simply an attempt to keep Latin American countries in a state of subservience (and governments that acquiesced in the demands of the United States were charged with being subservient to foreign interests).

The inter-American bank was partly designed to bridge these conflicting points of view. But it had deficiencies of its own, and clearly could be useful only if it had no obvious competitor and there were no obvious alternatives to the policies it recommended. The Cuban Revolution was a spectacular example of a possible shortcut to industrialization, independence, and reform. And when the Soviet Union, in July 1960, began to support the Cuban government in its dispute with the United States, it began to appear that not only were there alternatives to the policies recommended by the United States, but there was a competitor who might support those alternatives.[57]

Suddenly it was more difficult to expect that many Latin American governments could find support for the sorts of programs the United States was advocating, unless there was more evidence that the programs would yield immediate gains as well as long-term ones. It was also more difficult to expect those governments to find popular support for following the lead of the United States in dealing with Cuba. In short, just when the United States government most needed political support from the governments of Latin America (and when it was therefore most vulnerable to demands for economic concessions), the price of such support went up, and the objectives it had been pursuing in Latin America were threatened.

In light of the Cuban Revolution and the Soviet Union's support of it, it looked as if further innovations were needed in the United States' policies toward Latin America; but it was not entirely clear either how the United States' foreign economic policy was related to the causes of the Cuban Revolution or how it might be used to prevent similar occurrences elsewhere. Unlike the Guatemala affair, the Cuban Revolution seemed to be directed as much against the United States as against any opponents within Cuba. Castro seems to have wanted a break with the United States government and to have sought the backing of the Cuban Communist Party and the Soviet Union as much for that reason as for their ability to support his domestic goals.[58] If this was so, then Castro evidently believed that the foreign economic policies of the United States were not in harmony with the domestic objectives of the revolution, and that these objectives could not be achieved in association with the United States.

Some members of the Eisenhower administration were becoming interested in social development projects that were directly relevant to the sort of conditions which had led to revolution in Cuba. Their interest was based on the fear that economic development could itself give rise to inequalities and tensions that might invite Communist influence. Cuba's situation strikingly demonstrated the point. Cuba was one of the most highly developed countries in Latin America,[59] and it had developed unevenly. Unequal distribution of incomes, enormous differences between urban and rural living conditions, constraints on economic growth, which particularly frustrated the middle class, prominent foreign investments and the resultant tensions, and a high rate of unemployment among the professional class (of which Fidel Castro was a member) all provided occasions for discontent and potential supporters for a revolution.[60]

These seemed to be reasons for thinking that the Cuban Revolution might have been prevented, and that other such revolutions could and should be quickly anticipated. But there are three important qualifications that must be made to this reasoning. These concern the limitations of the Cuban example as a model for other countries, the limitations on Soviet support, and the political characteristics of Cuba that help account for the occurrence and success of Castro's revolution.

It was the connection between domestic and international objectives in Cuba that limited its attractiveness as a model. Some people in Latin America wanted to share the domestic objectives that the Cubans seemed to be on the verge of attaining in 1961, while avoiding the cost of broken relations with the United States. Castro was probably correct in thinking this impossible. The United States would not have provided sufficient financial support, and a split with the United States might well have been indispensable as a means of eliminating the main sources of domestic opposition.[61] Other Latin Americans would undoubtedly have liked to diversify their international position somewhat, and use closer relations with the Soviet Union to influence the United States (without necessarily going as far as Cuba had gone), while avoiding a domestic revolution. But the Soviet Union had no real incentive to substantially support a move toward independence, unless it could be expected to yield as much support for Soviet objectives in Latin America as the Cubans had undertaken, probably including a willingness to create trouble in other countries. And only the desire for an internal revolution could have provided sufficient incentive for Latin Americans to exchange dependence on the United States for a commitment to such Soviet objectives.

If the severity of the Cuban cure had not been enough to limit its relevance to Latin America, the drain on the resources of the Soviet Union would soon have been. For the Soviet Union was probably unable (or at least so nearly unable as to be unwilling) to support an extensive number of economic dependents in the Western Hemisphere. The United States, by attempting to make the Cuban government almost wholly dependent on the Soviet Union, has undoubtedly tried to demonstrate at once to the Soviet Union the costliness of acquiring client states in the Western Hemisphere, and to Latin Americans the limitations on the achievements possible independent of the United States. Given these limitations, it is likely that Soviet support for Castro's objectives was reluctant, and that it resulted partly from Castro's ability to exploit some of the influences on policy makers in the Soviet Union.[62]

The significance of the Cuban Revolution for the United States would have been limited whether there were further innovations in United States economic policies or not. And one might seriously question whether any innovations (including the ones contemplated in 1960 and 1961) could have won additional support for allies of the United States in Latin American politics. One must consider that President Batista's policies had left him with insufficient support to cope with Castro's uprising; that the political institutions of Cuba quickly dissolved; and that to a considerable extent the basis for the authority of the new regime was the person of Fidel Castro. These are all symptoms of such a low level of political institutionalization that one wonders how social tensions could have been reduced to the point where the political system would have been capable of handling them.[63]

But these last considerations are more relevant to the question whether the Cuban Revolution could or should have been prevented than to the problems it created for the United States government. The innovations in policy that followed might—where accompanied by the requisite indigenous effort—provide the means of enabling political institutions and economic programs to withstand the pressures accentuated by the Cuban Revolution. It is important to emphasize that there seemed to be a greater likelihood that the indigenous components of such programs would be supplied in Latin America in 1960 than had been true of Batista's Cuba—or of most of Latin America—in 1954. And as Castro began to turn against even the progressive governments of Latin America, support for domestic reform probably increased.[64]

Whatever the limitations on the ability of the Soviet Union to play an important role in Latin America, the United States government had every reason to want to avoid placing the Soviet Union in such a tempting situation again, for this would complicate Soviet-American relations elsewhere and increase the likelihood of direct Soviet-American conflict. In short, it now seemed more likely that the Soviet Union would be tempted to play an active role in Latin America, and at the same time it seemed more nearly possible than before for the United States to cooperate with Latin American governments to prevent future revolutions. If a revolution had not happened, it would have been much more difficult to demonstrate the limitations of Soviet power in Latin America; but once it had happened, it was necessary to minimize its consequences and seek to prevent its recurrence. This, then, was the context in which the Act of Bogotá and the Alliance for Progress were introduced.

The Act of Bogotá and the Alliance for Progress

The Act of Bogotá, which was negotiated in September 1960, contained a series of multilateral commitments to support the United States government's interest in financing social development in Latin America. Its main objectives were improvements in rural living and land use, housing and community facilities, and public health, and it emphasized the responsibility of Latin American governments to mobilize their own resources toward those ends. The Eisenhower administration proposed to finance the projects that came under the Act through the inter-American bank. The Act also provided for measures to strengthen the Inter-American Economic and Social Council so that it might serve as a forum for the annual review of social and economic developments in Latin America.[65]

The incoming Kennedy administration accepted these innovations, and quickly added its own as part of its overall reform of the entire foreign aid program to Latin America. The new administration, like the old, hoped to establish a closer connection between planning projects and administering funds. It chose means that had been avoided by the Eisenhower administration, however: overall economic planning in underdeveloped countries through the use of country-wide economic development programs, and the commitment of long-term financial support to encourage more long-range planning and clear the way for the removal of many of the obstacles to economic growth. In addition the Kennedy administration gave much greater emphasis to economic development as a goal of United States foreign policy, and less to the use of public assistance as a means of influencing other nations' policies toward private investment.

When applied to Latin America, these general emphases were translated into a commitment to supply foreign aid funds "in sufficient quantities" for ten years in return for the establishment of procedures for screening development programs, and for a commitment to undertake specific domestic reforms.[66] The Kennedy administration also expanded the military assistance program to help prevent guerrilla activities of the Cuban variety. And it was much more willing than the Eisenhower administration to participate in commodity agreements. These were the main components of the Alliance for Progress.

To many people in both the United States and Latin America, the most significant aspect of the Alliance for Progress was its promise of greatly increased aid funds on less stringent terms. But the most important innovation was not the increase of aid funds but the willingness of the United States government to use public funds in an effort to increase the capacity of Latin American countries to absorb them. As Hollis Chenery said of the Kennedy aid program:

The main problem is to raise the productivity of aid to countries in these regions by helping them to make better use of their own resources as well as of those that we provide. This is one of the basic objectives of the Alliance for Progress. At the present time, development loans and grants to most countries in Latin America . . . are limited more by the ability of these countries to use external resources effectively . . . than by a shortage of funds from the United States and other sources.[67]

This point of view contrasted sharply with the policy of the Eisenhower administration, which had agreed with the estimate of Eugene Black:

Either South America develops governmental institutions and policies which allow local capital to be invested productively or both local and foreign capital will simply stay away. . . . There is little that outsiders can do about these shortcomings other than to withhold support until tolerable conditions exist.[68]

In the early 1950's, President Eisenhower's advisers had doubted that financial inducements to reform, even if accompanied by technical assistance in policy making at the highest levels, would yield higher productivity than the pressures that resulted from withholding aid funds. After 1954, these pressures seemed to have increasingly worse results, and the penalties of relying on them increased as well. Then, in the late 1950's, conditions began to seem more favorable to foreign investment as progressive, reform-minded regimes appeared in a number of Latin American countries. As Lincoln Gordon said in defending the Kennedy administration's program: "We obviously can't say we are going to dictate the land reform legislation of another country but we can provide help where the right kind of legislation is forthcoming and refrain from providing help where it doesn't."[69] The same point was made more directly by Adolf Berle: "President Kennedy's plan would have been meaningless if most Latin American governments were still cast in the mold of the ousted Argentine dictator, Juan Domingo Perón."[70]

The most important conflicts between the United States and the governments of Latin America over economic issues did not disappear, but they were obscured for a time by the furore over the Cuban Revolution and by the willingness of the Kennedy administration to experiment with new techniques for negotiating. The conflicts will be seen more clearly after the events already described have been examined from a Latin American perspective (in Chapter 2). They have been exacerbated by disagreements over the causes of Latin America's economic and political problems, and by their implications in the domestic politics of both the

United States and the countries of Latin America. For the moment it will be helpful to reiterate two constant themes in the behavior of the United States government. It has judged the relevance of any proposed form of inter-American cooperation in the light of its central concern, namely, preventing any event that might invite a challenge to United States military power in the Western Hemisphere. And it has attempted to accomplish this objective with the smallest possible drain on its political and economic resources. The governments of Latin America obviously place other objectives higher on their list of priorities than these.

2. United States Economic Policies and Inter-American Politics

It is important not to assume that there is a single Latin American set of interests that can be summarized and contrasted with the interests of the United States government. One problem Latin American governments have is precisely that of coordinating their policies so as to bring maximum pressure to bear on the United States. But their association with the United States has affected them all in similar ways, and consequently there are important similarities in their responses and in the attitudes toward the association that prevail in Latin American public opinion.[1] Differences in the responses of Latin American governments have resulted from a variety of factors, among them differences in the extent to which their countries have been affected by United States policy in the past, differences in the way United States policies affect their political goals (both domestic and international), differences in the significance that has been attributed to United States influence (a matter powerfully affected by ideology), and differences in the capacities of Latin American leaders to form a view of these problems independently of the advice of the United States government.

The Latin American Experience of Economic Dependence

Every country in Latin America is to some degree dependent on the economic power of the United States and has good reason to fear the exercise of that power. Because of this dependence on the international economy, most major political goals in Latin America affect and are affected by the ability to earn foreign exchange and to attract foreign capital, both public and private. The availability of these resources is substantially affected by what goes on in the United States, either as a consequence of governmental decisions or as a consequence of the play of forces over which the United States government could, if it chose, exercise some control. Many Latin Americans greatly exaggerate the extent to which the United States government has controlled or could have controlled the working of these economic forces. And many also, in the opinion of the United States government and many American economists, overemphasize the dependence of their domestic objectives on these external forces.[2] But these are differences in the interpretation of what is an undeniable fact—that the way the United States exercises its economic power, both public and private, is of fundamental importance to the economic life of most of Latin America.

Three points can be made about this fact independently of the various interpretations woven around it in both the United States and Latin America. First, the present degree of dependence on the United States, having largely developed since 1930, is a relatively recent phenomenon to which all parties have had to make some adjustment. Second, the way that the United States government has managed this relationship has often seemed not very stable or reliable. Third, the responsibilities of the United States elsewhere in the world and within its own borders have led it to make decisions that have seemed flatly contrary to the economic interests of many Latin American countries. It will be useful to examine these statements before considering the opportunities that have been available to Latin American governments to influence United States policies and the implications of these issues in domestic politics in the United States.

World War I temporarily disrupted some of Latin America's economic relationships with Europe.[3] But, together, the great depression of the 1930's and World War II produced a major, long-lasting change in the international position of Latin America. The depression forcibly emphasized the dependence of Latin American countries on economic forces they could not control. It accelerated the demand for autarky in Latin America, as it did in the industrial countries, but Latin American governments lacked the power to attain that goal. World War II produced further great economic changes, made the countries of Latin America even more vulnerable to changes in United States policy, and aroused hopes for economic advancement that were subsequently disappointed.

Before the United States entered World War II, it fairly successfully absorbed Latin American surpluses created by the war and provided an alternative source of goods and capital. But the participation of the United States in the war created problems that have continued, in some form, ever since. The first noticeable effect was the reduced supply of American goods available.

The United States could no longer provide goods on the same scale as before, because its resources were pressed to the limit. This provided enormous encouragement—not to say necessity— for developing domestic industries in Latin America, but much of this new industry was threatened by the reappearance of competition after the war. Naturally the Latin Americans were anxious to protect the gains they had made, but the United States chose to press for the lowering of trade restrictions after the war, without which these industries could not survive.

The reduced flow of goods from the United States produced large dollar balances in favor of the Latin Americans and large-scale inflation. The pent-up demand for imports had to be met after the war, when American prices were no longer controlled. Thus, by postponing their expenditures, the Latin Americans gained less from their exports than they would have gained had they been able to spend the dollars they earned earlier.

A second effect of the United States participation in the war was that its war effort created an unusual demand for many Latin American raw materials, which did not continue when the war ended. Special purchase arrangements concluded in wartime, under which production of essential raw materials was encouraged, were allowed to lapse, and in several instances the former tariffs on them were even restored. In addition, not only did the United States begin purchasing materials from other parts of the world again, but the United States government promoted raw materials production elsewhere as part of its attempt to restore the economies of Europe.[4]

By discontinuing assistance to Latin America so soon after the war, the United States government exposed itself to the charge of being an unreliable ally.[5] It seems unlikely, however, that the problems of reconversion in Latin America could have been separated from broader conflicts of interest in any case. For the Latin Americans were plainly anxious to transform their international economic position, and that ambition implied many conflicts with the United States government. In the absence of agreement on the nature of the long-range relationship desired, it would have been difficult to agree on the adequacy of measures designed to deal simply with the transition period.[6]

The seriousness of Latin America's basic economic problems did not become obvious for several years after the war—by which time the demand for many Latin American exports began to decline in earnest, and the large foreign exchange reserves built up during the war had disappeared, spent largely for consumption rather than capital investment.[7] When Latin American governments demanded economic assistance, the United States emphasized their past failure to institute sufficient economic controls to make good use of their foreign exchange reserves.[8] Thus began a persistent pattern in inter-American politics: Latin American demands for economic assistance, followed by a lecture from the United States government on how the need for assistance could be lessened by proper management of native resources.

By this time, of course, the full extent of other demands on the United States' resources was beginning to be obvious. I argued earlier that the broad outlines of United States policy toward Latin America were not significantly affected by these demands. Nevertheless, the drain on the United States' resources produced first by the Marshall Plan and then by the Korean War did present problems.

United States policy makers were convinced that the recovery of Europe was essential for the economic well-being of Latin America and therefore believed that the Marshall Plan would indirectly benefit the Latin Americans. Many Latin Americans, however, were dubious about any immediate gains and were also afraid that a revival of Europe and Europe's colonies, without some prior measures to secure the markets for Latin America's products, would be as much a menace as a benefit.

When the Marshall Plan was being devised, government officials anticipated that its demands on American production would lead to some shortages and consequently to the reduction of the supply of capital equipment available to non-European countries. Thus it was expected that the pace of industrialization in Latin America would be slowed somewhat and that gains would come instead through the traditional exchange of raw materials for industrial goods from Europe. The United States government undertook merely to help secure some essential goods from the United States.[9]

The House Select Committee on Foreign Aid (known as the Herter Committee) was especially anxious that no part of the Marshall Plan funds be used, even indirectly, for the benefit of Latin America. This position was probably necessary to secure public support for the Marshall Plan in the United States, and it was undoubtedly reinforced by the mandate and the independence of the special agency that was set up to administer the European Recovery Program, namely the Economic Cooperation Administration.[10] Indeed, the Herter Committee not only insisted that no Marshall Plan funds be used indirectly (through offshore purchases, for example) to assist Latin America, but also turned the question around the other way. "The question becomes," it said, "what more can Latin America do to assist in European recovery?"[11] It concluded that several Latin American countries were capable of extending credits to Europe.[12]

The Marshall Plan was regarded within the Truman administration as a temporary interruption of the long-range plans the government was making for economic cooperation with Latin America. In 1948 President Truman had asked for an increase of $500 million in the lending authority of the Export-Import Bank specifically for economic development in Latin America;[13] and though Congress did not act at once on this request, it was assumed that it would do so eventually, even though the administration was beginning to realize that more funds would not have much effect unless the quality of the projects for which the funds were used was improved.[14] Then the Korean War and the related reassessment of the demands that competition with the Soviet Union would make on United States resources led to still further postponement of the time when the United States could freely contribute to economic development in Latin America. When the resources available to the Export-Import Bank were next expanded, it was in order to finance the production of raw materials needed for the Korean War and to promote the development of the Philippines, Japan, and the Middle East.[15]

By the time the Korean War began, the balance-of-payments crises of most Latin American countries were over. The report on foreign economic policies submitted to President Truman by Gordon Gray in November 1950 was optimistic about the immediate prospects for Latin American exports and maintained that there were good prospects there for the investment of both public and private capital.[16]

The increased demand for raw materials that the Korean War produced was expected to yield additional benefits for Latin America. But the Korean War also created scarcities in the United States, inflation in Latin America, and a fear among many Latin Americans that once again after the war both the value of their dollar holdings and the demand for their goods, which was temporarily stimulated, would decline. This time Latin American governments wanted a guarantee of the value of the foreign exchange they would earn during the war and measures to stabilize the prices of their raw materials. But the United States government merely insisted once again that it was the Latin Americans' responsibility to institute the proper governmental controls so that gains from the war could be productively used thereafter.

The United States' responsibility for some of these problems was recognized, however, by the Assistant Secretary of State for Latin American Affairs, William Miller. He compared these problems to the ones that followed World War II and urged that we "profit from the errors and lessons of the past," carefully considering the needs of Latin American economies when allocating scarce materials and manufactured goods. It was important, Miller said, not only to maintain a reasonable level of economic activity, but also to allow economic growth. Furthermore, he said,

We must not lose sight of the objective of bringing about a greater degree of stability in world markets for specific commodities. As we stimulate expansion of production of individual commodities, we must look to the day when demand for those commodities may decline and attempt to safeguard the investment and effort of the producer and to soften the shock of the emergence of burdensome surpluses following an abrupt change in the supply-demand equation.[17]

Thus the Korean War reemphasized the difficult position of the United States in Latin America.[18] And whereas World War II involved a clear threat to Latin American security, and European recovery could plausibly be argued to be important to Latin America as well as to Europe and the United States, the Korean War seemed to have little direct relevance to the vital interests of the countries of Latin America—yet they were expected to make sacrifices on its account.

The United States government, in attempting to secure the cooperation of the Latin Americans in controlling raw materials prices, used the language of international alliances and burden-sharing. In a speech before the Inter-American Economic and Social Council in September 1951, Assistant Secretary Miller said that the sacrifices presently required of citizens of the United States were being undertaken "not in our own national interest alone but in the interest of the collective cause of peace and security, to which we have all pledged our mutual cooperation." Obviously, therefore, the problem of monetary reserves and other aspects of inflationary and financial problems had to be considered "in the light of the total emergency situation which we collectively confront."[19] But the sacrifices to be made by Latin American countries, if they did prove to be sacrifices, were not voluntary. The joint military planning begun at this time helped give some appearance of cooperation in a common cause and may have contributed to the willingness of some governments to acquiesce in the economic arrangements desired by the United States.[20] But given the unfortunate symbolic role of the military in Latin America, and the fact that many Latin Americans could claim they were being exploited by the United States, it may have been unwise in the long run to couple economic and defense issues.[21]

Other conflicts between the United States and Latin America over commodity prices were not so directly the result of the war. Coffee and copper can be taken as representative examples. In 1950 a report by the Senate Agricultural Committee accused Brazil and Colombia of having begun a campaign to raise coffee prices. The committee recommended that a representative of the Department of Justice attend meetings of the Special Commission on Coffee of the Inter-American Economic and Social Council, that special precautions be taken in giving loans to coffee-producing countries in Latin America, and that the Economic Cooperation Administration cease dollar purchases of coffee there. This report was published just when it was becoming obvious to Latin Americans that the Marshall Plan would provide them little direct assistance, and it aroused great resentment.[22]

The rise in coffee prices seems to have come about because supplies lagged behind the increased demand that followed World War II. From 1948 to 1951 production remained virtually constant, and prices rose from 26.6 to 55.5 cents per pound.[23] Although coffee production caught up briefly with demand in 1952, in July 1953 a frost in the coffee plantations of Paraná, Brazil, led to speculation on the coffee market, causing an even larger increase in coffee prices in the United States.[24] The result was organized consumer resistance in the United States and an investigation of the coffee market by the Federal Trade Commission. This provoked more Latin American protests; but more important, it also led to a decrease in the consumption of coffee in the United States.[25] And the high prices of these years helped stimulate the increased production that in 1958 would force the United States government to reconsider its policies concerning international commodity agreements.

Similar conflicts over the price of copper complicated the relations between the United States and Chile, with the difference that in this instance the United States is both a producer and a consumer, since the companies that produce copper in Chile also produce in the United States. To add to the confusing conflicts of interest that this situation created, the United States was anxious to persuade Chile not to sell copper to the Soviet Union, a restriction for which many Chileans felt inadequately compensated.

During the Korean War the United States' efforts to keep copper prices down led to protests from Chile, and the United States government subsequently agreed to pay a premium for Chilean copper. Chile agreed at the same time not to sell to the Soviet Union, and to withhold for her own use no more than twenty percent of the output of the American companies. In the spring of 1952, the Chilean government became dissatisfied once again, as the world price rose still higher, and the agreement was cancelled. After further disputes over sales to the Soviet Union and the treatment of the American-owned companies in Chile, the United States government finally agreed to import copper at the world price in 1953 (which meant that the United States government was purchasing copper from Chile at a price above the ceiling set for its own domestic market).[26]

These and other controversies over commodities during the Truman years were dominated by the problem of rising prices, and the administration was under strong pressure to protect the interests of United States consumers. The Eisenhower administration coincided with a period of falling commodity prices, during which the interests of United States producers seemed better represented in the government's decisions than the interests of Latin America. Some of these prices fell when demand for the commodities declined after the Korean War.

At the same time, the way the Eisenhower administration reviewed its commitments to Latin America, and the pressure on the administration to emphasize domestic objectives over foreign policy ones, raised serious questions about the stability of United States policies. John M. Cabot, Assistant Secretary of State for Latin American Affairs, said in October 1953 that "at the moment the question appears to be whether we can continue to do as much as we have been doing rather than whether we can do more."[27] There were indications that the administration intended to curtail the Export-Import Bank's rate of lending in Latin America,[28] and the broad outlines of the United States government's commercial policies, embodied in reciprocal trade agreements legislation dating from the 1930's, were threatened by the Republican majority in Congress.[29] The Randall Commission, which was given the task of reviewing the whole range of United States foreign economic policies, left the impression that foreign policy problems were considered implicitly or not at all.* The report was slanted in this way chiefly because Clarence Randall wanted to win the support of enough isolationists on the commission to split the forces of the isolationist opposition in Congress.[30] Thus the main emphasis of the Eisenhower administration seemed to be on compromising with its domestic political opponents.

By 1954 there was therefore considerable reason to doubt that the increased responsibility of the United States government for the economic life of Latin America had been sufficiently institutionalized. In addition, there were at that time greater doubts among Latin Americans about their own economic future than ex-

---

* As one contemporary critic of the commission's report said: "One of the major functions of foreign economic policy is to support American foreign policy. The foreign policy of the United States is concerned, among other things, with the economic health of our principal allies and, to some extent, with the economic health of the underdeveloped countries. There is little of this in the Report. There is almost no sense at all that the problem is more than one of the rest of the world's trade and payments with the United States." H. Van B. Cleveland, in Klaus Knorr and Gardner Patterson, *A Critique of the Randall Commission Report* (Princeton: International Finance Section, Princeton University, 1954), p. 65.

isted in the United States. The United Nations Economic Commission for Latin America summarized the worries of Latin Americans:

One must beware of facile illusions. Latin America has undergone a very high rate of development in recent years. Average per capita income rose by 3.3 percent annually during the period 1945–52 as compared with a rate of 1.9 percent recorded in the historical growth of the United States. If a similar rate could be steadily maintained, the Latin American countries could double their present standard of living in twenty-one years. But unfortunately the factors which stimulated this growth were exceptional and show no signs of repetition. The principal factor was the improvement in the terms of trade, which had a favorable effect upon income, both directly and indirectly, by stimulating investment. But the outlook has been changing for the worse and the slight effect which may still persist is being absorbed by the obstinate tendency of consumption to take advantage of any available margin of product for its own benefit.

The anxiety aroused by these events in responsible Latin Americans is clear to see.[31]

Partly because of the Guatemala crisis in 1954 and Latin American demands, the Eisenhower administration decided to expand rather than restrict the lending of the Export-Import Bank in Latin America and to support the creation of an International Finance Corporation as an affiliate of the World Bank. But because the Randall Commission recommended against participating in international commodity agreements or buying buffer stocks to stabilize prices of raw materials, the government refused even to participate in discussions of these measures.[32] The efforts of the Eisenhower administration to cope with commodity surpluses were therefore restricted to attempting to stave off the demands of United States producers for import restrictions, which, in effect, would have shifted more of the burden of surplus supplies onto foreign producers, including Latin Americans. The administration's ability to do this depended on its ability to stave off the demand for protection by balancing one domestic interest against another, or to find an alternative means of meeting the demand. The future of the existing trade agreements legislation was in doubt throughout both Eisenhower administrations, and its continuation was bought at the price of agreeing to protection for a number of commodities.[33]

Through the use of purchases for the stockpile, the administration was able to put off demands for import restrictions on lead and zinc for five years. The Suez crisis and conflicts among the oil companies enabled the administration to avoid import restrictions on oil during the same period. By 1958, however, these efforts finally failed, and the United States government increased its import restrictions on a number of Latin American commodities at a time of general crisis for Latin American exports.

By encouraging the development of mineral resources in Latin America during times of scarcity and then restricting the market for them when supply outran demand, the United States government risked being considered by Latin Americans to have designed its economic policies to benefit its own citizens at the expense of Latin Americans. It was possible similarly to interpret the government's response to the coffee problem.

The sharply rising coffee prices of the early 1950's led to a large increase in coffee planting, particularly in Africa. The supply of coffee can be adjusted to rising demand only slowly, because of the period of time required to plant trees and bring them into production. These new plantings came into production in the early 1950's, and soon supply began to overtake demand. There is probably a tendency for this to happen over the long run, because the demand for coffee does not increase with production in industrial countries, while coffee is easily produced and the returns to individual producers are quite large.

Between 1954 and 1962 the average wholesale price for coffee fell by more than 50 percent. By 1962, Brazil alone held sufficient stocks of coffee to supply the world for over a year.[34] In addition, the Latin Americans found their share of the market being steadily infringed on by African producers—a problem that would be greatly aggravated if African producers won preferential treatment in the European Common Market. These trends were a threat to the economic future of many Latin American countries. In 1961 coffee exports accounted for the following percentages of their export earnings: Colombia, 71 percent; Guatemala, 60 percent; El Salvador, 59 percent; Brazil, 51 percent; Costa Rica, 49 percent; Haiti, 41 percent. In some of these countries, taxes on coffee production provided as much as twenty percent of government revenues.[35]

Before 1958, the United States government was not prepared to do more than attempt to reduce fluctuations in the coffee market by improving the collection of information about the state of the market.[36] Late in 1955, Assistant Secretary of State Henry Holland noted that some Latin American countries were interested in reaching an agreement among themselves. "In view of our own price stabilization programs," he remarked, "we could not disagree in principle if the coffee-producing countries try to accomplish the same objective, as long as the actions they contemplate would not hurt the consumers in this country."[37] But not until there were further market declines did any government take action. Then seven producers, who were together responsible for 94 percent of the United States' coffee supply, signed an agreement in Mexico City, in October 1957, allocating quarterly export quotas to each participating country. This agreement failed to curb exports sufficiently, however, and also did not include African producers.[38]

In attempting to regulate the market by forming an agreement among producing countries (as Brazil had been trying to do alone since well before World War II), these countries were doing much the same thing the United States had done in protecting the interests of its agricultural producers. First, prices were supported by government purchases and other auxiliary arrangements. When Brazil found this impossible to do single-handedly, it tried to persuade other Latin American countries to cooperate. Brazil and Colombia initially bore the main burden of stockpiling coffee and then persuaded others to join, hoping that they could later pressure the newcomers into bearing part of the costs. The same tactics were later applied to African producers, with some success. Completely successful regulation of the market, however, could only be guaranteed if the consuming countries—principally the United States—would force all producers into the agreement by denying the market to nonmembers.[39]

Despite its various expressions of faith in an unfettered international economy after World War II, the United States government had already participated in schemes for regulating the international market for sugar and wheat and had instituted import restrictions in order to achieve a unilateral advantage.[40] And it had earlier used its market power to drive down the prices of coffee and minerals. Now it was reluctant to sustain prices merely to benefit Latin America; but by 1958 the relation of these problems to United States security seemed sufficiently obvious to warrant a change in policy.

It should be clear, then, that the behavior of the United States government exhibited great fluctuations, some of them perceived as harmful by public opinion in Latin America. But it should also be clear that the problem of minimizing the damage to Latin America resulting from United States policies was made more difficult by the desire of Latin Americans to maximize the benefits they might receive from those policies.

Economic Conflict and Cooperation

Before 1958, the interests of the United States government and the governments of Latin America in general economic policies could not be said to overlap, except to the extent that there was some undefined level below which the United States government was not willing to allow economic growth in Latin America to drop. The level had not been defined because the main concerns of the United States government provided no clear criteria for estimating it. These were fostering economic growth in Latin America over the long run and preventing any extension of Soviet influence in the meantime. And though the government hoped the detrimental effects of its economic policies would be minimized, its failure to be cooperative was very unlikely to raise a serious threat to its interests.

The range of common interest could not be greatly expanded, since there was little further the Latin Americans might offer the United States that was of interest and nothing they were already providing that they could afford to withhold for a higher price.

Moreover, such common interests as existed were obscured by the fact that there were alternative paths to any given goal (for example, a certain rate of economic growth) and the costs of pursuing any objective were distributed differently according to the path chosen. A conflict over who was to bear the cost was superimposed on every common interest, however meager.

The refusal to cooperate proved to be an effective way, for each side at different times, to force the burden of providing for the common goal onto the other side. The United States government, usually having the less intense interest in the common goal, more often held the stronger bargaining position. It sought to minimize its own costs by providing no public aid for purposes that could be financed by foreign private investment or by local savings or tax revenues; and sought to minimize the burdens of its producers and consumers (and thereby to reduce its own political burdens) by refusing to support artificially the market for commodities produced in Latin America. In both instances its refusal to cooperate was reinforced by doubts that any more economic assistance would contribute to either its own military security or the economic independence of the Latin American countries.

Reducing the costs to the United States necessarily increased the costs to Latin American governments, since greater use of indigenous resources meant higher taxes, increased investment at the expense of consumption, more efficient use of land, and a shift in the pattern of local investment so as to increase its contribution both to economic growth and to the country's ability to earn foreign exchange. And increased reliance on foreign private investment, which was necessary without public aid, left governments vulnerable to the criticisms of nationalists.

Because the United States wished to avoid participating in any relationship with any Latin American country or group of countries that might weaken the credibility of its refusal to liberalize its lending policies and its commercial policies, or that might increase the opportunities for Latin American governments to apply pressure to that end, it was inhibited in its efforts to cooperate even within the framework of the policies it had chosen. Through the Export-Import Bank and technical assistance programs, it tried to help Latin Americans attain domestic prosperity and the capacity to earn sufficient foreign exchange to liberate themselves from special international credit arrangements. But it was difficult to relate technical assistance to the Export-Import Bank loans and still more difficult to assess the contribution of either form of assistance to the objective of economic development. This was partly due to the organization of the United States government. The technical assistance program brought together disparate activities managed by different governmental agencies with scarcely any coordination among them. It required several reorganizations to enable the agency responsible for technical assistance to gain sufficient control over its elements to apply any comprehensive criteria to the choice of programs. There had to be a similar transformation in field operations, where, in the beginning, officials were not accustomed to thinking in terms of overall economic development.[41] The Export-Import Bank, the only direct source of capital from the United States government, remained an autonomous agency.

But this lack of coordination was a less serious problem than the conflict between the United States government and most Latin American governments over what aspects of development were most important and what means were suitable. The Act for International Development, which translated into law President Truman's Point Four proposal, provided for the establishment of joint economic development commissions to negotiate overall sets of objectives for the aid being offered (including technical assistance in Latin America). The Office of the Coordinator of Inter-American Affairs had developed this idea during World War II and had used it to promote economic development in Mexico after 1943.[42] A joint Brazil–United States Technical Commission had also been established, in 1948. The *New York Times* reported then that the "success of this mission, according to views in foreign trade quarters, may also form the pattern for similar joint technical and economic commissions for other countries now developing industrially, including Mexico, Chile, Colombia, possibly Argen-

tina, India, and China."[43] But the work of the Brazilian-American
Commission quickly exposed disagreements between the Americans and the Brazilians over the relative attention to be given to
industrial development and agriculture.[44] And similar but more
serious disagreements eventually disrupted the joint commission
for economic development established under the authorization of
the Act for International Development.

The authorization of the joint commissions, as Philip Glick has
said, represented "no less than a suggestion that the government
of the United States and the government of the host country
might attempt the joint administration of a central programming
agency for the host country."[45] Only three countries requested
such commissions: Brazil, Paraguay, and Liberia. The Paraguayan
commission was never well organized. The Brazilian commission
failed because the Brazilian government attempted to use it to
obtain more financial aid. Rather than submit to such pressure,
the United States government simply discontinued the commission at the beginning of the first Eisenhower administration.[46]

From this point on, the United States government ceased trying
to influence the overall process of economic planning in Latin
America. The technical assistance program gradually began to
concern itself with the technical aspects of public administration, but it avoided the subject of broad economic planning and
the preparation of projects for which governmental assistance
would be asked.[47] And the Export-Import Bank never developed
a more intimate relationship with any Latin American country
than was required to assess the technical merits of a proposed
project and to form some estimate of the country's likely willingness and capacity to repay in dollars. Both of these unfortunate
situations developed because the Eisenhower administration did
not want to make a prior commitment of economic assistance, except in special circumstances.[48]

There were only three exceptions: Guatemala, Bolivia, and
Haiti. In each of these countries the likely consequences of not
providing grant aid seemed unacceptable, and therefore in these
three very different countries the government did attempt to in-

fluence the overall course of economic planning. Aid to Guatemala was offered to shore up the regime of Castillo Armas. Aid to Bolivia was given to prevent a famine and to support the revolutionary government there. And aid to Haiti was given to avert financial collapse after a hurricane in 1959. But once the programs were begun, the objectives rapidly grew in number, and thus the assistance was continued beyond the end of the original emergencies that had prompted it.[49]

In the rest of Latin America, the technical assistance program seems to have been ideally designed to enable the United States to assist in economic development without confronting the many intergovernmental problems that would have been involved in a grant aid program. Emphasis was placed on isolated projects in the fields of health, agriculture, and education, which were normally the province of technicians and which were judged by technicians' standards. The institution that administered each project was the *servicio*, an agency jointly managed by the United States and a Latin American official. This agency was isolated from the government of the recipient country, and thus tended to maintain its stability even through radical political changes.[50] In theory, the servicio, after reaching a certain stage, was expected to pass the project along to some regular government agency and then initiate a new program in cooperation with the United States. But there seems to have been some reluctance to do this, largely because of fears that the project would suffer at the hands of the local government.[51] Far from overcoming the political obstacles to economic cooperation between nations, then, the technical assistance program may have reinforced them. It may have increased the demands made on the local government without increasing its capacity to meet them.[52]

Like the technical assistance program, the Export-Import Bank had for many years been active in Latin America, and its operations also reflected a desire to protect itself from the demands on its resources that might follow from involvement in Latin American politics.[53] This orientation was reflected in the bank's criteria for lending money and in its preference for financing individual projects. The bank insisted that the projects make a measurable contribution to economic development (which ruled out schools, hospitals, and housing); that loans be given only to countries with a capacity to repay in dollars at nearly commercial rates of interest (although when United States foreign policy has demanded it, the bank has made loans to avoid the threat of a country's defaulting on loans already made); and that loans be made only for the foreign currency costs of development projects.

These restrictions prevented any significant increase in lending to Latin American countries and made the government's promise in 1954 that the bank would be more active in Latin America seem hollow.[54] One of the presumed virtues of the Inter-American Development Bank, which the United States government finally agreed to establish in 1958, was to have been its ability to escape from these limitations without increasing the strain on the United States government's purse strings.

Bargaining over Economic Policies

The United States' strategy of noncooperation eventually had to be abandoned, partly because it was not completely successful, and partly because the government's interest in the economic growth of Latin America intensified as the Soviet Union played a more active role there. There were only four courses of action open to Latin American governments that might have had some effect on United States policy. They could appeal to public opinion in the United States; make economic assistance the price of cooperation in other activities in which the United States government was momentarily interested; refuse to meet the terms of the United States government, driving economic performance even below the level that the government was willing to tolerate; or implicate the Soviet Union in their economic problems. All four of these methods were tried, and all were eventually successful. But their success depended partly on extraneous factors.

The United States government's membership in the OAS and its desire to maintain that organization as a device for legitimizing its own necessarily dominant role in Latin America periodically exposed it to pressure exerted indirectly by Latin American governments through public opinion in the United States. The United States government was vulnerable to this kind of pressure for two reasons: first, New Deal policies toward Latin America had shaped the American public's image of the proper role of the United States there; second, the public expected that international conferences would have concrete results and would minimize conflicts. It was no doubt partly for these reasons that the United States government resisted the calling of an inter-American conference to deal with economic issues during President Truman's administration— in spite of the fact that such a conference had been scheduled shortly after the war.

An economic conference was finally held, in Rio de Janeiro in 1954, because the Guatemala crisis made it impossible for the United States to avoid one any longer. This crisis forced the United States government to seek the approval of OAS members for its policies toward Guatemala. Thus for a brief moment the United States government actually required the cooperation of Latin American governments. The price for that cooperation was the convening of a special conference devoted to economic issues, which increased the pressures on the new Eisenhower administration to liberalize its economic policies toward Latin America.

The inter-American conference at Caracas in 1954, at which the United States government sought a resolution that would condemn by implication the government of Guatemala, was the tenth regularly scheduled inter-American conference, and the first since the OAS was created at Bogotá in 1948. Thorsten Kalijarvi, the Deputy Assistant Secretary of State for Economic Affairs, made the following frank report:

Our principal objective at Caracas was to obtain the concrete expression of hemispheric solidarity that was embodied in the anti-Communist resolution. It was made perfectly clear to us, however, that the willingness of some of the Latin American countries to follow our lead in political matters was directly dependent upon concrete evidence of U.S. willingness to contribute more fully to the solution of the major economic problems confronting the area. It was in recognition of this sentiment that Secretary Dulles devoted almost two-thirds of his speech in the plenary to economic matters and in addition made a personal appearance before the Economic Committee. United States acceptance of the suggestion of a special economic conference to be held later this year in Rio de Janeiro was also widely interpreted as an acknowledgement of U.S. interest in the problems of trade and economic development which are of central concern in Latin America. Our preparations for the Rio Conference have provided us with the occasion for a searching reexamination of our economic policy toward Latin America.[55]

Between the Caracas conference and the economic conference at Rio de Janeiro, the Arbenz government in Guatemala was overthrown. It is interesting to speculate whether the necessity of dealing with a firmly established Communist regime in Guatemala would have prompted the United States to undertake a much more radical review of its policies than the one it actually conducted.[56] Regardless of the answer, it seems clear that the two innovations in United States policy presented at Rio, insignificant as they seemed to the Latin Americans, were almost entirely the result of the pressure Latin American governments were able to exercise through the OAS.*

From 1954 through 1961, the United States government engaged in periodic negotiations with Latin American governments over economic issues. Each occasion created indirect pressures on the United States government to modify its policies. These pressures increased greatly in the aftermath of the demonstrations against Vice-President Nixon.[57] The next major opportunity for the Latin American governments to make substantial economic assistance the price of their cooperation was, of course, presented by the Cuban Revolution. The statements of several progressive Latin American governments at the conference of foreign ministers of the OAS at San José, Costa Rica, in August 1960, indicated clearly that they regarded the differences between the United States and Cuba as a problem strictly concerning those two countries, and they were prepared to do no more than mediate.[58] It quickly became obvious that economic concessions were the price of a more

---

* This is discussed further on pp. 130–34. The two innovations were the creation of the International Finance Corporation and the attempt to expand Export-Import Bank lending in Latin America.

cooperative attitude. As Adlai Stevenson said of the Punta del Este conference of 1961: "It was generally and strongly felt that no collective action [against Cuba] could be officially considered until the economic conference was concluded and had demonstrated its success as a major step toward economic and social development."[59] It was widely assumed, said Stevenson, that collective action would be useless unless supported by two of the three largest Latin American countries: Argentina, Brazil, and Mexico. The concurrence of Mexico was unlikely. The possibility of Argentine and Brazilian concurrence depended largely on "developments" in the immediate future.[60] A favorable attitude on the part of the United States toward commodity agreements would be helpful, he thought. It might soften slightly the disappointment these two countries would feel concerning the actual volume of aid funds they would receive.

Most Latin American governments refused to conform completely to the United States government's conditions for public loans (e.g., the control of inflation). Their refusal was, of course, only partly a conscious bargaining tactic. Their noncooperation is primarily to be explained by the political penalties they would have incurred at home for doing otherwise and by the prevailing conceptions of economic requirements among Latin Americans who thought about such problems. But during the second Eisenhower administration, as the Soviet Union began to play a more active role in Latin America, the Brazilian government demonstrated some of the potentialities of a conscious tactic of noncooperation.

The loans provided by the United States government to several Latin American countries in 1958 to compensate for the effects of the export crisis were carefully coordinated with the International Monetary Fund, which made stabilization programs to control inflation the precondition for granting loans. In 1958 and 1959 the Brazilian government rejected the conditions set by the IMF and turned to the United States for direct assistance. Thus President Eisenhower and his advisers had to choose between pursuing their own foreign policy objectives in Brazil (which meant staying on

good terms with the Brazilian government) and supporting the
IMF (which meant supporting the whole system of international
controls over financial policies in underdeveloped countries).

In June 1959, the United States found a way out of its dilemma:
it postponed the payments due on Brazil's foreign debt. This still
left Brazil severely constrained by its foreign debt, however, and
unable to contract for any new foreign loans. Brazil ignored this
offer of a moratorium and would not come to terms with the IMF.[61]
Late in 1959 slightly higher coffee prices helped temporarily to
support Brazil's independent position.[62] A decision by the IMF to
acquiesce in Brazil's resistance would have helped undermine the
position of the IMF with respect to other countries. It might also
arouse domestic agitation against the governments of those countries that did conform to the IMF's demands. Among these was
Brazil's neighbor Argentina.[63] If the United States were generous
in this instance, it might be taken advantage of later on. If it were
not generous, irreparable damage might be done both to Brazil's
economy and to the United States' international relations. This
dispute accentuated the need of the United States government to
build a base of support in Latin America for its position on this
issue, and the ineffectiveness of its noncooperation. As Raymond
Mikesell said:

It is in the interest of both the IMF and the U.S. Government to create
a more favorable image of the Fund and to place it in the eyes of the
public squarely on the side of broadly based economic reforms, and not
identify it with financial orthodoxy for its own sake or with economic
and social reaction.[64]

This need for a better image was further accentuated by the
new interest in Latin America that the Soviet Union exhibited.
The governments of Latin America could not easily exploit this
interest, partly because the Soviet Union had limited economic
capabilities and no special wish to compensate for its limitations
before the Cuban Revolution,[65] and partly because their relations
with the United States government and with private American
investors, though not wholly satisfactory, were still too important
to jeopardize by cultivating too close relations with the Soviet

bloc. Nevertheless they were conscious that some trade, properly publicized, might improve their strength in bargaining with the United States. To quote one study of the subject, published in 1959:

Latin American countries have not shied away from publicity about Soviet and East European offers of trade and credit, partly because of the hope that the United States will be more sympathetic. Indeed, there has been a tendency to call attention to such transactions. This has not been done with the specific hope or expectation that the United States would feel compelled to follow suit, but with the rather general anticipation that if the United States is fully conscious of the details of the transactions and the fact that Latin American countries feel it necessary to consider seriously such economic relations, then the United States will tend to take the area's problems more seriously, and will try to be as helpful as possible.[66]

There probably would have been innovations in United States economic policies, given the influences just described and the enthusiasm of American intellectuals for devising new institutional frameworks for economic cooperation with underdeveloped countries, even if the Cuban Revolution had not occurred.* But for several years the Cuban Revolution greatly increased the bargaining power of the governments of Latin America. And it probably impelled the United States government to play a more active role in Latin American domestic politics than it would otherwise have wanted to play. Indeed, its activities were probably a good deal more than many Latin Americans had bargained for.

The Cuban Revolution, and the innovations in United States policy that followed it, inaugurated a period in inter-American politics that was different in several respects from the one just examined. Since there was a fairly high probability that the Soviet Union would participate in future political conflicts in Latin America and that such conflicts would occur—owing in part to the

---

* Over the long run, the Cuban Revolution may have helped solidify support in Latin America for United States policies, lessening the demand for innovations, since it eventually threatened the stability of even progressive governments in Latin America and diminished the appeal of the Soviet Union as an alternative source of economic aid. See Ernst Halperin, "Why Castro Can't Be Neutral," *New Republic*, Nov. 27, 1961, pp. 11–13.

Cuban example—the United States government became considerably interested in preventing them, if possible, and in insulating them, where they occurred, from the influence of any group that might implicate the Soviet Union. It was therefore interested in forms of intergovernmental cooperation that would allow it to influence the ways Latin American political conflicts were controlled—and that meant, primarily, new programs of military and economic assistance. Further incentives to participate in new forms of economic assistance were the poor performance of Latin American economies and the growing belief that a cooperative attitude would elicit greater indigenous efforts to eliminate the obstacles to growth than a noncooperative one.

The extent of the changes in inter-American politics caused by the Cuban Revolution was probably exaggerated by many people at the time. This question will be discussed in Chapter 7. But first it is necessary to examine the ways in which the conflicts already analyzed have been influenced by domestic politics in the United States. There can be no question that domestic politics has had a powerful effect, but the nature and extent of the effect have been a matter of great controversy and are by no means easy to estimate.

Part II. Domestic Politics

3. United States Domestic Politics and Economic Policy Toward Latin America

There have been three persistent lines of criticism of United States foreign policy toward Latin America, all of which concentrate on the influence of the domestic political process. These criticisms allege that the national interest has been made subservient to the interests of United States businessmen here and abroad; that the government has failed to coordinate its many arms of policy to produce a coherent and desirable effect; and that the government has been unable to innovate policies and programs in time to forestall problems, and as a consequence has had to react hastily, and perhaps inappropriately, to crises.

Before the government's commercial and financial policies became important, the first criticism predominated. The entire unpleasant story of United States military intervention in Latin America is probably thought by most people who have any thoughts at all on the subject to be the result of the United States government's desire to serve the interests of American private investors, in spite of the number of scholarly studies that show this was not the case. It is less common to hear the policies of these early years of the century criticized for lack of coherence or for inconstancy (resulting from the inability to sustain public support or coordinate the government's efforts), although it is certainly possible in retrospect to make such criticisms.

These other criticisms became as important as the first, however, with the appearance of the Reciprocal Trade Agreements Program,

the Export-Import Bank, the technical assistance programs, and
other emergency economic measures developed during World
War II. In the early stages of these efforts one of Roosevelt's aides
complained, "the main 'headache' of our cooperation with South
America has been the faultiness of our internal mechanism—in
other words, the clash of personalities and the disagreements between the interested agencies of our Government."[1] It was in response to such difficulties that the Office of the Coordinator of
Inter-American Affairs was created. This agency was the seat of
most of the Roosevelt administration's ambitions to initiate programs of inter-American economic cooperation. The programs
were supposed to deal with basic, chronic problems as well as the
wartime emergency, but the agency was not conspicuously successful in these aims, and it finally disappeared without having
made a large or a permanent impact on United States policies. The
official history of this office explains that the office was formed
when the war seemed imminent, partly in preparation for meeting
that danger, and its long-range objectives were inevitably subor-
dinated to programs more directly concerned with the war emergency.[2] It should not have been surprising that the imperfections of
the political process in the United States would be given a large
share of the blame by those who were interested in doing something about the problems of Latin America.[3]

By the early 1950's, the conflicts between the United States
government and the governments of Latin America analyzed in
Chapter 2 had led to a renewed public debate in the United States
over what were appropriate policies. Criticisms were revived by
persons who had been active in Latin American affairs during the
Roosevelt years, Nelson Rockefeller and Adolf Berle, among others.[4] The mounting resentment of the United States in Latin America became a campaign issue in 1952. Nelson Rockefeller accused
the Truman administration of neglecting Latin America, and this
criticism was echoed by other Republicans, including John Foster
Dulles, who wrote about the subject before the Eisenhower administration was elected to office, and gave it considerable attention in his early weeks as Secretary of State.[5] It was widely assumed,

again, that the problem of policy making lay in the structure of United States government. As the *New York Times* said in an editorial on the subject:

> The difficulty could not be that Mr. Acheson has any less appreciation of the importance of Latin America to the United States than the others; it would be that the burden of his work forces him to choose those tasks he considers the most urgent, to the neglect of the others. If that is the case, then there ought to be a Secretary of Inter-American Affairs with Cabinet rank. The affairs of the hemisphere cannot be neglected, and the problems must be presented to Congress with authority and insistence. If that is not happening now—and it does not seem to be—then Mr. Rockefeller is correct in his general criticisms. . . . Many of the signposts in Latin America are pointing toward trouble. The next few years threaten to be exceptionally disturbing.[6]

The Eisenhower administration came into office with the apparent intention of raising the consideration of Latin America's problems to a higher level within the executive than it had held under President Truman. Eight years later, in the context of another presidential campaign and the Cuban Revolution, the program for supporting social change offered by the Eisenhower administration (which led to the Act of Bogotá) was criticized by Democrats in Congress as too little too late, and once again the organization of government, specifically the executive, was given a large share of the blame. Senator Mansfield, one of the more outspoken critics, said: "As I understand it, this [proposal] is the result of negotiations that have been carried on within our own government to a large extent for a number of years. . . . It has taken a long time, too long for a proposal of this nature."[7] His criticism of the Eisenhower administration's proposal was therefore accompanied by demands for reorganization of the executive:

> Regardless of the adequacy of our concepts with respect to these relations [i.e. with Latin America], regardless of our willingness to revamp our policies, we are not likely to do what needs to be done, given the present administrative structure for the conduct of these relations. Apart from a serious lack of outstanding citizens dedicated and skilled in inter-American affairs, we are seeking to act through a creaky, confused, and jumbled machinery of administration. . . . Policies are determined or influenced not only by the President and the Secretary of State, but also by various other sources of power in the executive branch . . . without adequate central control or direction.[8]

Thus the Eisenhower administration ended by being criticized for the same defects it had attributed to its predecessors.[9]

Characteristics of the American Political System

The above criticisms, and the many others like them that have been leveled at United States policies, are all directed at important characteristics of the American political system. Before the fairness of the criticisms can be assessed, it is necessary to describe these characteristics carefully, and see how they affect the formulation of foreign policies. There are two mutually supporting characteristics that are important for this analysis: the decentralization and fragmentation of political power in the United States; and a relative lack of differentiation between the political system and other aspects of society.[10]

The first of these, and its effects, has been most clearly summarized by Warner Schilling. He has described the policy-making structure as consisting of "an elite structure characterized by a large number of autonomous and competing groups; and a mass structure characterized by a small, informed stratum, attentive to elite discussions and conflict, and a much larger base normally ignorant of and indifferent to policy and policy-making."[11] From these general attributes Schilling infers that the conflict among elite groups may lead to stalemate—hence no policy at all—or to compromised, unstable, contradictory, or "paper" (i.e. unenforceable) policies. The policy-making process tends to be blind or directionless, slow, and indecisive. The policies made tend to persist until a crisis induces a change.[12]

These attributes of policy making, if they accurately describe the American political system, are the result of competition among independent individuals and groups who have to cooperate if they are to make decisions. But in creating a policy, more is necessary than just the decisions that officeholders make. These officeholders must obtain support for their policies from outside the government. At a minimum this support must include tax funds, votes for the officeholders, and a continuing supply of personnel to implement the policies. More is usually required, as for example, in the case of economic policies, the cooperation of bankers and private business-men in providing information and adjusting their activities to conform more closely to the goals of the political leaders.

The fragmentation of political power implies that outside sup-port is necessary not only for maintaining the decision-making sys-tem and implementing the policies but for enabling participants in the process of collective decision-making to withstand each other's influence to some extent. Conversely, by undermining, influencing, or overwhelming the support for one's institutional antagonist, it is possible to influence the terms on which he is willing to compro-mise. For example, a member of the Joint Chiefs of Staff who is dissatisfied with a presidential decision can attempt to modify it by appealing to a congressional committee, or to public opinion, thereby making it more difficult for the President to acquire the support he needs from these quarters without meeting some of the demands of the military.

This reliance on outside support in turn reinforces the decentral-ization and fragmentation of political power. Because of the de-centralized structure of government, the President cannot guaran-tee to all members of the bureaucracy or of his party in Congress all the support they need to carry out their tasks. This makes it difficult for him to control them, because they are required to find support where they can, often from people whose aims are opposed to those of the President. Their finding other support renders them still more capable of resisting the President's influ-ence and makes the President even less capable of guaranteeing them the requisite support.[13]

The same process helps reduce the extent to which the political system is differentiated from the rest of the social order in the United States. The autonomy of the political system is reduced at all levels as a result of the constant, competitive search for sup-port from outside it by all of its members. As mentioned before, because the President is unable to guarantee sufficient support to the bureaucracy, bureaucrats find it necessary to seek support else-where. As a result, the bureaucracy not only is resistant to presi-dential influence, but is divided within itself, making it more difficult to develop a career civil service with its own set of goals. Therefore the bureaucracy is staffed by people whose careers and orientations are developed as much outside it as within it, and it becomes difficult at times to distinguish the agency regulating a type of business activity, for example, from the businessmen being regulated.

Similar influences are at work in the party system. Because the party cannot guarantee adequate financial and campaign support to candidates, they are forced to seek it elsewhere. As a result it is difficult to distinguish politicians from their sources of support and political careers from other kinds of careers. Thus, with parties as with the bureaucracy, goals and orientations formed outside the political system find their way in, with very little modification in the process. The lower one descends in the system, the less differentiated is the polity from the society. But because of the fragmentation and decentralization of political power and because of the predominantly local base of most congressional political careers, political influences and orientations important at the "grass roots" can be extended directly to the highest levels of government. Thus political leaders' autonomy and the coherence of their goals are diminished because they are unable to control the terms on which the society will give them political support.

It is because of the relentless competitive quest for political support that the American political process is so open and such diverse interests are represented in it. Information of all sorts, favorable publicity, votes, campaign funds, manpower, and all other forms of support are, for each participant, so scarce that anyone who can provide some small amount is able to participate in the political process. But at the same time, so long as several groups must cooperate to make a political decision, few can be said to have truly large amounts of power. Where cooperation is not necessary, of course, groups may acquire vast power to be used essentially for their own ends. This possibility helps account for the penchant of politicians in the United States for dividing political issues into their component parts, which enables them to give everyone as much as possible of what he wants. This helps make the task of coordination more difficult. Where the subdivision of issues is not possible, inaction is the most likely result.[14]

Any political goal without a firm extra-political base of support of its own will tend to be de-emphasized by policy makers. This is a consequence of the nature of the American political process— one that has led many people to despair of the ability of the makers of foreign policy to acquire sufficient political resources to attain their goals without distorting them. Because foreign policy goals are collective goals rather than the goals of some specifiable group, they will tend to be short-changed. The Department of State has no domestic constituency; nor has the foreign aid program. Their budgets are therefore vulnerable to political opposition.[15] The Defense Department, on the other hand, by distributing its spending among key congressional constituencies and by developing reserve officer and veterans organizations to support the demands of the services for funds, has become a much more secure government department.[16]

These characteristics of the political system in the United States, which must be understood if one is to understand the decisions of the government, are all well documented. Whether they represent a complete description of the workings of the system is another matter. But they have been the basis for most criticisms of the way United States foreign policy has been made. And because these characteristics are well confirmed, the criticisms must be taken seriously.

Since many of those who participate in making foreign policy are more or less independent of each other and have conflicting views, it is possible that the government will undo with one hand what it is trying to do with the other, and it is likely that it will do nothing that departs from past decisions (usually compromises) until forced to do so, thereby sacrificing the advantages of prompt action. It also may fail to elicit adequate support for important goals or may purchase support at the price of seriously compromising them. Finally, because the process of policy making necessarily involves a great deal of public argument and incorporates many different ideas of the nature of the problems and of the national interest, the original intentions of an administration may be obscured, even to itself. It may thus mislead other governments, arouse unrealistic or dangerous expectations at home and abroad, and become the prisoner of domestic ideologies or parochial points of view.

In the case of policies concerning Latin America, such characteristics of the American political process may account for what many people consider political ineptitude, the failure to anticipate problems, the sensitivity of the government to the interests of businessmen in spite of the antagonism this arouses in Latin America, and the influence that both liberal and conservative ideologies have been able to exert on United States policies toward that area.

It is important to remember, however, that another effect of the nature of the political process in the United States is to make accusations like those above, and arguments like those of Nelson Rockefeller and Senator Mike Mansfield quoted earlier, part of the process of political influence that produces the policies. The political process may have corrupted the government's foreign policies; but it is equally possible that the same process has corrupted the judgment of those who make these allegations. The criticisms must be taken seriously, then, but they cannot be taken at face value without extremely careful scrutiny. But before scrutinizing these criticisms it is necessary to analyze independently, as I did in Chapter 1, what was attempted and what was possible. It will be necessary to return to that analysis later. First, it will be useful to specify how the above generalizations about United States politics apply to economic policies toward Latin America.

Economic Policies: The Fragmentation of Power

Decisions about economic issues that were of concern to the countries of Latin America required a perspective encompassing such diverse agencies and programs of the United States government as foreign aid, both financial and technical, the Export-Import Bank, the international lending agencies of which the United States was a member, government purchasing programs such as the stockpile, and the several institutional components of policies concerning import restrictions and commodity agreements. Though all of these could be considered part of a single system for allocating resources to Latin America, each agency or program was also involved in other allocation systems that had other goals, many of them domestic ones. Even though within each system the gains and losses that might result from any given change could be readily seen, it was difficult to estimate the relative importance of the goals of the different systems.[17]

Technical assistance, for example, was meant to be part of comprehensive economic development programs; this required some coordination with the main sources of capital assistance, namely the Export-Import Bank of the United States and the World Bank, both of which were outside the foreign aid program. Beginning in 1951, the technical assistance program began to be progressively integrated into the foreign aid agency (then called the Mutual Security Administration). This may have raised the prospect that technical assistance would be part of a comprehensive economic development program in any country receiving grant aid. But it did not serve to connect technical assistance more closely to the main sources of capital in Latin America. Some people feared that the reorganization would mean that technical assistance would have to compete more directly with other parts of the foreign aid program for tax funds and would hence be affected both by the increasing use of aid for strictly military purposes and by the increasing pressures to discontinue the foreign aid program entirely.[18]

The World Bank, of course, had its own resources and criteria for allocating funds, which were subject only to marginal influence by the United States government. The Export-Import Bank competed with the World Bank, and it was necessary to coordinate the activities of the United States agency with those of the international one in order to ensure that the former did not interfere with the objectives of the latter.[19] The Export-Import Bank represented a drain on the United States Treasury, since it acquired its funds by borrowing from the Treasury, within statutory limits. It had close ties with Congress, where it was quite popular. Congress probably reflected to a certain extent the interests of United States exporters and United States producers of commodities for use at home and abroad that competed with Latin American products. Both of these groups had an interest in the use of the Export-Import Bank's funds. It seems clear that the bank's lending policies were affected by all these influences.[20]

Decisions about import restrictions were made within the authority of the reciprocal trade agreements program that had been initiated in 1933. The basic legislation supporting this program was steadily undermined as changes were made in the international goals the program was supposed to serve and Congress threatened to act to protect United States producers hurt by imports.[21] Since World War II, the continuity of the program has been secured only at the price of compromising with many of the interests affected by it. By prescribing the administrative procedures and by keeping the program on a fairly short legislative leash, Congress has been able to maintain considerable influence over its operation.[22]

The government stockpile was primarily designed to ensure the supply of raw materials necessary to national defense against disruptions in normal lines of supply in time of war. Yet the same objective could have been reached by other means, for example, by giving preference to domestic rather than foreign sources of supply during peacetime, in order to preserve a lively domestic industry, or by doing the opposite, in order to preserve scarce natural resources. Furthermore, because the reliability of foreign sources of supply may be affected by relations with other governments, and because commodity policies may affect such relations, it might have been in the interest of the United States government to take the preferences of other governments into account in managing the stockpile and its other commercial policies.[23]

Two questions have thus arisen about the stockpiling of commodities in the United States. First, to what extent should the desire of American producers for high and stable prices be satisfied? Second, to what extent should the interests of foreign producers and their governments be taken into account? Both questions are related to decisions about import restrictions. For if the market for commodities could be supported by government purchases, then import restrictions could be lessened.

The history of the basic stockpile legislation showed that Congress intended the stockpile to serve the interests of domestic producers.[24] And the Department of the Interior could be expected to provide some support within the executive branch for congressional interests. The State Department, however, was able to make claims for foreign interests mainly when there was a clear threat of a crisis in relations with another country.[25]

As time passed, more institutions became involved in decisions relevant to Latin America. The foreign aid program began to be more active, especially after the Development Loan Fund was created. The Inter-American Development Bank added a new international institution that had to be taken account of. And the decision to dispose of commodity surpluses by transforming them into foreign aid in kind brought in the Department of Agriculture.

The problem of coordinating United States policies toward Latin America was clearly severe. One of the most important instruments of coordination in the United States government is the annual budget, which provides a regular occasion when many agencies of government compete for funds. But it should be obvious from the above description that many components of foreign economic policies are outside the budget; therefore coordination is accomplished through *ad hoc* procedures. The nature of the circumstances that prompt a review of policy helps determine the weight given to the views of the participants in the decision-making process. But unless these circumstances elicit the interest of the President, they are not likely to lead to an effective review. As a study published in 1955 said:

Foreign economic policy can, at best, be brought into manageable "chunks" of related functions. . . . But, it is apparently impossible to give a comprehensive span of policy and administrative control—such as would be involved in the unification of all foreign economic policy—to any person short of the President.[26]

Clearly, then, if there is any countervailing influence to be found to the fissiparous tendencies of the American political process, it must come from the President.

The process by which United States economic policies toward Latin America were formulated seems to have been characterized by the same fragmentation of power and difficulty of achieving a set of political goals insulated from the demands of private groups that characterize the rest of American politics. In the next three chapters I will be concerned with whether the effects of these attributes have been the ones alleged by most critics of United States policies.

Politics and Policy: Basic Questions

The international environment in which the major postwar decisions affecting the countries of Latin America have been made has been described above. Some of the decisions themselves will now be scrutinized in order to discover the motions made by the internal mechanism of government. The following three questions about these decisions are derived from the generalizations just offered about the political process in the United States. (1) How successfully did the United States government maintain some overall conception of the relation between what it was doing in Latin America and what was in its best interest to do, and how well did it manage to coordinate its efforts within the framework of policies once they were decided? (2) By what means did the government acquire sufficient domestic support to maintain its policies, and to what extent were the policies corrupted by the process of gaining support for them? (3) How successfully did the government anticipate problems and devise new programs and policies to cope with them?

Although these questions are distinct, in any concrete case any procedure will serve more than one of the purposes they imply. For example, the government will attempt to build support for its policies at the same time that it is reviewing them; and it may find simultaneously that it cannot maintain an acceptable relation between means and ends within the established framework of policy and so be moved to invent new policies and new institutions to administer them. Nonetheless, the distinctions are important, for the government may do one task well while failing at another; and an imperfect performance of one task may be justified by the need to perform another, more important one, at the same time.

The distinction between performance within a framework of policies and the innovation of a new framework of policies is of considerable importance, and it merits some elaboration. It is an instance of the distinction between institutionalized and non-institutionalized political power.[27] The notion of institutionalization is difficult to speak about precisely, but it is enough for my purposes to say that it refers to a relation among political goals, the environment that political leaders hope to influence, the organization of tasks among political leaders, and the provision of support necessary to maintain the leadership and to pursue the goals decided on. Political leadership may be said to be institutionalized when its internal organization is stable, complex, and routinized, and when the requisite external support is diverse, and provided by a stable, routinized process.

In order to achieve and maintain such a state, the political leadership must successfully pursue a set of goals acceptable to its sources of support (although it may pursue its own goals at the same time). The main threats to its ability to do this will come from changes in its environment that make it impossible to achieve its goals by the established methods, or changes in its sources of support that, for one reason or another, make support less available. The leadership has two main defenses against such threats. The first is its own adaptability in devising new sets of goals and appealing to new sources of support. This ability is influenced by its own pattern of organization. The second is the availability of generalized support, which can be used in a flexible fashion.[28] These last two qualities are themselves the result of the successful institutionalization of political leadership. Institutionalization, then, is a cumulative process, with each successful effort to overcome external stress leaving the leadership in a better position to overcome such stress in the future.

As institutions become more adaptable, one may expect that the difference between decisions made within an established set of policies and decisions to innovate policies requiring new forms of organization and new types of external support will diminish. Even so, it is clearly unrealistic as a rule to expect the same level of performance in both types of situation. Policies that require the creation of new institutional forms will involve more direct bargaining between the leadership and its sources of support and some confusion as a result of internal reorganization and the need to clarify and refine the new goals. They will be resisted for a time, because of the investment that has been made in established institutions. One may compare the capacities of two political systems to create new institutional forms or their performances within the context of established policies. But it is not very informative to compare decisions in one system that require institutional reform with decisions in another that do not. For whether or not decisions require institutional change will be partly determined by the novelty of the problems they deal with, and that is not determined by the institutions.

Rapid transformations in the international environment have required a high rate of institutional innovation in the United States since the end of World War II. And new foreign policy goals have required more domestic support, and a greater variety of support, than had ever been required before. In the case of foreign economic policies, these requirements have been accompanied by considerable controversy about both the ends that should be pursued and the efficacy of various means to those ends. Therefore the most important questions about the effects of the domestic political process on the United States government's policies toward Latin America up to the Alliance for Progress concern the way new goals were developed and institutions were adapted to implement them.

4. Coordination and Review of United States Latin American Policy

About the time of the Korean War, the United States government began to pay more serious attention to the way it was allocating its resources among the various claims made on them by the cold war. As President Truman said at the time:

Certain choices have to be made—hard choices based on the best judgment we can bring to bear—as to how we shall allocate our great but limited resources between use at home and use abroad, between use in various areas of the world, and between various types of programs designed primarily to strengthen our defenses, strengthen the free world economies, or strengthen the political and social forces that are working generally for the preservation and extension of freedom. . . . The questions that arise concern mainly the relationship of the Mutual Security Program to our over-all political, military, and economic policies; the magnitude of the Program; the proper balance between military, economic and technical assistance; the proper emphasis of effort by geographic area; and the choices involved between the relatively short-term results and the relatively long-term results that we are seeking.[1]

The adequacy of the procedures for making these choices has been questioned ever since.

At times the choices were made particularly with regard to Latin America; and at other times they affected Latin America indirectly. In the reviews of policy that accompanied the development of the Mutual Security Program, at the time President Truman's statement was made, the attention of the government was focused on other parts of the world—southern Asia, for example. The value it placed on economic development in these areas increased greatly at the time of the Korean War compared to the value it placed on development in Latin America. But before it made this evaluation, the government had already decided that the productivity of public funds spent in Latin America, measured in terms of economic development, was rather low compared to that of private funds. In other parts of the world, these conditions were reversed.[2]

The distinction between value judgments and estimates of the productivity of various forms of economic assistance is important in assessing the merits of the claim that the United States government paid insufficient attention to the countries of Latin America during the Truman administration and the first Eisenhower administration. Charles Wolf has said:

It is probably a reasonable assumption that in the case of foreign aid, as in most other government programs, Congress tends to concern itself more with the "higher-level" value judgments than with the "lower-level" productivity judgments: more with the desirability of A, B, C . . . as effects or consequences of proposed government programs, than with their physical effects.[3]

The same is undoubtedly true of public controversies about United States policies toward Latin America.

It is difficult to estimate the relative importance of these value judgments compared to judgments about productivity in decisions about allocating aid to Latin America. Both clearly were important in the report on foreign economic policies prepared by Gordon Gray in 1950, and the recommendations of this report were influential in the administration's planning for the Mutual Security Program in 1951. The Gray report said that "private investment should be considered as the most desirable means of providing capital and its scope should be widened as far as possible."[4] It recommended new forms of public economic assistance for India, Pakistan, and Southeast Asia, but none for Latin America.[5] As Thomas Cabot, Director of International Security Affairs in the Department of State, stated in hearings on the proposed Mutual Security Program, it was necessary to consider all possible sources of aid, and compare them with all possible claims on it, in order to achieve the "minimum net demand on our own wealth."[6] He went on to say that

in some areas, development capital is available from local sources, from outside private investment, or from public lending institutions, such as the Export-Import Bank and the International Bank. In those countries the form of organization [i.e. the kind of United States agency] required is one which can lay out jointly with the country authorities an effective economic development program and can then supply the essential ingredient of technical know-how.[7]

That was what the technical assistance program was supposed to accomplish. Since technical assistance programs were already functioning in Latin America, no changes in existing plans for that area were considered necessary or desirable.

From 1951 on, the pressure of events in other parts of the world on increasingly scarce foreign aid funds was undoubtedly added to the other reasons I have mentioned for pursuing limited, orthodox economic objectives in Latin America. Departures from these policies would have required the leadership of the President. The use of foreign aid funds in support of political objectives, for example, would have required modifications in the principles for economizing on the use of public funds, in which the Treasury took a keen interest, and an attempt to muster sufficient political support for increased foreign aid appropriations. Thus the procedures the United States government followed in reviewing the policies it had adopted around 1950 were of some importance, for the burdens on them were great.

The First Eisenhower Review

In 1953 the new Republican administration undertook a major review of economic policies toward Latin America, spurred by the President's wish to take a fresh look at foreign policy in general, the end of the Marshall Plan, the end of the Korean War, and the congressional attack on existing reciprocal trade agreements legislation.[8] Many administrators and Congressmen alike expected that with the end of the Korean War and the completion of the Marshall Plan the entire foreign aid program would come to an end as well.[9] If this were not to happen, then support for continuing special assistance programs had to be sought. Furthermore, there had been controversy over the adequacy of the government's policies toward Latin America. This, together with the Guatemala affair, provided yet another incentive for a review of policy.

Even if the previous administration had had greater resources to devote to the economic development of Latin America, it would not have wanted to do much more than it did. But if it had wanted to pursue less orthodox economic objectives, it would have been prevented from doing so until the end of the Marshall Plan and the Korean War by these more pressing demands. By about 1953, these pressures were relieved, and expectations of innovation in United States economic policies were increased by the Guatemala affair and the demands of Latin American governments presented at Caracas and Rio de Janeiro, which were received sympathetically by many opinion leaders in the United States.

Before examining the process followed by the United States government in choosing among the alternatives presented to it by these new developments, it is important to notice that signs that the government was reconsidering its policies helped arouse expectations that changes would be made. During the presidential campaign of 1952, the Republicans freely criticized the Truman administration for paying inadequate attention to the problems of Latin America. In the hearings on his nomination as Secretary of State, and in his first major speech in that office, John Foster Dulles returned to this theme.[10] When, in the face of all this, the Eisenhower administration changed policies hardly at all and constantly emphasized the limitations under which it would operate, it brought serious criticism on itself, perhaps more than it deserved. Both the criticisms of past policies and the argument that change was prevented by more urgent domestic objectives were partly the result of the search for political support. The criticisms were the product of the contest for the presidency. The emphasis on competing domestic objectives was partly the product of seeking political support once that office had been won.

The members of the first Eisenhower administration were intent on reducing the amount of competition between foreign policy and domestic objectives (especially private domestic objectives). But this goal was actually pursued much more intently by Congress than by the executive. Moreover, the administration's need to appeal to its supporters in Congress helped shape the language that was used to describe and justify its policies.

The most comprehensive review of foreign economic policies was made by the Commission on Foreign Economic Policies, otherwise known as the Randall Commission. The commission was proposed by the President and was authorized by Congress in action renewing the trade agreements legislation provisionally, for one year. Its purposes were first, to build congressional support for the President's trade program, especially among the isolationist members of the President's own party, and second, to review the whole range of foreign economic policies.

The character of the political context in which the commission did its work required that foreign economic policies be made compatible with the domestic interests represented by several members of the commission. Randall hoped to persuade enough of these isolationist members to support his final recommendations to be able to split the forces of the isolationists in Congress.[11] As a result of this effort to compromise, the commission left the impression that it had barely considered foreign policy problems at all.[12] In attempting to strike a balance between foreign and domestic claims on the government's resources, it had defined foreign policy in strictly economic terms, assigned the use of public aid funds and the manipulation of world markets to objectives directly related to national defense, and shifted the burden of dealing with any remaining problems onto the private sector of the economy.[13] To many people, this method seemed more likely to satisfy domestic objectives than foreign policy ones.

Was this a fair assessment of the implications of the commission's findings? Was it true specifically with regard to Latin America? To determine the answers to these questions, it is necessary to examine another review of policies toward Latin America that took place at the same time. This review proceeded through two stages, the first managed by Dr. Milton Eisenhower, and the second managed from within the government, under the stimulus of the Guatemala affair and the economic demands made at Caracas and Rio de Janeiro.

By 1953, earlier optimism about the future demand for Latin America's exports was being replaced by doubts, especially among Latin Americans. This was the problem on which attention was focused in the United States government. "We soon decided," Dr. Eisenhower has since written, "that the great economic problem which dominated all others was that of the changing relationship between raw commodity prices and the prices of industrial goods."[14] His study group concentrated on finding "general methods to speed orthodox economic assistance."[15] The final report included a tentative suggestion that the government stockpile be used to support the prices of some commodities, but most members of the Eisenhower administration obviously thought this method less desirable than the indirect method of compensatory financial assistance.[16]

The domestic political milieu in 1953 was undoubtedly enough to prevent any more direct attack on Latin America's commodity problems than this. The Randall Commission's report opposed even the limited use of buffer stocks that was suggested in Dr. Eisenhower's report.[17] But there were other reasons why the government did not use this method of assistance. There were many conflicts of interest between the United States government and Latin American governments over the purposes for which aid was to be used. Financial assistance provided a better means of negotiating about such conflicts than did the management of commodity markets. Furthermore, the extent and probable duration of Latin America's commodity problems were still not well established.

The possibility of using economic assistance for any purpose other than promoting industrialization over the long run seems not to have been contemplated. Dr. Eisenhower has written of his trip to Latin America in 1953:

I want to emphasize as strongly as I can that both United States and Latin American leaders were then thinking solely in terms of orthodox economic aid to Latin America as the solution to perplexing problems. By the end of the trip I personally had become painfully aware of the need for social reform. . . . But except for an uneasiness and a feeling of compassion, I did not relate this to what we were doing and should do officially, except to hope that our efforts might aid countries to improve production and thus provide funds for internal social development. Certainly instigating internal social change did not seem to be the responsibility of the United States.[18]

But there were even difficult questions about the terms on which direct financial assistance should be offered, and this complication postponed any increase in the flow of aid. Furthermore, these difficulties at the level of intergovernmental relations were made harder to resolve by the desire of the Eisenhower administration to reduce governmental expenditures.

The Truman administration's conception of the United States' interests in Latin America implied that the Export-Import Bank, the World Bank, and private investment ought to provide sufficient foreign capital for Latin America. The Eisenhower administration, by attempting to reduce governmental expenditures, endangered the existence of the Export-Import Bank's future as an independent lending institution. Those officials responsible for policies toward Latin America had to resist the desire of Secretary of the Treasury George Humphrey to bring the bank under his control at least partly in order to curtail its activities.[19] In his report to the President, Dr. Eisenhower recommended that the Export-Import Bank continue its independent role, if necessary by acquiring funds from the private capital market rather than by borrowing from the Treasury.[20] The Randall report provided further support for the existing role of the Export-Import Bank, and the Guatemala affair and the conference on economic problems at Rio de Janeiro added reinforcement.

Except for recommendations that the stockpile program be used for price stabilization and that surplus foods be given "in very unusual circumstances," very little in Dr. Eisenhower's report could be regarded as innovative.[21] Significantly, however, the report acknowledged that existing policies and programs, such as the Export-Import Bank loans and the policy of seeking lower trade barriers for Latin American exports, were threatened.

Between the Caracas conference and the conference on economic problems at Rio de Janeiro in November 1954, President Eisenhower adopted the Randall Commission report as the basic framework for his foreign economic policies. A special review of the government's policies toward Latin America was begun in April 1954 in preparation for the economic conference at Rio. It was managed by Henry Holland, the Assistant Secretary of State for Latin American Affairs. Under his chairmanship, a sub-Cabinet committee met twice a week to review policies and make recommendations. Its work was completed in August.[22] By November, when the conference convened, the basic framework of the administration's policies toward Latin America had been fixed.

Three main forms of assistance had been demanded by Latin American governments since World War II: stable commodity prices, low United States tariffs, and more financial aid for economic development.[23] The United States government was prepared to deal with the first problem only through the government stockpile.[24] A special Cabinet committee on mineral policy had recommended an increase in government stockpiling to support the prices of some minerals.* With regard to the second demand, the government was not willing to lower its tariffs unilaterally, even though it admitted that the problem some Latin American countries faced was a result of "almost continuous threats of tariff increases or other restrictions" on a number of important commodities, including petroleum, lead, and zinc. A government official recommended that some other means of protecting American pro-

* An administration official reported: "The President has announced the initiation of a new 'long-term' stockpiling program and has directed the Office of Defense Mobilization to review objectives for 35 to 40 minerals. . . . In acquiring metals and minerals under this new security program, preference will be given to newly mined metals and minerals of domestic origin. The program will, nevertheless, have indirect benefits to the mining industries of other areas, including Latin America. To the degree that the U.S. government buys and stockpiles domestic materials, these materials will be withheld from exerting a generally depressing effect on world commodity markets." Department of State, *Bulletin*, XXI (July 19, 1954), 81.

ducers be found besides tariffs,[25] but one of the most useful ways of doing this—giving direct compensatory financial aid to communities or firms to enable them to adjust to competition—had been explicitly rejected by the Randall Commission.[26] And the administration, needing congressional support for its trade legislation, was hardly in a position to resist demands for protection.

In late October 1954, the United States government announced a concession designed to cope with the third Latin American demand, that of increased financial aid. Assistant Secretary Holland reported that the United States would expand the activities of the Export-Import Bank. "Through it we shall do our utmost to satisfy all applications for economic development loans that fulfill certain sound and logical standards. . . . After thoughtful consideration, we believe that the bank's capacity is and will continue to be adequate fully to support this policy. In reaching this conclusion we are entirely aware that this policy implies a substantial increase in the bank's activities."[27] In early November the administration announced a further concession: it would support the creation of an International Finance Corporation (as an affiliate of the World Bank) to directly assist private enterprise in underdeveloped countries. It was hoped that these two concessions would offset demands for a new regional bank at the forthcoming conference in Rio.[28]

These decisions were the outcome of heated debates within the administration. There were newspaper reports that John Moors Cabot, who resigned as Assistant Secretary of State for Latin American Affairs, had done so because of the controversies over economic assistance to Latin America.[29] As his successor Henry Holland said of the basic decisions that finally emerged, they were "a compromise between the sincere convictions of those within our Government who would not have gone so far and those who would have gone farther."[30]

This compromise was made without any objective certainty about the problems that lay ahead. In its public statements, the administration expressed optimism about the economic future of Latin America; but the economic forecasts contained in a report prepared by the Foreign Operations Administration (the foreign aid agency) were much more pessimistic. The report said, for example:

For Latin America, faced with an annual population rate of growth of 2.5 percent, the fundamental problem is to expand output at a faster rate than population growth if a higher standard of living for the people is to be achieved. During 1953, the very rapid rate of economic growth experienced in the region after World War II declined. . . . There was less than a one percent increase in the per capita gross product, which was almost entirely due to the favorable terms of trade.[31]

During the same year private investment in Latin America dropped considerably, and Latin America's mining output declined owing to "adverse effects stemming from a decline in world prices and demand."[32]

The report was not optimistic about the prospects for increasing the flow of capital to Latin America in the future. It concluded that "although more effective use of the resources of the International Bank and the Export-Import Bank could probably be made, the volume of operations of these institutions is not likely to affect substantially the outlook for foreign investment in Latin America in the future."[33] Barring any major innovations that might increase the quantity of development capital available, the countries of Latin America would have to depend primarily on domestic savings and foreign private investment. Yet the report concluded that because of political obstacles neither of these sources looked promising.[34]

Such investment will increase only to the extent to which the Latin American governments, by their policies and administrative actions, succeed in creating a climate favorable to foreign investment. The United States Investment Guaranty Program has not proven particularly suited to Latin America because of historical and psychological considerations. Lacking a substantial improvement in the climate for international investment, capital from foreign private sources and existing international lending institutions will probably not provide more than the recent average of 5–10 percent of Latin America's total investment.[35]

The report concluded that "an enormous gap" existed "between the needs and the resources available to fill the needs,"[36] and because sufficient outside help would not be forthcoming, the gap could be filled only by mobilizing resources within Latin America. How was that to be accomplished? Obviously a fundamental requirement was political stability.[37] It was also fairly obvious that "the political climate in many of the countries is influenced greatly by the economic conditions existing there." The report described the situation as follows:

> While economic considerations may not by themselves determine the complexion of the government in Latin America, any government unlucky enough to become saddled with responsibility or blame for an economic disaster or chaos, more severe and damaging than the normal economic crises many Latin American governments are habitually faced with, . . . pays the price for its failure by . . . a palace revolution or a "coup d'état."[38]

Thus political stability and strong governments were necessary for economic development; yet without healthy economies, governments would be undermined. The report did not resolve this dilemma. One might reason that more foreign aid would help to stabilize Latin American governments by enabling them to undertake essential domestic measures; or that foreign aid would be of little use until political conditions improved, and that offering it prematurely would remove a useful incentive for reform. The conclusion to be drawn depended not only on prejudice and ideology but on the intentions and capabilities of the government concerned. Would governments favored by increased economic aid be able to do their part in maintaining their stability? It was not obvious that many could. Just as the United States government was prevented by domestic political pressures from granting Latin America all the economic assistance it needed, Latin American governments were constrained by their internal political difficulties from taking steps to control inflation, stimulate industrialization, and do the other things the United States government considered necessary for accelerating their economic development. Unfortunately, awareness of the constraints on Latin American governments diminished the United States government's incentives to overcome the constraints on its own actions.[39]

It was still possible in 1954 for policy makers to believe either that the economic future of Latin America (whose performance had recently been comparatively favorable) would prove quite acceptable; or that the problems were so deep-seated that there was little the United States government could do to correct them. In short, if one were to advocate radical changes in policy, it was necessary to be able confidently to predict an economic and political crisis in Latin America and at the same time to be convinced that it could be prevented.

Execution of the basic decisions made in 1954 presented difficult problems of coordination. The management of the stockpile and the use of other forms of special assistance to United States producers in a way that would support the market for Latin American minerals and avoid demands for import restrictions required the intrusion of foreign policy considerations into a process of coordination that was weighted in favor of domestic interests. Interdepartmental committees, such as the Trade Policy Committee (chaired by the Department of Commerce) and the Council on Foreign Economic Policy (chaired by the President's Special Assistant for Foreign Economic Policy), were charged with this function.[40] But the main burden of the staff work fell on individual departments that had close connections with domestic interests; and therefore the initiative in making policy remained with them.[41]

Similarly the administration was able for a time to meet its commitment not to increase import restrictions primarily because it was able to elicit support from several kinds of private producing groups in the United States. Lead and zinc producers, for example, agreed to the use of the government stockpile to support the prices of those commodities.[42] And agricultural groups approved a program to barter surplus agricultural commodities for strategic materials produced abroad, which would be placed in a supplemental stockpile.[43] By 1957, however, the limits of the stockpile's capacity for such use had been reached, and support for the supplemental stockpile had begun to diminish.[44] At that point the limitations of the process of coordinating decisions began to be apparent. For the administration first supported the efforts of the lead and zinc industries to persuade Congress to limit imports of those commodities, and only after Democrats in Congress balked at this, switched to support for a direct subsidy to the mining industry as a way of avoiding import restrictions.[45] The latter proposal seems to have been the fruit of the efforts of Douglas Dillon to improve the co-ordination of economic policies with foreign policy objectives.[46] It failed to pass Congress, however, and the administration then set quotas on the importation of lead and zinc.[47] Restrictions on oil imports were also avoided by the administration for several years, but in this case it was the blockage of the Suez Canal in 1956 rather than the government's ingenuity that was responsible for the delay.[48] In 1957 the President initiated a system of voluntary quotas for crude oil imports; the quotas were made compulsory in 1959.

The execution of the decision to expand the role of the Export-Import Bank, on the other hand, required improvement in the planning of projects by Latin Americans. As Randolph Burgess, deputy to the Secretary of the Treasury, admitted in 1954 when an expansion of the bank's activities was being discussed: "In practice, the real limit on lending by this institution is not its legal authority. The limitations are rather in the quality of the loans, to make sure that they are in the interests of both the American exporter or importer and the foreign borrower."[49] In order to remove this sort of obstacle to increased lending, it was necessary to bring the influence of the United States government to bear on the planning of projects for which loans were requested. This required in turn both a change in the decision-making mechanism of the United States government (to improve the coordination of the Export-Import Bank's activities with the foreign aid program) and the development of new procedures by which the United States government might share in economic planning in Latin America.

But at this very time the United States government was liquidating one of the primary means for joint planning—the Joint Brazil–United States Economic Development Commission. This clearly made it difficult to implement the promised expansion of Export-Import Bank loans to Latin America. Assistant Secretary Holland testified in 1956: "If we make more money available for loans, we would not increase the volume of our loans. The money that the

Export-Import Bank has available to lend today very substantially exceeds the aggregate of all applications on hand."[50] A more direct United States role in the planning of applications would probably have increased their number.

The Second Eisenhower Review

The next major occasion for comparing what the United States government was doing in Latin America with what would best serve its interests as it saw them was the controversy over what was referred to as the "Sino-Soviet economic offensive" and the adequacy of the United States' response.* Little attention was given to Latin America in this debate, but two studies commissioned by the Senate Special Committee to Study the Foreign Aid Program did deal with Latin America. They tended to support the administration's earlier view that no major innovations were required.[51] It is true that a study of Central America prepared for the Senate Foreign Relations Committee contended that the United States was not doing enough there, but this contention was not supported by any very specific recommendations and did not present a very convincing argument for change.[52]

In 1957, then, there was still agreement among many people both in the government and outside it that any improvement in economic conditions in Latin America would come through existing orthodox methods, chief among them foreign private investment.[53] A report prepared by the Center for International Affairs at the Massachusetts Institute of Technology, however, implied the need for a change in the government's foreign aid policies without explicitly mentioning Latin America. It said:

Where bottlenecks are numerous and the difficulties great, a feeling of hopelessness and resignation may prevail. The removal of one bottleneck, capital shortage, and the contribution of technical assistance may overcome apathy and release new hope and energy. Realization of in-

---

* "Sino-Soviet economic offensive" was a phrase frequently used to refer to the increased emphasis that Soviet foreign policy, under Khrushchev, was placing on relations with underdeveloped countries and on the use of economic assistance and special commercial arrangements as means of fostering those relations.

adequacies in the domestic effort may then be a stimulus to action. Aid should be made conditional on and synchronized with agreed-upon targets of domestic performance. It is neither necessary nor useful to say: "You perform first, then aid will follow."[54]

Yet this is of course precisely what the United States government had been saying to the governments of Latin America all along.

The relevance of this recommendation to relations with Latin America was not discussed when it was made. The debate on the aid program concentrated on how to provide capital to some underdeveloped countries on more lenient terms rather than on how to improve joint planning, which the Eisenhower administration was not enthusiastic about. But it presaged innovations that were to come.

At the same time, the manner in which economic policies, foreign and domestic, were coordinated in the executive branch was subjected to critical scrutiny.[55] The Senate Special Committee to Study the Foreign Aid Program and the Senate Foreign Relations Committee both urged that the role of the Department of State in developing foreign economic policies be strengthened.[56] Partly as a result, the Secretary of State, by executive order of the President, was given more coordinating power over the aid program. In practice, this power was exercised by the Deputy Under Secretary of State for Economic Affairs, Douglas Dillon, who began to participate in a series of reviews of economic policy that were to have great significance for the countries of Latin America.[57]

In the years between the first and second comprehensive reviews of United States policies toward Latin America by the Eisenhower administration, there were several attempts from within the administration to reconsider various elements of its policies. Dr. Milton Eisenhower has written that as early as the winter of 1956–57, at a meeting of presidential representatives of the OAS, he attempted to persuade officials of the United States Treasury to alter their opposition to an inter-American bank.[58] There also was growing interest within the administration in using United States aid funds to support welfare projects, such as public housing, in Latin America.[59] Finally, as the evidence of serious economic difficulties in Latin America began to mount in 1957 and 1958, and as the administration's efforts to avoid further restrictions on Latin American imports began to fail, there was renewed interest in some form of direct attack on Latin America's commodity problems.[60]

Interest in social reform measures in Latin America provided the main stimulus for the next ad hoc review of United States policies organized by Dr. Eisenhower.[61] Trips to Mexico in August 1957 and to Central America in the summer of 1958 accompanied this review. The second Eisenhower report reached the President in December 1958 and was published in January 1959. It was delayed in reaching the President by disputes within the administration about the use of foreign aid funds to support public welfare programs.[62]

By the time this report had been completed, the administration had already announced its willingness to help establish an inter-American bank. The report recommended that the new bank be used to foster a closer connection between the planning of projects and the provision of funds, and that the United States government again attempt joint economic planning with Latin American countries. The report failed to recommend a major departure in the financing of public housing in Latin America (this had been successfully opposed by the Treasury). It did, however, recommend supporting the creation of common markets in Latin America. Little else in the report was new.[63]

Despite the lack of progress, interest in supporting social reform did not die, and early in 1960 a group of State Department officials began seriously to consider some proposals.[64] Their discussions finally resulted in the Act of Bogotá in the fall of 1960. The Kennedy administration accepted the Act of Bogotá, but, like the first Eisenhower administration, was interested in taking its own look at the whole range of policies toward Latin America.*

* This was organized primarily by a task force appointed by President Kennedy and was headed by Adolf Berle. Berle's role in policy making led to some tension with the Department of State and made it difficult to find an Assistant Secretary of State for Latin American Affairs. *New York Times*, 1961: May 21, p. 12; June 23, p. 8; July 24, p. 1. See also Arthur Schlesinger, Jr., *A Thousand Days* (Boston: Houghton Mifflin, 1965), pp. 186–205.

The Role of Congress

In the meantime, reviews of policy in the executive branch had been accompanied by increasingly critical examinations of policy by congressional committees, especially the Senate Foreign Relations Committee. When the Eisenhower administration introduced the proposals for social development which led to the Act of Bogotá in the summer of 1960, Democrats in Congress accused it of having long rejected similar programs urged on it by the Congress. This charge is not borne out by the record. Criticism of policy proceeded at about the same pace in Congress as within the executive branch.

In 1954 congressional interest in Latin America was largely concentrated in the Senate Banking and Currency Committee.[65] The questions asked by members of the Senate Foreign Relations Committee were tentative and not well informed.[66] During the next three years, the most vocal champion of the Latin American countries in Congress was Senator Smathers of Florida. He eventually succeeded in persuading the Senate Foreign Relations Committee to add to the foreign aid bill, over the protests of the administration, a small amount of money to be used for economic development and social reform in Latin America. This special provision, called "the Smathers amendment," was first added to the foreign aid bill in 1956. Although the administration had at first opposed the amendment, it later admitted that the funds had been useful.[67] Eventually the administration made $15 million in loans and grants available for such projects as an anti-malaria campaign in Panama, a children's hospital in Costa Rica, resettlement of Indians in Peru, and agricultural research by the OAS.[68]

With the creation of the Development Loan Fund in 1957, the efforts of Smathers to extend these small programs were merged with and eventually replaced by the efforts of a number of Congressmen to see that funds from the DLF were available for use in Latin America.[69] These efforts began with the creation of the fund itself. The Senate Foreign Relations Committee report on the bill that created the fund said:

The Committee wishes to stress its understanding that every consideration will be given to Latin America in the use of the fund. It emphasizes
that the resources of the fund, where appropriate, will be made available for Latin America notwithstanding the special provision of $25
million for assistance to that region contained in section 8(a) of this
bill.[70]

This provision was in part the result of some concern over the difficulties the government was expected to face at an economic conference scheduled to be held at Buenos Aires in 1957.[71] Although
the administration continued to emphasize that there was little
need for the type of loans that the new fund was to provide in
Latin America, in the next year or two it began to change its position.

Senator Wayne Morse soon became the chief congressional
critic of United States policies in Latin America. Morse combined
a desire to promote democracy in Latin America with a critical
attitude toward the military assistance program and a suspicious
one regarding the relationship between the government and American businessmen in Latin America. It was largely as a result of
his efforts that most of the criticism of United States policies between 1957 and the Act of Bogotá that occupied the attention of
the Senate Foreign Relations Committee concerned the size of
the military assistance program.[72] As Morse later said, "there are
many causes for the deterioration of American–Latin American
relations; but, in my judgment, the most important cause—the
major one, the one at the head of the list—is American military aid
to Latin America."[73] As a result of the criticisms of Morse and a
number of other Senators, notably Frank Church, the administration became increasingly defensive about the political effects of
military assistance to Latin America.

From about 1957 on, in short, the administration was criticized
in Congress for supporting reactionary regimes in Latin America,
for being unduly responsive to the interests of American businessmen there, for stifling social reform through military assistance,
and for neglecting the area in its programs of economic assistance.
These criticisms originated primarily in the Senate Foreign Relations Committee and gradually attracted the support of such influential Senators as William Fulbright and Hubert Humphrey.

Given impetus by the Nixon riots in 1958, this criticism became more widespread and vocal and was supported by influential elements of the American press. Finally, with the campaign of 1960, these criticisms reached their peak, reinforced by the Cuban Revolution.

As the Eisenhower administration began to modify its economic policies toward Latin America, congressional criticism, especially from these influential Democratic senators, tended to be that the administration was doing too little, and that something more nearly like what came to be called the Alliance for Progress was needed. Earlier, however, the most important criticism concerned the military assistance program. Of the presuppositions that lay behind this criticism, unquestionably the most important was the notion that the interests of the United States lay with the Latin American left, and that the United States government had thus far acted in such a way as to suppress reformist politicians in Latin America.

The growing interest within the executive branch in financing social development in Latin America won support in Congress during late 1959 and early 1960. Senator George Aiken made a study mission to Latin America, and reported back favorably on using funds for that purpose. According to Senator Mike Mansfield, Senator Aiken's championship of social development programs helped persuade the Development Loan Fund to support a Peruvian housing project.[74] Approval was given for a small loan in March 1960.

During the same month Senators Smathers and Morse introduced bills to amend the Home Owners Loan Act of 1933 and the Mutual Security Act of 1951 to provide the authority to establish "pilot projects in housing for the Latin American area."[75] At that time Senator Smathers said:

There is, within the administration and within the Congress, little doubt about the contribution which housing development makes to social stability. However, opponents of Latin American housing have two fears: first, that the launching of a housing program would bring a deluge of applications beyond the resources of the United States government to meet, and second, that housing would not have the cumulative economic effect which is the primary objective of our assistance program to underdeveloped areas.[76]

Yet, he argued, political and social stability, which would be promoted by housing projects, were necessary for economic growth.

But the administration remained cool to further requests for a more liberal attitude on the part of the Development Loan Fund toward projects that would not directly expand the economy. It was not until President Eisenhower decided on the proposals to be made in Bogotá that this attitude changed. Later in the same month the President announced the decision to extend another, larger loan to Peru for housing and land development, a loan explicitly associated with the larger program that the administration was about to propose.[77]

Senator Fulbright, in introducing the administration's program before the Senate, said:

My sense of justice is injured by the President's proposal. It has been a long time since I have felt so torn between my sense of duty and my sense of fairness regarding a proper assignment of praise and blame. For a good many years responsible citizens and legislators, predominantly Democrats, have been calling for a really adequate, long-term program of assistance for economic development in Latin America. For eight years of this administration these recommendations have been ignored. . . . Now, at the eleventh hour, as the last dying gasp of this administration, we have received a request for a special authorization for economic aid to Latin America. The administration deserves little credit for this proposal. It has been forced on them.[78]

Against the background of the congressional activity sketched above, these remarks seem somewhat overstated.

Conclusions

What is to be learned from this summary account of the United States government's reviews of its policies toward Latin America? First, although ad hoc procedures were required for comprehensive reviews of policy, there was no lack of them. If the Eisenhower administration failed to adopt some programs that it might have adopted, it did not fail to do so inadvertently, but consciously rejected them. Second, the decisions made were not always in accord with the preferences of the officials most directly concerned with Latin America. The dispute about aid to Latin America in the first few months of the first Eisenhower administration, the long discussion of an inter-American bank and of support for social development projects before their approval in the second Eisenhower administration, and the struggle against import restrictions, which eventually failed, could all be taken as evidence that the decision-making process gave undue weight to other factors besides those pertaining to the interests of the United States government in Latin America.

The nature of these other factors is evident from the preceding discussion. They were the desire to make private investment the main source of foreign capital in Latin America, the desire to keep governmental expenditures to a minimum, and the desire to protect United States producers from the same adverse market trends that were affecting Latin American producers. Although it was the decentralization of the executive branch that allowed the institutional proponents of these views to resist the demands of others, it was clearly the way extra-governmental support for policies was organized that accounts for the views themselves. It is therefore necessary to examine the problem of finding support for United States foreign policy objectives without corrupting them.

5. Institutionalization of United States Latin American Policy

Private economic groups may acquire an interest in a government's relations with other countries in three different ways. Some foreign economic programs may conflict with private interests; for example, the provision of public funds for industrial development abroad competes with private investors (and may weaken their position in conflicts with the governments of underdeveloped countries) and with producers of competitive products in the United States. Groups affected by economic developments abroad may attempt to persuade the government to protect their interests by setting tariffs to preserve their markets or by protecting their enterprises from nationalization. Finally, the government and private interest groups may cooperate for strictly domestic purposes in ways that incidentally lead to conflicts with other governments over economic policies. Agricultural protection schemes and the pursuit of full employment can have such effects.

Because the government itself has competing objectives (e.g., the management of the overall balance of payments and the maintenance of the value of the dollar versus a flexible aid program), it will have to settle for less in one area in order to maintain an acceptable position in another. Its choices will also be influenced by its need for the support of other groups, which may have objectives that conflict with its own. In the United States, the President needs many types of support from many different groups; of chief importance is the support of Congress and, by implication, the support of the groups and individuals that Congressmen are dependent on. Congressional authority over the collection and appropriation of governmental revenue is the key to the participation of many groups in the process of making foreign economic policy.

Because the President is electorally independent of Congress, he can use the prerogatives of his office in exchange for congressional support on many issues. He also has the ties of party loyalty to rely on, backed up by some common electoral interests. Finally, when foreign policy decisions are related to military security, the President can seek to assert the obvious collective interest over individual or group interests.

But there is a limit to the first two kinds of presidential assets: they are apparently not adequate to support all the desires of the President. And rarely, in the case of foreign economic policies, especially as they have concerned Latin America, have the demands of the collective interest been sufficiently compelling or obvious to eliminate the claims of persistent interested groups. When the government is dependent on these groups for support, it is impossible to ignore their demands. Since the representation of interested groups in the political process is considered legitimate by both the government and citizens, a search for compromise between the demands of foreign policy and the demands of groups with special interests is also set in motion for reasons independent of calculations concerning political power.

Rather than simply abandon foreign policy objectives in order to satisfy domestic groups, policy makers attempt to find a formula that renders the two sets of goals consistent, and if possible, mutually supporting. Goals of least importance will be abandoned, and the means of carrying out a controversial policy may be altered in order to save the policy itself from attack; possibly conflict will be obscured by ambiguous rhetoric designed to capture support while postponing conflicts or transferring them to another arena. These techniques make the task of analyzing policy making difficult because they obscure the real preferences of the people involved and thus obscure the amount of conflict and compromise among them. Furthermore, once the relationships of interested persons and groups become institutionalized, they will continue to exist much longer than the circumstances that originally called for the compromise.

The Export-Import Bank

The history of the Export-Import Bank demonstrates these propositions well. Unlike many other foreign aid programs of the United States, the bank has been a stable institution. From the beginning it was intended to serve the purposes of both domestic groups and the makers of foreign policy.[1] It was established in 1934 to encourage United States exports, which were lagging because of the depression, and to handle trade agreements that the Roosevelt administration was seeking with the Soviet Union.* Its use to promote economic development in Latin America began almost accidentally, before World War II, in Haiti. When unsuccessful attempts by French creditors to recover their investments in Haiti led the French government to prohibit imports of Haitian coffee, the Export-Import Bank extended funds to meet the emergency, and the money was used primarily for public works, especially road building. Shortly afterward, funds were used for similar purposes in Paraguay and Nicaragua.[2] In September 1940, the bank's lending authority was increased from $200 million to $700 million, and its life was extended to 1947. The legislation accomplishing this provided that the bank could make loans to governments and/or their central banks "to assist in the development of the resources, the stabilization of the economies, and the orderly marketing of the products of the countries of the Western Hemisphere."[3]

During the war, the bank made loans for specific projects and extended lines of credit to foreign governments. It also participated in joint development corporations set up in Bolivia, Ecuador, and Haiti just before the war. These joint corporations received dollar credits from the Export-Import Bank of Washington and

* A similar institution was created to finance commercial relations with Cuba. The two banks were later consolidated and their resources greatly expanded in order to deal with the wartime emergency in Latin America.

local currencies from the Latin American governments. Each had a board of directors composed of local and United States officials, with a general manager from the United States. Their work was handicapped by the shortage of materials during the war, and their activities, like other programs of the Export-Import Bank, came to be directed primarily at problems directly connected with the war effort, either increasing the production of needed materials or assisting the recipient government in dealing with the dislocations of war. Naturally this led to some disappointment; and the fact that the corporations were managed by United States citizens apparently led to some resentment as well.[4] But the bank did make major loans to Brazil for the development of its iron ore resources and for the Volta Redonda steel mill.[5]

The lending criteria adopted by the bank were a successful formula that combined the objectives of both the Department of State and the domestic groups interested in the bank's operations. Consequently domestic support for some of the government's foreign policy objectives was secured. The bank insisted: (1) that the projects it supported be directly productive (which ruled out schools, hospitals, and housing); (2) that the funds loaned be spent in the United States; (3) that loans not be given to industries that were directly competitive with certain declining industries in the United States; (4) that loans be given only to countries with the capacity to repay in dollars at nearly commercial rates of interest (although when the larger interests of the United States have demanded it, the bank has made loans to avoid the threat of default on earlier ones, both public and private); (5) that loans be made only for the foreign currency costs of development projects. Besides these self-imposed criteria, limits were imposed by the lack of any mechanism for joint planning with the recipient governments. Such a mechanism would have enabled the bank to assist in planning projects or formulating applications for assistance; instead it only processed the applications made by others.

The bank's judgment of what was a productive investment was undoubtedly affected by the desires of interested United States citizens, especially those represented by the banking and currency committees of Congress, on which the Export-Import Bank depended for legislative support. As Raymond Mikesell has said: "Nor is the Bank specifically prohibited from financing certain types of projects, i.e., schools, hospitals, etc., which it normally avoids. However, one finds ample justification for the general policies of the Bank in the Congressional committee hearings and committee reports relative to the Bank's operation."[6] For example, these committees probed carefully for evidence that the bank had assisted some enterprise that competed with a declining American industry, and the bank's sensitivity on this point can undoubtedly be attributed to this fact.[7]

Of all the restrictions on the bank's lending, the most important were probably the denial of support for social overhead projects, the requirement that the recipient be able to repay in dollars at nearly commercial rates of interest, and the dependence of the bank on projects formulated by others. They were established in part to reduce the number of claims on public funds, and to maintain as many incentives as possible for the governments of underdeveloped countries to be solicitous of private capital. These two objectives were obviously related. Some people were probably most interested in strengthening the position of private investors abroad; others, in economizing on the use of public funds. The bank's reluctance to finance the operations of state petroleum corporations which competed with private investors, for example, was probably motivated by both these aims. Congressional hearings concerning the Export-Import Bank were full of admonitions that the bank not compete with private capital in any way.[8]

The bank's judgment about its investments was also influenced by the United States government's earlier experience with debtor-creditor relationships with the countries of Latin America. There was a distrust of the ability of Latin Americans to use funds lent more freely for purposes serving genuinely mutual interests, a distrust that developed in the climate of inter-American relations in which the bank had its origins, the 1930's.[9] Many people with experience believed that it was important to insulate the activities of the bank from Latin American politics, rather than to adapt it to the purposes of Latin American politicians. Thus a particular pattern of responsibility to domestic interests and a particular conception of the nature of the United States interest in Latin American politics were mutually reinforcing factors in determining the lending criteria of the bank. The result was the creation of a stable institution with a strong domestic base of support, whose influence on the bank's policies it is difficult to estimate.

Although the State Department was never very successful in persuading the bank to violate its conception of what constituted a sound loan, it was able to insist that loans not be given if they would violate some foreign policy interest of the United States. Through close informal relations with the bank it could also see that loans were granted where they would further foreign policy objectives, so long as they were sound.[10] The bank was most easily used for foreign policy purposes when the interests of the State Department and of exporters coincided, as they did, for example, shortly before World War II, when both had reason to try to compete with German commercial activities in Latin America.[11]

As new foreign assistance programs were gradually developed to meet difficulties in various parts of the world after World War II, the role of the bank as an instrument of foreign policy declined. But since Latin America was the last area for which new foreign aid legislation was especially designed, the importance of the Export-Import Bank for that area increased rather than diminished during these years.[12] In 1945 the lending authority of the bank was increased to $3.5 billion, and it was made an independent agency with indefinite life. The government gave the bank a prominent place in its statements about economic assistance to Latin America, and after the Bogotá conference in 1948 President Truman asked Congress to increase its lending authority by $500 million specifically to finance economic development in Latin America.[13] Although Congress failed to act on the request at that time, it was expected that the bank would continue to be the main instrument for providing public funds for economic development in Latin America.

The relationship among goals, internal organization, and bases of support that was institutionalized in the Export-Import Bank was quite stable, as Secretary of the Treasury Humphrey learned when he tried to extend his control over the bank's operations in the early days of the first Eisenhower administration. As an independent corporation, the bank was a drain on the Treasury that was difficult to control. However, by attempting to subordinate it to the Treasury Department, Humphrey aroused people both inside and outside the government whose main interest was in improving relations between the United States and the countries of Latin America. He also provoked United States exporters, who were disturbed by increasing competition from European countries for Latin American markets. The complaints from all these people found a sympathetic audience in Congress, particularly in the Senate Banking and Currency Committee, on which the Export-Import Bank depended for legislative authorization; and in the end, the independence of the bank was reaffirmed, and an attempt was made to expand its activities in Latin America.

The first in the series of maneuvers that took place was the announcement of the administration's intention to reorganize the bank. Reorganization Plan Number 5, which was made public in 1953, transferred all functions of the board of directors of the bank to a new managing director. (The Secretary of State had been a member of the old board.) The advisory board of the bank was abolished, the representation of the bank on the National Advisory Council was eliminated, and the NAC, already empowered to coordinate the lending activities of the bank with those of other agencies of the government and with the World Bank, appeared to have been given broader control.[14]

The effects to be expected from these changes were subject to some dispute, because it was clear that the informal ways of establishing the bank's policies had always been more important than the letter of the statutes.[15] The power to coordinate the activities of the bank with those of other agencies had, in fact, always been interpreted rather broadly by the Treasury, which managed the work of the NAC.[16] Yet in practice the bank had managed to maintain a position of relative independence and a close working relationship with the Department of State. Its independence of Treasury control was strengthened by the presence of its representative on the NAC. As a study prepared by the staff of the Senate Committee on Government Operations reported, "if the Bank's representative on the Council indicates that the Bank feels very strongly about a particular matter, the Council does not interfere."[17] Humphrey's proposed reorganization seemed intended to strengthen the Treasury's control, and diminish the influence of the State Department.

There were two main objectives behind the proposed changes. One was to give the World Bank a clear field in development lending. This had been recommended four years earlier by the Hoover Commission in the report on its investigation of the organization of the executive branch of the government.[18] The other was, in Humphrey's words, to assist in "bringing about a balanced budget . . . making possible an eventual reduction in Federal taxation."[19] It was strongly implied that the bank's role would be restricted mainly to short-term assistance to United States exporters and that the amount of its lending would be reduced. These objectives governed the administration from August 1953 to August 1954.[20] Their final defeat was brought about by the passage of the Export-Import Bank Act of 1954, which not only reaffirmed the independent status of the bank but emphasized its role as a source of development capital for Latin America.

Naturally, the objectives of the Treasury Department were opposed by the State Department staff members who were responsible for coping with demands from the countries of Latin America. Perhaps of greater interest is the extent of congressional opposition to them. Senator Homer Capehart, chairman of the Senate Banking and Currency Committee, led a vigorous effort to restore the bank to its original position and to ensure that it would contribute development capital to the countries of Latin America. His committee conducted an extensive series of hearings on the operations of the World Bank and the Export-Import Bank, solicited the opinions of a large number of United States bankers and businessmen through both questionnaires and direct testimony, invited the opinions of many Latin American leaders, and conducted a study tour of Latin America. The findings of the committee, published in a large volume as an interim report, clearly favored continuing the bank's active role in development lending.[21]

Senator Capehart was not the only member of Congress to suddenly exhibit concern about the direction that policies toward Latin America seemed to be taking. Congressman Fulton of Pennsylvania, at the economic conference in Rio de Janeiro in November 1954, publicly criticized the position his government was taking at the conference, and called for a large program of development loans for Latin America.[22] Senator George Smathers of Florida also began at about this time his personal campaign for greater economic assistance to Latin America.

It was abundantly clear from the public record that the main concern in Congress at the time was the likely increase of competition from European businessmen for Latin American markets. As the president of the Export-Import Bank testified in 1955:

Within the last two years the situation in the foreign trade field has changed from a seller's market to a buyer's market. Manufacturers of other countries, principally the countries of Western Europe and Japan, are now offering extended terms of payment to potential foreign customers. In many instances they are able to do this only because of financial assistance from their own government in the form of export credit insurance.[23]

United States exporters, seeing this, demanded comparable assistance from the Export-Import Bank.

Many Congressmen supported them. In May 1954 Senators Smathers and Maybank had jointly called attention to these developments from the floor of the Senate.[24] In June 1954 Senator John Kennedy had expressed concern over the curtailment of the bank's operations, "not only because the bank is an important instrument of our foreign policy, particularly in the critical area of Latin America, but also because the bank increases the foreign markets so desperately needed by the manufacturers of machinery and other products manufactured in New England and the United States."[25] Representative Fulton stated that he believed the government should act to help nations that had been good customers in the past, and to promote full employment in industrial areas of the United States, such as his own, by granting funds that would be used to purchase equipment from the United States. He wanted the Export-Import Bank to authorize a billion dollars' worth of new projects in Latin America because it would help steer a good portion of Latin America's business to the United States, rather than allowing it to go to Germany, Japan, France, Britain, and Italy. "We in the United States," he said, "should aim to keep a fair share of business in South and Central America."[26]

It is not necessary to believe that Congressmen were subjected to great pressures from businessmen to understand these statements. Perhaps a more credible explanation is simply that the bank's constituency in Congress and outside it had grown accustomed to its activities and still believed the justification of them originally set forth during the 1930's. The decentralization of Congress and the party system allowed them to resist any changes.

It is difficult to estimate the importance of this congressional support for the maintenance of the Export-Import Bank's active role in Latin America. But it is striking in light of the amount of opposition in Congress to the aid program at the same time. It probably strengthened the hand of those in the executive branch who wanted to resist the efforts to curtail the bank's lending.[27]

A necessary, and perhaps sufficient, condition for a reaffirmation of the idea that the bank had a role in Latin America was a presidential decision, announced at the Caracas conference by Secretary Dulles, that the bank would continue to make long-term development loans. Newspaper accounts suggested that the President's decision was stimulated by the approach of that conference. Support for the continued use of the bank for development lending had also come from both the minority and majority reports of the Randall Commission, and by then the Capehart committee had begun to indicate the nature of its views on the subject.[28] Between the Caracas conference and the economic conference at Rio de Janeiro, the government announced that it would actually attempt to expand the development lending of the Export-Import Bank, as well as increase its responsiveness to requests for assistance from

American exporters.[29] At a conference at the White House attended by all the principal parties to the dispute, the administration announced its support for legislation shortly to be introduced in Congress by Senators Capehart and Maybank and Representative Wolcott.[30] This legislation, when passed, increased the lending authority of the bank by $500 million and created a five-member bipartisan board of directors to manage the bank. The chairman of the board was to be the president of the bank, and would be represented on the National Advisory Council. A nine-man advisory committee was authorized, its members to be drawn from production, commerce, finance, agriculture, and labor.

The legislative history of the Export-Import Bank Act of 1954 virtually instructed the bank to be more aggressive both in direct assistance to United States exporters and in long-term development assistance to the countries of Latin America. As an example, Senator Capehart said in the course of the hearings, "it is the intention of this Congress" that the bank "make more loans and be more active" than it had been in the last twelve months, and that it "become a very active and aggressive organization" not only to assist United States exporters but "to assist friendly countries in building up their production."[31] With regard to Latin American countries, he believed that the bank should make long-term loans for capital goods to enable those countries to industrialize, reduce their unemployment, and "pull themselves up by their own bootstraps."[32]

Samuel Waugh was Assistant Secretary of State for Economic Affairs when the new policies for the Export-Import Bank were devised. He then became president of the bank to see that they were carried out. During the hearing on his nomination, Mr. Waugh was asked to assure Congress that the Export-Import Bank would remain independent of the Treasury Department. He was asked by Senator Douglas, "Suppose the intent of Congress is clear, as I believe it is, that a liberal lending policy is to be followed by the Export-Import Bank, but the Secretary of the Treasury and the National Advisory Council should advise against it. Whose opinion should be controlling? . . ." Mr. Waugh replied,

"I feel very definitely . . . that the intent of Congress, when it is clear—and it is clear—should be followed unequivocally."[33]

Thus, at the very time when congressional support for a long-term program of economic assistance to underdeveloped countries was in great doubt, Congress was attempting to strengthen the Export-Import Bank, which had very similar objectives. The explanation seems to be that the bank provided benefits both to the Department of State and to some United States businessmen; that conflicts of interest were resolved in ways acceptable to all of these parties; and that this relationship was mediated by an independent congressional committee, which effectively isolated the bank from the broader controversies about foreign policy that other foreign aid programs tended to get involved in.

The Technical Assistance Program

A similar attempt to find common ground between the foreign policy objectives of the executive and the private interests of some American citizens characterized the technical assistance program. In this instance the foreign relations committees of Congress served as mediators. Once again, there proved to be much in common between policymakers and their extragovernmental sources of support. But the mingling of the objectives of technical assistance with broader foreign policy concerns led to a slightly greater threat to the institutionalization of technical assistance programs.

The technical assistance given the countries of Latin America during World War II was largely devoted to specific, isolated projects that were chosen by using disparate and often unclear criteria. This mode of operation was encouraged by the way the United States government was organized to handle such projects. The procedures for high-level review and coordination were minimal, and the many participating government agencies had considerable influence in shaping the programs. This had the effect of placing greatest emphasis on programs that the government was already equipped to handle, such as agricultural development, public health, and education. These were activities in which the United States was thought to have an obvious advantage over the

Latin Americans, and, since the needs of Latin America were so overwhelming, there was little need to think further about priorities. These programs therefore raised few questions of interest to other American citizens, chiefly businessmen, with a stake in Latin American affairs. And their low cost, together with the fact that they made use of existing organizations and skills already available to the government, helped secure their domestic base of support.

In theory, the Act for International Development, which resulted from President Truman's famous fourth point, changed all this. It provided the government with the statutory authority for providing technical and financial assistance to the countries of Latin America as part of a long-term coordinated effort. This seemed to presage programs that would cost more money, mobilize new, more relevant skills, and intrude into areas of Latin American economic life of concern to American investors.

As a result, many business groups with interests in underdeveloped countries, especially Latin America, were initially not enthusiastic about President Truman's proposal. The National Council on Foreign Trade, the United States Chamber of Commerce, and the American members of the International Chamber of Commerce expressed their concern that these proposals would remove some of the incentives that underdeveloped countries had for being hospitable to foreign capitalists. Congressman Christian Herter was primarily responsible for mediating between the administration and these business groups. A compromise was reached, and these groups then announced their support for the revised legislation.[34] The changes were designed to reemphasize that public capital should not supplant private capital, and that participating countries had an obligation to attempt to create domestic conditions conducive to private investment from abroad.

But these changes did not represent a substantial modification of the desires of the administration, which doubted the efficacy of most alternatives to private investment and was anxious to economize on the use of public funds. Indeed, the Point Four program was partly designed to deflect the demands made by underdeveloped countries for capital assistance programs. As James Webb, acting Secretary of State, testified in 1949:

> We hope that some of the nations that have been coming to us to talk about government-to-government loans . . . or grants and other types of assistance will fall in line with the program. You understand, they will have to do a large part of the job themselves. There is the technical assistance plus the investment guaranties, which will encourage the flow of private capital and will permit them to move ahead with certain projects which we can agree to.[35]

Thus it was not too difficult to find a position acceptable to both the executive branch and interested private groups, and the technical assistance program proved to be a stable and popular form of foreign aid.

Since this program was administered by institutions that also dealt with other aspects of foreign policy, however, it was subjected to greater strains than was the Export-Import Bank. Eventually it was absorbed into the broader foreign aid program, a program justified as a set of temporary measures to further "mutual security." There was some danger, therefore, that it might be molded to serve the ends of the broader program and be subjected to the same criticisms that the broader program was subjected to.

This did not happen, however, since the demands of the Mutual Security Program did not, evidently, reduce the funds available for technical assistance, and Congress was careful to distinguish between the provision of technical assistance and capital assistance, thereby avoiding the controversies associated with the latter.[36] The technical assistance programs persisted, therefore, with relatively little disruption.

Commercial Policies

The stability of the commercial policies of the United States government also had to be secured through compromises between the executive and interested private groups. There were many more conflicts of interest in this case, however, and as a result there was much greater strain on the stability of these policies. Congressional support for renewing legislative authorization of the Trade Agreements Program declined markedly during the early

1950's. Renewal had to be purchased by the executive branch through concessions to especially well-represented producers of specific commodities.

In 1953 Congress could be persuaded to renew the legislation for only one year, during which time foreign economic policies were to be reviewed by the Randall Commission. But the following year Congress could be persuaded to do no more than renew the program for one more year, even though the Randall Commission had recommended a three-year extension of the law, with peril point and escape clause provisions included.[87] In 1955, therefore, the administration tried once again to achieve a three-year extension of the law, and it was in the course of this attempt that the President made the promise that "this program . . . must be, and will be, administered to the benefit of the Nation's economic strength and not to its detriment. No American industry will be placed in jeopardy by the administration of this measure."[38]

The identity of the industries in question was made clear in the course of the legislative controversy. During Senate debate on the administration's bill, in 1955, a number of amendments were advanced to protect specific commodities. Foremost among them were crude and residual oil. Rather than recommend legislation designed to protect such specific industries, the Senate committee recommended an amendment to the administration's bill authorizing the President to impose quotas or any other type of import restrictions whenever, in his judgment, imports were injuring industries essential to national security. The assumption was that the President would use such authorization to impose quotas on oil imports.[39] During the floor debate on the bill, this assumption was extended by Senator Milliken to cover a number of other minerals.[40]

Foreign policy makers were constrained not only by the need to accommodate the demands of industries subject to foreign competition, but also by the need to adopt the methods of assistance those industries most preferred. A possible alternative to import restrictions, for example, was some form of direct financial assistance, taken out of tax revenues, to declining industries or communities. But even when the administration persuaded itself to support such a scheme (as it did in the case of minerals in 1958), the industries' belief that the support was likely to be impermanent helped generate opposition to it in Congress and probably contributed to its failure.[41]

Another alternative was more acceptable, however, and it was employed for some time. This was large-scale government purchases of minerals for the government stockpile. Previously the main objective of the stockpile had been "to make up for anticipated loss of, or serious interference with, foreign sources of strategic materials in a five-year war period."[42] As a result of the recommendations of a special Cabinet Committee on Minerals Policy, however, and with the support of the Senate Interior and Insular Affairs Committee, these objectives were broadened to place greater emphasis on maintaining a strong domestic mineral industry rather than simply keeping an adequate stock of minerals on hand to deal with a war emergency.[43] This enabled the President to increase government purchases of lead and zinc mined in the United States, ostensibly to "strengthen the domestic mobilization base," but actually to provide assistance to a mining industry in trouble.[44]

Soon the administration acquired still further authority to purchase minerals, as a result of an effort to assist yet another domestic interest, in this case farmers. The Agricultural Trade Development and Assistance Act of 1954 (P.L. 480) authorized the President to enter into agreements with foreign countries to use the foreign currencies that accrued to the United States from the sale of surplus agricultural products abroad to purchase strategic and critical materials (within the terms of the Strategic and Critical Materials Stockpile Act) for a supplemental stockpile. The President could make advance payment contracts for supply extending over periods up to ten years.[45] The same Act directed the Secretary of Agriculture to barter agricultural commodities for strategic materials "entailing less risk of loss through deterioration or substantially less storage charges," whenever he "has reason to believe that . . . there may be opportunity to protect the funds and assets of the Commodity Credit Corporation" by doing so.[46] Thus the government could now purchase minerals abroad, as well as at home, through the expanded stockpile program; and by this method the Eisenhower administration managed to stave off demands for import restrictions on lead and zinc for a number of years.[47] But the rejection by Congress of the administration's plan for subsidies to the mining industry precipitated the imposition of import restrictions, in the form of quotas, in September 1958.[48]

Once again, then, the extensive decentralization of the United States government allowed economic groups with intense interests to participate in shaping foreign economic policies. Whether because the industries concerned were especially prominent in certain states and congressional districts, or because they were favored by the Congressmen and Senators who represented them, the many diverse groups across the country that shared some interest in protection against imports were represented with significant numerical strength in Congress. Furthermore, the committees concerned with these interests were more than usually responsive to their constituents' pleas.

Similarly, the executive departments that dealt with these problems (e.g., Interior and Agriculture) had close ties to the main interest groups concerned and to members of Congress with similar ties. The initiative in making policy in the executive branch seems to have lain with these departments. Two interdepartmental committees were primarily responsible for the coordination of policies concerning tariffs: the Trade Policy Committee, chaired by the Department of Commerce, which advised the President on Tariff Commission cases; and the Council on Foreign Economic Policy, chaired by the President's Special Assistant for Foreign Economic Policy. The latter body was set up by presidential directive and given the authority to take up any matter affecting foreign economic policy, recommending either approval or modification of any agency's actions.[49] But clearly the staff work involved must have been undertaken by the departments concerned, particularly for any such complicated scheme as the mineral subsidies proposal.

The conflict between the President and the interested groups was not very intense, however. For example, the preference of the industries for indirect and permanent forms of assistance (import restrictions) over direct financial aid was shared at the highest levels of the administration.* Thus the way in which policies were coordinated was partly determined by the Eisenhower administration's conception of the relevant range of alternatives. When this changed (as it began to do in the late 1950's) there was a greater effort at centralization. This effort was directed by Douglas Dillon, who began, during the later years of the Eisenhower administration, to improve the coordination of economic policies with foreign policy objectives.[50]

Conclusions

In each of the three instances of the institutionalization of foreign economic policy that I have described, institutional decentralization allowed interested nongovernmental groups and individuals to participate in policy making. Not only were these groups able to shape policy in conformity with their interests, but by resisting efforts to centralize policy making they were able to preserve their freedom to influence policy in the future. The reinforced autonomy of the Export-Import Bank and of the foreign aid program (if not the technical assistance program itself) and the limited authorization for the trade agreements program secured both these objectives.

At the same time, there was not much conflict between the objectives of the main centralizing force—the President—and these interested groups. Even on the issue of greatest conflict, import restrictions, the overall commercial policies of the United States government were not really threatened. Certainly the significance of any individual case, such as lead and zinc, was not very great for the President's foreign policy. Import restrictions reinforced the widespread belief in Latin America that United States foreign policy was designed to protect American business interests, but those beliefs would have continued to exist anyway. Furthermore, the

---

* This was in contrast to the Kennedy administration, which committed itself to finding alternatives to import restrictions. See H. Bradford Westerfield, *The Instruments of America's Foreign Policy* (New York: Thomas Crowell, 1963), pp. 306–7.

significance of trade restrictions, when they came, was dwarfed by the general economic crisis in Latin America and the other measures the United States government initiated at the time to deal with them.

Of course, the lack of conflict between the President and the other interested parties to these decisions can be explained as simply a lagged effect of institutional decentralization. One might argue that the decentralization of the bureaucracy prevented the development of views very much contrary to those of interested private groups and that the decentralized party system prevented the emergence of a chief executive with strong independent views.

This argument is no doubt at least partly true. The question it raises is a difficult one, which concerns the value of certain international objectives seen in the light of their costs to domestic interests. Even if two observers assess the international benefits identically, they may yet differ in their evaluation of policy because they evaluate the domestic costs differently. The discussion above provides some information about how the political process in the United States assigns values to those costs. It provides little help in criticizing the values thus assigned. Criticism of these values is itself a function performed by the political process, and to criticize them is to participate in politics.

The examples of the institutionalization of foreign economic policies given here help one understand the reasons behind the objections that were raised to the innovations in policy that the United States government finally adopted in the late 1950's and early 1960's. We see that every innovation not only altered existing commitments but also required changes in the formulas for reconciling public and private interests. The point is not that the new policies were clearly contrary to the interests of private groups, but that they called into question an existing set of formulas that both governmental and nongovernmental groups had become accustomed to, and that everyone felt comfortable with. Before policies could be changed, it was necessary to work out a new one, and then develop support for it.

Thus the true significance of the role of private interests in

United States foreign economic policies cannot be determined until we have examined the process of institutional change itself. In the next chapter I will discuss the process of innovation in detail, and then in the following chapter attempt to assess the effects of the domestic political context in which United States policies have been made.

6. Innovation in United States Latin American Policy

Serious questions have been raised about the adaptability of the United States political system to changes in the international environment. How one answers these questions depends in part on one's evaluation of the domestic costs of changing or not changing policies. But even assuming a given evaluation, one can question the ability of the system to recognize new conditions and adapt to them speedily.

How are these capacities, or the lack of them, related to the decentralization of the government? The complexity of communications and the need for agreement among many parties in a decentralized system, along with the natural desire to preserve the existing compromise rather than hammer out a new one, tend to retard action. Some would argue that action is usually delayed beyond the point when it might have done some good. These hindrances are overcome only when the cost of not acting is high and is visible to all participants; then a few key officials acquire the ability to make decisions. Usually this occurs in times of crisis.

The relationship between crises and decisions is well illustrated by the following episode. During a study trip to Latin America, Dr. Milton Eisenhower arrived in Panama with his party at a time of unrest. Relations between Panama and the United States were poor. The issues were numerous: apart from the general poverty of most Panamanians, for which they tended to blame the United States, the wages of those who worked for the Canal Company no longer seemed enough. Moreover the Panamanian government wanted to raise canal tolls, receive a larger percentage of the gross revenues of the Canal Company, and assert its residual sovereignty over the Canal Zone by flying the Panamanian flag there.

Dr. Eisenhower seems to have interpreted the impending crisis in the same terms he was beginning to apply to the rest of Latin America. The issues, he thought, no less than the anti-Americanism accompanying them, were really popular expressions of dissatisfaction with living conditions. If only national income could be redistributed more equitably, perhaps in the form of welfare projects, these manifestations would cease. He has since written:

We had ample opportunity to probe the details of the problems. In addition, President de la Guardia outlined Panama's need for capital to finance schools, roads, piers, and, above all, housing. He was especially interested in a project I had previously explored with the governor of the Zone and with representatives of Panamanian employees of the company. Some thirty-five hundred of these employees wished to build low-cost houses in Panama City; monthly payments to cover interest and amortization could be deducted from their salaries, making the loan from the United States for the total cost a fairly safe investment, since the United States was the employer. While this would be only a modest start in correcting the deplorable housing situation in the city, it would demonstrate our concern and might temper somewhat the passionate views about sovereignty, rental payments, wages, and flags.[1]

On returning to the United States, Dr. Eisenhower recommended concessions by the American government on most of the issues raised by the Panamanians. Most important, he thought, was a program of low-cost housing.[2]

Although he found support for most of his recommendations in the State Department, there were objections from the Defense Department, Congress, and the governor of the Canal Zone. And the Treasury and the lending agencies objected particularly to his proposal for United States support for low-cost housing projects. This proposal was therefore abandoned.[3] Later, in October of 1959, the Defense Department received reports that Panamanian students and some political leaders intended to march on the Canal Zone on the coming Independence Day to raise the Panamanian flag. Secretary of the Army Brucker consulted with Dr. Eisenhower, who later wrote: "Secretary Brucker then outlined a program of eight or nine actions which he felt we should and could take, without violating principle or provisions of existing treaties. I tried to appear placid as he presented a plan nearly identical to the one I had urgently proposed thirteen months before."[4]

The President hastily summoned representatives of the agencies chiefly involved, and a program was agreed on. But before it could be implemented, two thousand Panamanians invaded the Canal Zone. Accordingly the program was suspended once again, this time on the grounds that, if carried out, it would look like a response to the attack, and be interpreted as a sign of weakness.[5]

Here we see all the suspected inadequacies of decentralized decision-making, and the frustration experienced by one of the participants. Difficulties are foreseen and interpreted in the light of prevailing conceptions of their causes. Suggestions are made to cope with them, some of them by the parties with a grievance. These suggestions receive the support of the agency responsible for dealing most directly with the aggrieved parties, but are opposed by other agencies, whose tasks and patterns of responsibility lead them to give less weight to the objectives of the agency that "represents" the parties with a grievance. Then some crisis arises, the measures originally suggested are seized upon, and the opposition of other government agencies is broken.

There are several dangers involved in such behavior. One is that action may come too late. Another is that, in the heat of crisis, an inappropriate instrument may be seized and used merely because it is available and something has to be done. And another, illustrated by Dr. Eisenhower's story, is that crises are encouraged as the only means of getting policies changed.

There are, however, two warnings to be placed in the way of hasty criticism of the United States government's behavior. The first is that it may not be possible to have both a multiplicity of possible solutions from which to choose and immediate responsiveness. The same characteristics of the system that encourage one inhibit the other. The second is that the government has to deal with probabilities, not certainties. Possibly the dispute between the government and its critics grows out of their different attitudes toward risk. It may be that the characteristics of the political process that lead to a proliferation of proposals also lead to an exaggeration of the probability of their success by their proponents. Emergencies at least have the advantage of making the costs of inaction more nearly certain.

Much depends on what counts as a crisis. An examination of several instances of institutional innovation will reveal that at times merely the necessity of preparing a presidential speech or appearing at a difficult international conference will be sufficient to produce some innovation. This is especially true early in a new administration, when a president is anxious to put his own mark on decisions, and when he has an initial stock of political goodwill to back him up. Events of this sort can be counted on to occur often enough to provide ample occasions for innovation, if there is a desire for it. Nevertheless, one must suspect that the less critical the situation, the less radical the innovation it will call forth.

In this chapter I will examine several major innovations in United States economic policies toward Latin America. The relationship between crisis and innovation can be seen quite clearly in each case. But, let me repeat, the significance of this relationship is not so obvious as many critics of United States policy suggest. This matter will be dealt with more extensively in the next chapter; final judgment on the importance of these examples is therefore reserved until them.

The first major innovation in United States economic policies after the war that directly affected Latin America was the Point Four program. As applied to Latin America, of course, this program did not represent a startling break with the past; technical assistance had been given in the Western Hemisphere for some time. The act authorizing Point Four did, however, redefine the objectives of technical assistance programs and begin what proved to be a long process of reorganizing them. Even in Latin America, it represented much more than just a new name for old programs. It is interesting that the immediate cause of the decision to make this innovation seems to have been the need to fill President Truman's inaugural address with a sufficient amount of arresting material.[6]

As I tried to show earlier, this innovation lay well within the limits set on foreign economic policies by the conservative views of bankers and businessmen. At the time there were no great pressures to exceed these limits; the executive branch lacked influential advocates of radical policies, and there were no crises to call existing policies into serious question. Even if there had been radical demands, the pressure of the Korean War on scarce resources would have been sufficient to suppress them.

In the first Eisenhower administration, however, demands for more radical changes began to mount. The end of the Korean War both freed resources and created serious economic problems for the countries of Latin America. The realization that Communist influence in Guatemala had reached unacceptable proportions attracted high-level attention to the problems of that area. It was much easier then to extend the existing foreign aid program to the countries of Latin America than it would have been earlier to introduce an aid program especially for that region. Also, in the 1950's academic economists began to elaborate proposals for coping with the problems of underdeveloped countries, providing rather specific suggestions for innovations in United States policies. Therefore it is the pace of innovation from the first Eisenhower administration to the Alliance for Progress that will be scrutinized in the rest of this chapter.

The International Finance Corporation

The first institutional change in economic policies prompted by developments in Latin America was the creation of the International Finance Corporation, which was announced at the special economic conference in Rio de Janeiro in 1954.[7] The purpose of this institution was to directly support private enterprises in underdeveloped countries through purchases of stock issued by privately owned corporations. This idea had first been put forth by the International Development Advisory Board, headed by Nelson Rockefeller, in 1951.

As might be expected, the Treasury, the Federal Reserve Bank, and the Export-Import Bank opposed this proposal when it first appeared. A student of the process by which the IFC was finally approved has concluded:

There was nothing whimsical about this opposition. . . . It was consistent and inflexible. Suffice it to say that, as far as the Treasury Department was concerned, it opposed the IFC under both the Democratic and Republican administrations. If any change in this respect could be noticed after the advent of the Republican administration, it was only a certain hardening of the negative attitude.[8]

According to the same author, the most important reason for this opposition was "the strong conviction that participation of an intergovernmental institution in equity ownership of private enterprise essentially ran counter to the principles of the American economic system and therefore placed those principles in direct jeopardy." Further, "because of what came to be known as the 'equity aspect' of the proposed operations, the IFC proposal had provoked strong opposition from business circles fearful that the IFC proposal would encroach upon a field which rightly should be reserved for private enterprise."[9] The proposal had the "qualified approval" of the Department of State. "Again, as in the case of the Treasury Department, the change of administration had essentially no effect upon the basic policy pursued in this respect by the Department of State."[10]

Not only was the Treasury more dedicated in its opposition than the State Department in its support, but the Treasury also held a superior position from which to pursue its objectives:

The governmental policy on IFC was determined by the National Advisory Council, an interdepartmental agency in which the Treasury Department occupies an uncontested position of *primus inter pares*. The type and kind of problems upon which the National Advisory Council passes [i.e., international financial policies] belong beyond question to the domain of special, and, in a way, more exclusive interest of the Treasury. The interest in those problems that an agency such as the Department of State may have is, or is likely to appear to be, more of a subordinate or auxiliary nature. On the administrative side, for instance, this "special interest" of the Treasury is exemplified by the rule whereby the staff work of the National Advisory Council is always the responsibility of a representative of the Treasury Department.[11]

This combination of superior position and greater dedication meant that the Treasury was able to defeat the objectives of a larger group of people.

Support for the proposal was kept alive by the officials of the World Bank (the IFC was to be an affiliate of the bank), who persisted in trying to persuade the Treasury. In the end the World Bank was responsible for devising a compromise formula which the Treasury, in the face of other circumstances that I shall mention, was finally able to accept. This compromise included both a decrease in the extent to which the IFC would be involved in managing private corporations, and a reduction in the level of financial commitment expected from the United States. Continuous support also came from United States representatives on the United Nations Economic and Social Council, where the United States was under strong pressure to support a much more radical proposal, the Special United Nations Fund for Economic Development (SUNFED).

The Treasury argument that businessmen were opposed to the proposal seems to have been the result of selective perception. Bronislaw Matecki has reported that "the division on the IFC issue that existed in the government was broadly paralleled by one that split the ranks of the business community in the United States." When people in government gave as their reason for opposing the IFC "business was against it," virtually in all instances the assertion led to a reference to the strong position taken by the National Foreign Trade Council.[12] Yet during the public hearings on the bill to establish the IFC, the proposal was supported by a wide range of business organizations.

Finally the Treasury capitulated. The reason was apparently the approach of the international conference on economic policies at Rio de Janeiro. At the time the conference took place in 1954, the United States was simultaneously under pressure in the OAS and in the United Nations Economic and Social Council to support some drastic new measures to deal with the problems of underdeveloped countries. In the former the proposals of the United Nations Economic Commission for Latin America (ECLA) had attracted considerable support among Latin American countries; in the latter the SUNFED proposal was prominent. The United States was going to the Rio conference with no genuinely new proposals; and it was widely known that the Latin American governments were disappointed.[13] Then, on November 11, 1954, the United States announced its support for the IFC proposal.

Matecki, in his study of these events, has said:

> A high government official well-informed about the problem and in a position to influence its outcome has, in an interview with us, expressed his conviction that neither the persuasion exercised by the International Bank nor the pressures deriving from American participation in international institutions would have sufficed alone to cause the United States government to revise its policy on IFC "if they had not been accompanied by other important developments on the international scene." These developments included in the first instance the impending Rio de Janeiro Economic Conference, to which this government official referred quite openly.[14]

Another official said that "there was a great desire on our part to appease the Latin Americans."[15] The IFC seemed to be the least expensive and least objectionable way of doing so. An official of the State Department said that at the conference, "it was convenient for us to point to the decision of the government to support the establishment of the IFC." The United States delegates argued that, having decided to expand the activities of the Export-Import Bank and to contribute to the IFC, the government was not in a position to contribute to still another inter-American financial institution.[16]

Thus the stimulus of an international conference (against the background of the Guatemala affair) seems to have caused the normal process of policy making, institutionalized in the National Advisory Council, to be momentarily circumvented, and allowed the viewpoint of the Department of State to prevail. The result, however, was an innovation of exceedingly limited relevance to the problems of Latin America and to the problems faced by the United States government there. This was, to a great extent, the intention of the government, for all the reasons discussed previously. But this concession was of small value even for the limited goal of the Eisenhower administration, which was to take some of the pressures off the United States government.

If financial concessions were to be used for such a purpose, they should probably have been made at Caracas, rather than at Rio de Janeiro, several months later, at which time any benefits they might have provided had been offset by the clumsiness of the process through which the United States government had decided to offer them. Yet one can reasonably doubt that the administration's difficulties would have been appreciably reduced even if it had been able to combine its economic policy proposals and its demands concerning Guatemala into a coherent package and had presented them together at Caracas. It is quite possible that having done so, it would still have confronted increasingly strident demands from the Latin Americans, coordinated by the economists of ECLA.

This innovation was clearly stimulated by a crisis, but in this instance the crisis did not force a lethargic government belatedly to act in its best interests, but rather forced it to do something only marginally related to its interests. This case can therefore be said to constitute as much evidence for the proposition that even limited crises will lead to innovations (though not necessarily appropriate ones) as for the proposition that the government is too resistant to change.

The Inter-American Development Bank

A series of innovations appeared between 1958 and 1961 in two main stages, each apparently connected with what was interpreted to be a crisis in the relations between the United States and the countries of Latin America. The first major change was associated with the rough treatment given Vice-President Nixon during his visits to Peru and to Venezuela in 1958. Shortly thereafter the United States government agreed to the establishment of an inter-American development bank and began a series of discussions with the countries of Latin America concerning both international commodity agreements and the broad questions of economic development raised by the Brazilian proposal of an "Operation Pan America."

The second major change began in the summer of 1960, when the full dimensions of the problem presented by the Cuban Revolution became apparent, and continued into the first months of the new Kennedy administration. During this time the United States government initiated the discussions that resulted in the Act of Bogotá, and then opened a second round of discussions, which in August 1961 produced the Alliance for Progress. About the same time a definite decision was made by the Kennedy administration to sign an international agreement regulating the coffee market, and the United States government began to be more vociferous in its praise of political reform in Latin America than it had previously been.

These innovations were intended to bring policies of the United States more nearly in line with what government officials believed to be its interests; in this respect they differ from the creation of the IFC. One must ask whether they show that the innovation in 1954 was inadequate and whether they met appropriately the problems that elicited them.

An international bank for the Western Hemisphere had almost been created during World War II, and the idea had been suggested again by influential Latin American economists and political figures during the early 1950's. The source of its appeal to most Latin Americans was the hope that such an institution would provide a more stable and reliable commitment of United States public funds for investment in Latin America and would be more subject to Latin American influence than either United States institutions or other international ones.

In the United States a general interest in regional development banks began to grow in the early 1950's during the prolonged consideration of the economic problems of underdeveloped countries. Such institutions had been suggested to the director of the Mutual Security Program as early as 1953 by a government advisory committee and by a private study group.[17] And the report of the International Development Advisory Board prepared in 1957 in connection with the reexamination of the foreign aid program recommended that the United States participate in joint financial efforts with local investors and other institutions in underdeveloped countries. It said: "One vehicle for this which should be encouraged would be wisely-conceived regional development banks or operating corporations. Such institutions, with local initiative and resources, could effectively accelerate broad-scale development."[18] Such notions began to be developed more seriously from this time on, and thus became part of the pool of ideas that politicians with an interest in innovation could draw upon.

In addition to this general interest in regional banks, a particular interest in a bank for Latin Americans developed within the United States government around 1957. At a meeting of the presidents of the nations of the OAS in 1956, President Eisenhower proposed a conference of presidential representatives to consider ways of improving the OAS.[19] The only item suggested in advance for the consideration of this conference was methods of using nuclear energy in Latin America. Apparently the conference proposal was mainly another ceremonial gesture intended to indicate interest in the problems of Latin America. The only possible interest that the United States government might have had at the time in serious economic negotiations with Latin Americans was in improving the quality of the projects that were submitted to the Export-Import Bank and the World Bank.[20]

However the meeting had a result that was not anticipated. According to Milton Eisenhower, it was in the course of these deliberations that some members of the government, and Dr. Eisenhower himself, began to become interested in social reform in Latin America, and in using United States funds both to encourage reform and to finance it. Dr. Eisenhower has written:

I was stimulated to reach certain convictions by Pedro Beltrán of Peru, who made an eloquent plea for United States help in social development.

What we were doing in Latin America, he said, was well and good, but it was not enough, and it was doing too little for the people who needed housing, better diets, education, and health services. He urged that we finance such social projects in Latin America.[21]

An inter-American bank was mentioned as the instrument that might be used to finance such programs. Dr. Eisenhower's account continues:

I argued far into the night with United States officials that we give up our historical position and endorse this proposal for an inter-American bank. For twenty years . . . Latin American nations had been asking for the bank with the thought it would have a board of directors predomi-nantly from Latin American nations that would be more sympathetic to meeting their needs. It might surround loans with certain conditions which could bring about some slight change in the rigid social structure of Latin America.[22]

But at this time, he admits, none of the Latin American representa-tives seemed to realize that most of the reforms that were needed would have to come from within the countries themselves: "they were concerned only about more money from abroad for social projects."

High officials of the State and Treasury Departments had begun to be more sympathetic toward the idea of an inter-American de-velopment institution, but this was not made evident to the OAS presidential representatives.[23] The list of final recommendations devised at the meeting included further study of a regional bank at the coming economic conference in Buenos Aires, "creation of an inter-American technical agency to assist, when requested, in the study of 'bankable' projects for economic development," and fur-ther studies on methods of dealing with "the hemisphere's problem of housing."[24]

The question of an inter-American bank was indeed discussed at the economic conference in Buenos Aires in August of 1957. The primary outcome of the discussion was a provision for still further discussion, to which the United States agreed. Otherwise the posi-tion of the United States government remained the same.[25] The question of whether the United States government should support the creation of an inter-American bank was separate from the question of whether it should provide funds for projects that con-tributed to welfare but not directly to economic development. And the United States government answered yes to the first question two years before it acted on the second. Opposition to both pro-posals came from the same sources for the same reason. Both the Treasury and the Export-Import Bank wished not to weaken the terms on which the United States provided public funds to Latin

America. The division of opinion within the executive branch on these issues was therefore similar to the division over the IFC. The main difference was that the proponents of change had begun to think more specifically about the problems of Latin America and to consider these problems in social and political terms rather than merely financial ones. They had begun to think about using United States funds to support modest measures of social change in Latin America; and they had begun to think about the international political problems associated with the transfer of public funds to Latin America.

At the time of the economic conference in Buenos Aires, Robert Anderson had been Secretary of the Treasury only a short while. His stay at that conference was rather brief. In his absence Douglas Dillon was in charge of the United States delegation. He, too, was new to his post in the government. Thus the two men who would be most important for any major change in United States economic policies toward Latin America were, at this time, just beginning their official connection with the problems of this area.

One year after the conference, the United States government announced its support for an inter-American development bank. In the meantime there had been several significant developments. The extent of Latin America's economic difficulties began to be appreciated, and the United States government found it necessary to provide large amounts of compensatory financial assistance in order to prevent serious economic problems in Latin America. The delicate balancing act that the Eisenhower administration had performed to prevent restrictions on imports of important Latin American commodities collapsed. Dr. Eisenhower continued to reexamine United States policies in Latin America through study trips to Mexico and Central America (his report to the President was not made until after the inter-American bank was approved). And in May 1958 Vice-President Nixon made his eventful trip to South America.

In addition to efforts on the part of interested officials to engineer a few changes in United States policies, therefore, there were several events that might have served a triggering function. Critics of the Eisenhower administration were quick to point to the Nixon riots as the cause of the changes that came so quickly after them.[26] Certainly the riots had an enormous impact on Congress and on public opinion. They made Congress more receptive to new ideas about policies concerning Latin America and gave added impetus to the critical examination of the administration's policies that was already going on.

But the events that seem to have precipitated the actual decision to support an inter-American bank took place in the Middle East, not in Latin America. In August 1958 President Eisenhower decided to make a speech to the United Nations concerning events in the Middle East. He intended to announce, on that occasion, that the United States government would support the creation of a regional development bank. It would have been extremely awkward for the government to support such a bank in the Middle East and to continue to oppose one in the Western Hemisphere. Consequently, the day before Eisenhower appeared at the United Nations, a meeting of the Inter-American Economic and Social Council was called in Washington, and Douglas Dillon there announced that the United States had altered its position and would support a regional bank for the Western Hemisphere and contribute to its operations.[27]

Commodity Agreements

The change of policy most directly influenced by the Nixon riots seems to have been that concerning commodity agreements. Until the spring of 1958 the Eisenhower administration had refused even to participate in talks with other governments about such agreements. Then in April, James Reston commented in the *New York Times*:

The administration is deeply worried about the future of its foreign trade program—so much so that the State Department is now seriously considering a revision of two of this Government's pet economic doctrines.

These are its long-standing opposition to the principles of international commodity agreements, and its opposition to prolonged Government purchases of such things as domestic-produced lead and zinc.[28]

He reported that the State Department was urging a new government buying program for domestic lead and zinc, and was discussing the feasibility of an international coffee agreement. The argument was that "it would undoubtedly be cheaper and safer in the long run to revise our theory about commodity agreements than to deal with the economic and political consequences of a financial crisis" in coffee-producing countries. However, he foresaw serious opposition to this line of thought within the administration: "Some officials think the controversy over commodity agreements and stockpiling payments for lead and zinc will be the major issue within the executive branch of the Government in the next three months."

The concern over lead and zinc, of course, was caused by the administration's fears for the fate of the reciprocal trade agreements program at the hands of Congress. It chose to support a program of subsidies rather than government purchases of minerals, but in the end it was forced to resort to import restrictions.[29]

The decision to enter into discussions about a coffee agreement was made very close to Vice-President Nixon's trip to Latin America. On March 5, 1958, Assistant Secretary Rubottom testified that a task force in the State Department was deliberating on the commodity problems faced by the Latin American countries.[30] On July 31, Thomas Mann, then Assistant Secretary of State for Economic Affairs, testified that "some two months ago, we got permission from the Council on Foreign Economic Policy to conduct what we call a coffee study group" with representatives of coffee producing and consuming countries from around the world.[31] "Two months ago" would have been late in the month of May, when Nixon made his famous journey.

But more important than this event was the crisis in the coffee market. In the course of his trip, Vice-President Nixon spoke out in favor of fuller United States participation in the coffee organization that Latin Americans had created at Rio de Janeiro a few months earlier.[32] Evidently a decision to participate in discussions about a coffee agreement had preceded his trip. By the time the trip was over, if not before, the United States government had decided to organize in Washington the Coffee Study Group mentioned by Mann, thus beginning to take a more prominent role in the discussions. During the summer of 1958 it also decided to participate in the work of the United Nations Commission on International Commodity Trade. And as the problems of the lead and zinc industry accumulated, the government also began to participate in international conferences concerning those commodities.[33] It seems clear that the government had responded to a general economic crisis (and not just to the Nixon riots) with a general change in policy.[34]

There were severe limits to this change, however. The government was still officially skeptical that commodity agreements could be generally applied, and was officially opposed to any agreement that would "do more than provide time for sound policies by the affected countries themselves to become effective." Aid would be useless if it supported policies "which run counter to the fundamental forces of the market."[35] Dr. Eisenhower's second report on Latin America, which reached the President in December 1958, recommended that the United States, "if requested to do so, cooperate to the extent of furnishing such information as laws and regulations permit to assist the [coffee] producing countries in enforcing agreements upon marketing quotas." He did not believe the government should go beyond this.[36] This seems to have been the considered position of the United States government at the time.

The Act of Bogotá

By the end of 1958, a period of innovation in United States policy begun in that year had come to an end. The changes had included not only the decisions to create a development bank for the Western Hemisphere and to participate in discussions about the regulation of commodity markets, but also a decision to support the creation of common markets in Latin America and to press the Central American countries particularly to move in that direction. This decision was first made public in Dr. Eisenhower's second report, published in January 1959. Negotiations also began about this time to establish a common market in South America, but this was the result of a Latin American initiative, and the role of the United States government was mainly to monitor the negotiations to make sure that the resulting agreement did not unduly restrict imports from outside the area.

During a visit by Secretary of State Dulles to Brazil in August 1958, arrangements were made to hold a meeting of foreign ministers of the American states in Washington to take up the subject of Operation Pan America.[37] The meeting opened on September 23. By this time, the United States government had announced its decision to support an inter-American bank and had thereby aroused the expectation that the quantity of funds soon to be available to Latin America would be vastly increased; this helped produce a very friendly meeting in spite of the very recent decision by the United States to impose quotas on lead and zinc.[38] The foreign ministers recommended that a special committee of the Inter-American Economic and Social Council should be convened to establish the inter-American bank, that there should be intensified efforts to establish regional common markets, and that there should be continuing discussions about the markets for basic products. In addition they recommended that a special commission of the OAS should be created to study new measures for economic cooperation. This was the origin of what came to be called the Committee of Twenty-One.

The general satisfaction with which the foreign ministers' meeting ended was dispelled when the Committee of Twenty-One held its first meeting in November. It had become clear by then that the new inter-American bank did not represent as radical a change in policy as many Latin Americans had originally expected, and certainly did not signify any large increase in the quantity of development capital to be made available. Furthermore, the United States government was quick to object to the global, long-range planning that was part of the original Brazilian proposal. Assistant Secretary of State for Economic Affairs Thomas Mann stated that the United States preferred to follow a country-by-country method of planning to achieve concrete, short-term goals. The result was considerable criticism of the United States position by the Latin American delegates. But the whole issue was postponed until the special committee to create the inter-American development bank had completed its work.[39]

Thus, after the initial meeting of the Committee of Twenty-One, its business did not include questions concerning the new bank. By the time the full committee met again, the main issues surrounding the establishment of the bank had been resolved, essentially on the terms desired by the United States.[40] Until the United States government altered its policies once again, the Committee of Twenty-One remained merely another arena in which incompatible positions were stated, partly, at least, in order to appeal to public opinion in both Latin America and the United States.[41] Ultimately, the United States government placed before this committee its proposals for a new emphasis on social development, which led to the Act of Bogotá. But such proposals were not intended by the United States when the Committee of Twenty-One first began to meet regularly.

It is likely that some members of the United States government expected that the balance of payments crises of 1958 would eventually disappear, in which case the minor innovations made during this period would have served the purpose of maintaining the inter-American system relatively intact during a difficult period, while perhaps providing some marginal improvements in economic planning in Latin America. In testifying in 1960 on the proposals that became the Act of Bogotá, Under Secretary of State Dillon was asked if there had not been a need for such proposals earlier. He said:

It has become more acute as time has marched on. I think that there was a substantial change in the situation in Latin America beginning some three or four years ago at the time when the prices of Latin America's basic commodities dropped very substantially in world markets, and since then progress in Latin America has been very much slowed.

I think for a while people felt here this might be a temporary situation, but the general opinion now is that it is more permanent and that the situation in Latin America is certainly not as favorable as it looked in the early years of the 1950's.[42]

It was not only the passage of time that prompted such a reappraisal, but also what happened during that time. What happened, of course, was the Cuban Revolution.

In discussing the origins of the inter-American development bank, I have already mentioned the beginnings of at least Dr. Eisenhower's interest in what were called "social development" projects in Latin America. Interest in a regional development bank in the Western Hemisphere had been part of a general interest in regional development banks as a means of coping with problems of development finance in several parts of the world. Similarly, concern for the distribution of the gains from economic growth in Latin America merged with a general interest in that problem throughout the underdeveloped world among those who concerned themselves with the United States foreign aid program.[43]

These concerns as they applied to Latin America were made public for the first time in the testimony of officials in the foreign aid agency during April 1958. For example, on April 1, Rollin S. Atwood, the regional director for Latin American operations in the International Cooperation Administration (ICA), testified before the House Foreign Affairs Committee:

Our program in Latin America is a strong program. It is sincerely appreciated by the governments and by the people. It would be extremely difficult to convince the governments of Latin America to risk their bilateral programs with the United States in return for promises from Russia.

However, if concrete results consequent to the joint program are not convincing or do not produce the economic and social development demanded by the people, the situation in this hemisphere might change radically.[44]

The sorts of concrete results he had in mind became clearer in the course of his testimony. United States public assistance, dominated by the Export-Import Bank, had neglected such areas as housing, schools, public water supplies, and roads. Atwood estimated that there would continue to be for some years a serious shortage of capital funds available on long-term and medium-term bases to finance these neglected areas of economic and social development. He warned:

Advancement in these fields is essential if a balanced economic and social development is to take place, and failure to make this advance will not only postpone the development of a climate favorable to sound private investment, but it will also help to create a feeling of frustration among large segments of the population whose hopes and aspirations are not being fulfilled by the more spectacular industrialization in the form of steel mills, oil wells, mines, factories, and so forth.[45]

These statements represent a radical departure from the testimony the administration had offered in previous years in connection with the foreign aid program in Latin America.

The Development Loan Fund, which was established about this time, could have provided a means of financing such projects.[46] But the DLF's lending criteria, once they were established, were not sufficiently liberal to encompass everything that went by the name of "social development."[47] And given the scarcity of funds available to the DLF, other areas of the world were undoubtedly given priority over Latin America.[48] The new inter-American bank, which could have been a vehicle for such endeavors, emerged as little more than a regional version of existing international institutions.

Dr. Eisenhower's account of the background to his second report to the President makes clear that the opposition to financing social development projects within the executive branch came from familiar sources—the Treasury and others concerned with governmental lending.

Dr. Eisenhower had visited Mexico in August 1957 and shortly thereafter began planning a trip to Central America, which was to take place in the summer of 1958. Thus this second trip was being planned when Vice-President Nixon visited South America in May of that year. The objectives of the second trip were different from those of the first. Dr. Eisenhower believed that "no matter how successful we might be in helping promote economic growth within the prevailing order, this would not be enough. The masses did not benefit from prosperity; the gap between them and the privileged only widened."[49] This trip was to help develop ideas about how this could be changed. Public housing, which Dr. Eisenhower hoped might narrow the gap between rich and poor, was a project to which he devoted special attention. (His interest in housing in Panama was mentioned at the beginning of this chapter.) It was an aspect of "social development" that presented especially difficult financial problems. The opposition of the Treasury prevented the adoption of the proposals Dr. Eisenhower made after his trip to Central America, as he has since explained.

Under-Secretary Dillon coordinated the government-wide review of my report before its publication and transmittal to the President. Reluctantly, after receiving strong disapprovals from the lending agencies and the Treasury Department, he suggested that I modify the housing recommendation. So I altered the offending section.

On housing in Panama, I merely expressed the pious hope that private capital would help. On the larger issue, I adhered to the long-held orthodoxy that it would be preferable to increase the tempo of economic development so that wage earners themselves could build and finance their homes.[50]

But this position was wrong, he has since written; "the threat of revolution was rising, most of the Latin-American nations had not brought about changes to achieve economic justice, and the time had come for the United States to take the initiative in stimulating change."[51] As of January 1959, however, the United States government had rejected this recommendation.

By the winter of 1959 such concerns began to be taken much more seriously. In November the President followed one of the recommendations in Dr. Eisenhower's report by appointing a National Advisory Committee on Inter-American Affairs.[52] This committee held an organizational meeting in December, had two days of meetings and briefings in January, and accompanied President Eisenhower on his trip to Latin America in February and March, 1960.[53]

This committee provided a forum for exploring and debating questions about social reform in Latin America. Dr. Eisenhower reports:

The President had given us carte blanche to investigate whatever we felt to be relevant, and Secretary Herter and Assistant Secretary Rubottom had put the resources of the State Department at our disposal. We got all the ideas and facts we asked for—from the State Department, from the Development Loan Fund, from other lending agencies. The committee, with the full participation and creative leadership of Herter,

Dillon, and Rubottom, was coming to grips with the problem of stimulating social change. There can be no doubt that Castro's wicked influence in the hemisphere was spurring us onward, but we felt strongly that what we were considering was far too important to be distorted by emergency adaptations. . . . We wanted a procedure and legal authority which would permit the United States to help bring about social reform in ways that would not bring charges of unilateral intervention.

Early in 1960 a special technical group was organized to draft suggestions—on tax reform, land reform, tax administration, and other problems—for an inter-American conference to be held nine months later in Bogotá.[54] Whatever the precise role played by this committee, it seems clear that the Cuban Revolution was increasing the pressure for some dramatic innovation in United States economic policies, and making the concern of some officials in the State Department over the need for redistributing the gains of economic development in Latin America seem more pertinent.[55]

Anastas Mikoyan visited Cuba in February 1960 and made agreements for the Soviet Union to buy fixed quantities of Cuban sugar over the next four years, to lend Cuba $100 million at two and a half percent interest, and to provide technical assistance.[56] Shortly thereafter, President Eisenhower traveled to Argentina, Brazil, Chile, and Uruguay, amid declarations of support by the United States for reform in Latin America.[57] During the President's tour, the increasing evidence of Soviet interest in Latin America was often mentioned, with Eisenhower emphasizing the terms of the Rio Treaty concerning intervention in hemispheric affairs by a foreign power, and the Latin Americans emphasizing that more economic assistance from the United States was necessary to prevent further Communist encroachments.[58] While in Brazil, President Eisenhower agreed to a meeting of the working group of the Committee of Twenty-One to discuss any new proposals presented by the participating governments.[59]

It is not clear exactly when the plans that eventually were transformed into the Act of Bogotá received the President's approval. Though his speeches in all the countries he visited contained many references to the need for welfare measures in Latin America, Secretary Herter stated on his return that no new economic measures for Latin America were planned.[60] In late June of 1960, Under Secretary Dillon, as coordinator of the aid program, requested ICA missions in Latin America to suggest social development projects for possible inclusion in the program for the fiscal year 1962. An ICA official later testified: "At that particular time the administration was considering the utilization [for the social development projects] of a certain portion of special assistance funds which would be presented to Congress and justified to the Congress for a special Latin American program of somewhat more modest propositions." This proposed program was "supplanted and replaced by the Act of Bogotá."[61]

The meeting of the working group of the Committee of Twenty-One, arranged during President Eisenhower's trip to Brazil, took place in June 1960. According to the testimony of Under Secretary Dillon, it was

very clear when this meeting terminated, about the end of June . . . that further and substantial action in the social field was necessary.

The committee decided to call a meeting of the senior organizations— The Committee of Twenty-One—in Bogotá on the 5th of September, and it became obvious that we would have to submit a new program at that time.[62]

On July 8 a White House spokesman announced that the President and the State Department had been working for some time on a comprehensive plan, which they would submit to the Bogotá meeting of the Committee of Twenty-One in September. On July 11 the President himself announced that the United States would then have some new measures to propose. When questioned, he replied that, while new funds would be required, it was not yet clear how much, nor was it clear how the funds were to be administered. He mentioned that the inter-American bank might be used in some way.[63] The President's message on this subject went to Congress on August 8, 1960. In it he asked Congress to authorize the appropriation of new funds to finance social development projects in Latin America. Congress quickly obliged. And then at Bogotá, in September, the United States sought, and got, commitments from the Latin American governments to the domestic programs, such as tax and land reform, that were necessary complements to the money from the United States.

It is reasonable to hypothesize that the evidence of Soviet intentions to become involved in the deepening Cuban-American
dispute served to elicit the President's support for the argument
that "social development" was urgently needed in Latin America.
Such evidence began to be quite clear early in 1960. The full dimensions of the problem probably did not become clear until the
summer of that year, however, when the dispute between the
Cuban and United States governments over the nationalization of
the American oil refineries occurred, and when the Cuban government's appeal to the United Nations Security Council made a
meeting of the OAS necessary in order to forestall United Nations
action. At that point the United States government needed the
support of the Latin American governments in its dispute with
the Cubans.

Soviet aid to Cuba was negotiated in February. In March the
administration asked Congress for authority to alter sugar quotas
for individual countries, and President Eisenhower approved the
training and arming of Cuban rebels by the Central Intelligence
Agency.[64] In late June the oil refineries were expropriated; on July
6 the President authorized a cut in the Cuban sugar quota. The
Cubans then expropriated all property owned by United States
citizens in Cuba, and on July 9 Khrushchev announced his support
of the Cuban government in this dispute. President Eisenhower
issued a statement saying that this showed "the clear intention to
establish Cuba in a role serving Soviet purposes in this hemisphere."[65] On July 12 Khrushchev retaliated, pronouncing the
death of the Monroe Doctrine. On July 11 the Cuban government
appealed to the Security Council of the United Nations for a special meeting to consider aggressive actions by the United States.
On July 18 the council of the OAS voted to convene a meeting of
foreign ministers of that body, in San José, Costa Rica, in August,
in order to forestall United Nations action.

It does not really matter at what point in this chain of events a
decision was made to support social development in Latin America. The Cuban Revolution was not a momentary event, but a
prolonged crisis that deepened with the passage of time. The essential point is that at some stage it seems to have become a suffi-

cient stimulus to induce the President to overrule the opposition
of the Treasury and the lending agencies to financing social development projects in Latin America.

Conclusions

The Act of Bogotá was the last of the Eisenhower administration's marginal adjustments in the formula it had devised in 1953
and 1954 for balancing foreign and domestic claims on resources.
Each change was stimulated by a limited crisis that had the effect
of momentarily centralizing decision-making so that proposals
which had been made but blocked were adopted. The changes
made by the Kennedy administration were also adjustments and
were affected by the ongoing Cuban Revolution; but they were
also made in the context of a comprehensive review of United
States policies comparable to the one undertaken when President
Eisenhower first came into office. There were thus two centralizing forces at work: those produced by Cuba, and those produced
by a new presidential administration. Although the changes made
by the Kennedy administration were quickly grafted onto the
main body of United States economic policies toward Latin America, they were formulated to a greater extent outside the established executive departments. There were disagreements between
the task force on Latin American affairs and career State Department officials.[66] There had also been a comprehensive review of
policies at the beginning of the first Eisenhower administration,
but in that instance the pressure of external events was exerted in
a direction different from the one desired by the President. In 1961,
the pressure of events and the inclinations of the President were
moving policies in the same direction.

In both 1953 and 1961, new presidents criticized their predecessors for their ad hoc responses to crises. Each sought to organize the foreign aid programs of the United States in the light of
long-range goals, rather than expediency. Each believed that his
predecessor had lost some control over events by failing to take
a long-range, comprehensive view of the problems. In 1953 the
President emphasized conserving resources for domestic use,

mainly private use. In 1961 the President emphasized liberating resources for public use, both at home and abroad. Neither, however, followed a course of action as different from that of his predecessor as his rhetoric implied. And both, in introducing innovations, chose from a stock of suggestions, made both in the government and outside it, that were concerned with transferring resources to all underdeveloped countries. None was originally designed specifically for the problems of Latin America. The Alliance for Progress was a multilateral commitment to the principles that the Kennedy administration intended to reorganize the entire foreign aid program around.

Although the measures adopted by the United States government were chosen under the influence of what were perceived as crises, it would not be accurate to say that they were irrelevant to the problems the government faced in Latin America. During the second Eisenhower administration, the government sought more acceptable ways of imposing difficult conditions on Latin American governments as the price of financial aid. It also sought more effective methods of relating procedures by which economic planning was done, projects were devised, and financial assistance was sought by Latin American governments. Under the stimulus of the Cuban Revolution, these objectives were broadened to include an attempt to eliminate some of the major structural obstacles to faster economic growth in Latin America, as well as those sources of discontent that might lead to political violence. The Eisenhower administration remained convinced, however, that the major obstacle to economic growth in Latin America was not the limited availability of foreign capital, but conditions within Latin America. Its innovations in economic policies were primarily a means of achieving a mutually acceptable method of conducting negotiations about the need for financial assistance and the conditions that would go with it. The Alliance for Progress was another means of accomplishing the same end.

This increased willingness to risk commitments of public funds in order to increase their productivity was only partly the result of the activities of the Soviet Union. Before 1958 the value that the

United States government placed on economic development in other underdeveloped areas was probably greater than the value it placed on growth in Latin America. Moreover the government believed that the productivity of public funds was greater in other parts of the world (private capital, as has been mentioned, was believed to be more productive in Latin America). Gradually it was shown that the productivity of private investment and export earnings in Latin America, measured in terms of the United States' objectives there (chiefly, but not solely, economic growth), was not so high as had been believed. This in itself increased the incentives to provide public assistance to Latin America. Once the decision had been made to increase public assistance, the desire to economize on the use of public funds over time led to efforts to use such funds as an incentive for the recipients to undertake domestic measures that would eventually reduce their dependence on outside public funds.

The timing of the changes in United States policy was affected by both external and internal factors. There were serious disagreements between the United States government and the governments of most Latin American countries concerning priorities in economic policy. The government of the United States had doubts about the willingness of the governments of Latin America to use public assistance in ways that would serve the long-range interests of either the United States or the recipient countries. At the same time, the government of the United States and the governments of Latin America were engaged in attempts to influence each other. Latin American governments sought multilateral arrangements in economic affairs at least partly in order to increase their influence over such matters, and reduce that of the United States; and they used existing multilateral arrangements in order to bring pressure to bear on the United States. Therefore the United States government was not anxious to participate in multilateral economic negotiations with the Latin Americans. Nor was it anxious to reduce its bargaining power by granting to the governments of Latin America long-range claims on its funds.[67]

With regard to internal factors, decisions to commit resources to

Latin America required the cooperation of many different, semi-autonomous parts of the government. This decentralization had to be overcome in an ad hoc way. Apart from the inauguration of new administrations, the chief occasions for producing these compromises were events that, given the commitments of the government, had to be coped with. Such occasions were the economic conference at Rio de Janeiro in 1954 and associated events (especially the Guatemala affair), the economic crisis in Latin America in 1958, the Nixon riots, the crisis in the Middle East, and the Cuban Revolution.

These events were both necessary conditions for innovations, and among the reasons for innovation. They were necessary conditions because they momentarily centralized decision-making. They were among the reasons for change because they provided arguments for rejecting the views that had previously justified established policy. They did this in two main ways. First, the existence of a crisis meant that something had to be done. Innovations, which could be pointed to as positive action, were useful whatever their intrinsic merits. The establishment of the International Finance Corporation is the purest example of this. Second, the crisis could be pointed to as an instance of the problem that the proposed innovation was designed to correct. The Cuban Revolution is the purest example of this.

If a change in policy is probably a beneficial one, and is relevant to the crisis that evokes it, does this not imply that the change should have come earlier? To answer this question, and attempt a general assessment of the effects of politics on United States foreign economic policies during this period, in the next chapter I will place this discussion in the context of the analysis of United States policies and inter-American politics offered in the first two chapters.

Part III. Conclusions

7. The Effects of Domestic Politics on United States Latin American Policy

Whenever the United States government is faced with a serious foreign policy problem, many critics assume that the problem could have been prevented. Given such an assumption, the main problem for analysis is how to explain the government's failure to take the necessary preventive measures. A number of characteristics of the political process immediately suggest themselves as explanations. Criticism of this nature undoubtedly serves a useful purpose by sometimes forcing the government to justify itself in an area of policy in which governments can all too easily escape criticism. But for analytical (as opposed to practical) purposes, one cannot make an assumption of the government's omnipotence the basis for the study of United States foreign policy.

A second assumption often implied in criticisms of United States foreign policy is that foreign policies are made by individuals. Whenever foreign policy decisions differ from the decisions a rational, fully informed individual would have made, the government is assumed to be at fault, and the peculiarities of the political process are again offered as an explanation. This assumption, too, probably serves a useful purpose in focusing criticism on the government; but it is, of course, false, and it is therefore unrealistic to make it part of the groundwork for any serious analysis of the making of foreign policy. All foreign policy decisions are necessarily collective ones. They require the coordination of ever larger numbers of people. The relevant comparison, therefore, is not with the ratiocinative processes of individuals (which would be incapable of performing the tasks organizations perform), but rather with other organizations faced with similar problems.

Obviously neither a lack of complete success nor the exhibition of typical organizational behavior is sufficient evidence that United States foreign policy can be explained by the peculiarities of the domestic political process. Is there any such evidence? Clearly it can only come from an argument to the effect that given the identical situations, the decisions that another type of government could reasonably be expected to have made would have produced different and more favorable results. Such an argument grew out of the literature that sprang up after World War II on the relation between economic development and political stability. Most of the writings by Americans on foreign aid and economic development assert or imply that economic growth would solve the political problems in Latin America that have concerned the government of the United States. If this were true, it would seem reasonable to believe that a government that was better able to see its interests clearly would have acted much more quickly and decisively to promote economic growth in Latin America.

The popularity of this argument is greatly increased by the tendency to project viewpoints appropriate to domestic disputes onto international politics. In the case of liberals in the United States, two viewpoints are often projected. One is that international and domestic conflicts over economic questions are similar and can be resolved by similar policies.[1] The other is that the United States government's interest in the domestic conflicts of underdeveloped countries is similar to the national interest of the United States in its own domestic policies, as defined by American liberals, so that groups abroad with liberal objectives should be supported. This leads to some confusion, of course, about the merits of intervening in other countries' domestic politics. For though it may be necessary to provide support for deserving political groups, intervention violates the principle of international equality and the goal of international conciliation.

Conservatives, of course, are equally prone to project their conceptions of politics onto the international scene. And they, like liberals, tend to make common cause with what they believe to be sympathetic groups in other countries. This reinforces the notion that foreign policies have been largely determined by domestic interests with excessive political power.

The tendency to regard international issues as similar to domestic ones is especially important in the case of Latin America, for two reasons. First, the pressing demands of military conflict with a serious antagonist, which in other parts of the world compete with ideological interpretations of international politics, have been almost completely absent in the relations between the United States and Latin America. Therefore domestic analogies have had less competition as the basis for understanding the interests of the United States government there. Second, the New Deal and the Good Neighbor Policy provided a powerful example of what liberal conceptions of policy could accomplish in Latin America. They did not, however, provide an absolutely clear answer to the liberals' dilemma about intervention, as the controversy about Argentina showed.

Criticism of United States Policies

All these conditions have been bases for criticism of United States foreign policy in Latin America since the end of World War II, when the New Deal efforts at economic cooperation ceased. Sometimes the critics have merely demanded a large-scale program of economic assistance for Latin America, hoping that this would have indirect political effects. At other times they have demanded that the United States government intervene against Latin American dictatorships and in support of the democratic left. At all times, however, the success of the Roosevelt administration in Latin America has seemed to be an implicit criticism of the subsequent record of the United States government there.

Such criticism began shortly after the end of World War II, when Sumner Welles wrote:

The apparent indifference of Washington to its neighbors' difficulties and the unquestioned failure of the Department of State to live up to some of the commitments on economic policy which it made have created . . . serious ill-feeling toward the United States. What is . . . more immediately disquieting is that the economic dislocations will result in social and political upheavals in many parts of the Americas.[2]

He called for a program of economic cooperation that would have as its goal "the rapid industrialization of the other American nations."[3] In a book on United States relations with countries in the Caribbean, published in 1947, Dexter Perkins made a similar point:

It is the business of the United States to see to it that these republics enjoy the advantages of an expanding economy, that they are helped to a greater and greater degree of prosperity, that in all of them the condition of the masses is steadily improved, and that bit by bit the conditions are created in them which will lead in the direction, not of totalitarian dictatorship, but of liberal social democracy.[4]

This political transformation was to occur entirely indirectly. Perkins was careful to emphasize that the policy of nonintervention implied a neutral attitude toward internal politics in the countries concerned.[5]

As a result of the early crises of the cold war, many people were eventually persuaded that other claims on United States resources had priority over Latin America. By the end of the Korean War, however, it seemed to increasing numbers of interested people that the United States ought to try to begin rebuilding the cooperative relationships with the Latin Americans that the Roosevelt administration had shown were possible. The Cuban Revolution seemed to be definitive evidence that such an effort was overdue, and the Alliance for Progress a belated admission of the error.

But the New Deal's experience in Latin America was not a valid model, and the Cuban Revolution was not such definitive evidence of the inadequacies of United States policies. During World War II cooperation for collective security in the Western Hemisphere was both more important and more nearly possible than at any time before or since. And the economic dislocations of the war placed a premium on economic assistance as a means of promoting political stability. The result was that economic assistance was overemphasized as a means of promoting the United States' short- and medium-range objectives in Latin America.

This is not to suggest that the enthusiasts for closer economic cooperation with Latin America at the end of the war were unaware of the complexities involved in it. Laurence Duggan's *The Americas*, published in 1949, is a sensitive treatment of the basic problems of the area. But his was a vision of the very long run. And as such it underestimated the complexities of the short run: the differing priorities of the United States and the Latin American governments, the conflicting interpretations of what was required for economic development, and the difficulty of coping with political instability while seeking to bring about conditions that might eventually eliminate it.[6] In the short run all that the government could be fairly certain of accomplishing was to decrease slightly the dissatisfaction with its policies. Yet, with the end of the war, this could no longer be a sufficient criterion for United States foreign policy.

Because so many Americans have been anxious to repudiate the actions taken by the United States in the Central American and Caribbean areas prior to the Good Neighbor Policy, many have neglected one of the main lessons of that earlier experience: namely that in many instances a stable relationship with a government of a Latin American country was possible only if that government was itself stable. To undertake to stabilize it required a willingness to assume a much more direct political role within the country than the United States government, or other Latin American governments, would long be willing to tolerate.

Political change within a Latin American country might upset the relations between the government of that country and the government of the United States in a direct or an indirect way. For instance, a dissatisfied political group might seek support from another country in its attempt to gain power, or it might seek support for domestic objectives that it felt would be poorly served by the United States. In the early twentieth century it was not unknown for a dissident group to seek the direct military or financial support of a foreign power by offering a naval base in exchange.

The process of trading domestic support for international support has become more subtle since then. But such exchanges remain possible even now.

The same political change might also foster other conditions that would in turn lead to foreign intervention. Earlier in this century this danger primarily came about as a result of defaults on foreign loans; foreign powers then intervened in defense of private investors. Foreign support may also be and has been invoked when political instability has produced unacceptable economic conditions or civil war. In the one circumstance, the major country with which the unfortunate Latin American country is aligned may be blamed for the economic crisis, and a solution may be sought by inviting economic assistance on different terms from another country. In the other case, foreign involvement may result when a disadvantaged party seeks reinforcement from outside. In still another case, a politically insecure group may seek to increase its base of domestic support by encouraging an aggressive foreign policy, for which the assistance of a major foreign power might prove necessary.

Whether any of these things will happen, of course, is partly determined by the availability of external support and the means of retaliation open to the United States government. In both these respects the United States government has been in an extremely advantageous position since the end of World War II. But environmental constraints do not always physically prevent a government from pursuing a chosen policy, though they usually impose high costs for doing so. What seems too costly to one government may seem to another a price worth paying. And these evaluations will be affected by the domestic political situation each government faces.

The chief difficulty in trying to influence domestic politics in Latin America is that the conditions necessary for success are not really known. And were they known, one could not be sure that the governments assisted would be able to do their part in maintaining their own stability. If not, then the United States government would find itself on the losing side of a domestic political dispute, and its problems would be compounded rather than simplified.

Seen in this light, the possibility of preventing the Cuban Revolution may reasonably be doubted. What is more, one may doubt that it should have been prevented. Before the Cuban Revolution there was little to demonstrate the limitations of the Soviet Union's support for political and economic changes in the Western Hemisphere, and much to inflate its significance. In light of the many difficulties faced by Castro's regime once it was established, and the United States government's ability to force the Soviet Union to withdraw its missiles from Cuba, the position of the Soviet Union in Latin America has probably been weakened.[7]

The advantages of association with the United States of course have to be demonstrated too, in deeds rather than words; but the ability of the United States government to perform eloquent deeds is limited by the nature of the opportunities presented to it. It is undoubtedly important to emphasize that the United States government can be influenced by methods short of raising alarums about imminent financial collapse or invoking Soviet assistance. The countries of Latin America must have an incentive to play from strength rather than to exploit their own weaknesses. But for this there must be a certain amount of strength in Latin America for the United States to support.

Late in August 1960, in the course of the congressional debate on the Eisenhower administration's social development proposals, Representative Walter Judd asked:

Why did not the administration present such a bill earlier? The basic reason is that while we have given a good deal of aid in Latin America, some of it has not been too productive because some of those countries have not seen the necessity to make certain essential changes in their own laws, in their tax structure, in land tenure, and in legal procedures, without which changes significant improvement is not possible.

It is not useful or wise to expand aid programs in Latin America, or elsewhere, until the cooperating countries are willing to do certain things themselves. . . .

Some have called this the Castro bill. It can be thought of that way only in terms of what Castro's actions in Cuba have done to awaken the countries of this hemisphere to what is already happening and what can happen in the future. There is an increased realization that they cannot delay longer in making the changes necessary to make outside aid more effective than in the past.[8]

The same point was made by Under Secretary of State Douglas Dillon, who testified in support of the administration's proposals. "One can certainly question whether we should have reached this conclusion six months or a year ago," he said; but he doubted whether the proposals would have been practical much before that time. Then, Latin Americans were pressing for rapid industrialization—"they believed new factories would be a panacea for everything"—not recognizing the need for redistribution of land, social reforms, improved housing, and so forth. But now, he believed, there was a feeling in both the United States and Latin America that such improvements were vital.[9]

The Eisenhower administration's Democratic critics did not try to refute the contention that any such program introduced earlier would have resulted in few substantial changes. More to the point, virtually no one examined what purpose these few changes might have served. The critics seem to have assumed that such a program, introduced earlier and on a larger scale, might have prevented the Cuban Revolution. But if it had not, would the United States government have been in a better or worse position in the summer of 1960? Since it would still have been under great pressure to make concessions to the Latin Americans, its bargaining position on economic issues would probably have been worse.

In a statement that nicely illustrates how the congressional debate obscured the basic political problems involved, Senator Frank Church said:

It seems to me that we cannot possibly achieve our objective this way. Take, for example, our own country. We had great and meaningful reform programs that came as the result of the depression. If the depression had not been as extreme as it was, we probably would not have gotten the programs accomplished within our own Government, within our own electoral process, because it took that kind of a jolt to effect the kind of remedial legislation that was required.

Now, we go down to these countries, some of which are feudal countries, and everybody who goes to them knows that you have got to have land reform. That means taking the land away from a relatively small group of very wealthy people and distributing it to a great many peasants. That is an awfully hard thing to do when the government and the society in that country are controlled by those who own the land.

The same thing is true with tax reforms that are so badly needed. . . .

Now, I just do not see how you are going to get the kind of meaningful reform which is necessary if we are really going to have social progress in Latin America by taking $500 million and giving it to the Inter-American Development Bank.[10]

Senator Church's objections were persuasive. They were probably similar to the objections raised within the administration in opposition to the kind of assistance that the Cuban crisis finally persuaded it to adopt. They were, in fact, an argument for *not* preventing economic and political crises in Latin America. And such an argument implies that an attempt to prevent the economic crisis of 1958 or the Cuban Revolution would have had a conservative rather than a progressive effect on Latin America.

But in the summer of 1960, in the context of party competition and the Cuban Revolution, Senator Church reached the opposite conclusion:

It seems to me that if this thing is to accomplish its purpose, you must have a big program extended over a long period of years, a commitment on the part of the United States to do its part, with sufficient money there to form an inducement to these countries to come and sit down with us and work out an elaborate and meaningful extended multiyear program that is connected with the kind of basic tax and land reform programs that are necessary to accomplish the objective.[11]

The assumption of the administration's critics was that money would be sufficient inducement in the future, as it would have been in the past. But the view of Albert Hirschman is probably a more realistic one:

To paraphrase Marx, decentralized, unrequited violence is frequently found in the role of indispensable midwife to *reform.* To advocate reforms in Latin America without tolerating, accepting, and sometimes even welcoming and promoting the only kinds of pressures which have proven to be effective in getting reforms is to risk being accused of hypocrisy and deception.[12]

At the end of the last chapter I asked whether, by changing its policies under the stimulus of a crisis in a way that seems relevant to the causes of the crisis, the United States government does not implicitly convict itself of inexcusable delay in altering its policies. The answer, of course, is: No, not necessarily. The crisis may have been the most appropriate occasion for the government's decision. I have tried to suggest, both here and in Chapter 1, that there are, in fact, good reasons for believing this to be the case.

Organizational Structure and Policy Making

But the problem is not yet disposed of. If a crisis is not only the best reason for changing policy, but also a necessary condition for the government's being able to do it, is it not simply a fortunate accident that earlier, less appropriate situations did not lead to governmental action? Was the government not lucky rather than intelligent? What can be said about the effects of politics on United States policies, if not that they inhibited the development of intelligent policies? Do the decisions of the United States government show no effects of the peculiarities of its decision-making process?

To answer these questions, it will be convenient to treat the United States government as merely one organization in a world of organizations, and to make use of an article by James Q. Wilson called "Innovation in Organization: Notes Toward a Theory."[13] As Wilson employs the term, innovation means "a 'fundamental' change in a 'significant' number of tasks." What is fundamental and significant must be defined by the organization in question.[14] The change develops through three stages: conception or invention, proposal, and adoption and implementation.[15] The probability that each of these three stages will occur, Wilson suggests, is determined by the diversity of the organization. By diversity he means the complexity of the organization's task structure and incentive system.

The *task structure* (i.e., the sum of all tasks, or one-man duties, in the organization) increases in complexity as the number of different tasks increases and as the proportion of nonroutine tasks increases. . . . The *incentive system* (i.e., the sum of all rewards given to members) increases in complexity as the number of sources of incentives increases, and these in turn increase in number with an increase in the number of groups (both membership and reference groups, both inside and outside the formal organization) with which each member is affiliated.[16]

Utilizing these definitions, Wilson proposes three hypotheses:

Hypothesis 1: The greater the diversity of the organization, the greater the probability that members will conceive of major innovations.

Hypothesis 2: The greater the diversity of the organization, the greater the probability that major innovations will be proposed.

Hypothesis 3: The greater the diversity of the organization, the smaller the proportion of major innovative proposals that will be adopted.[17]

I propose to draw on these hypotheses in analyzing the foreign policy decisions I have summarized and in explaining some aspects of them. I will also employ some subsidiary hypotheses that Wilson infers from the three central ones just quoted, and for which he offers some additional evidence.

The first of these is: "If organizational diversity is directly proportional to the rate of proposals and inversely proportional to the rate of adoptions, little can be said about the total number (or the frequency) of adopted innovations in organizations."[18] A unitary organization that can easily adopt innovations but finds few suggested to it, and a highly diverse organization that receives many proposals but adopts few of them may be equally innovative. There ought, of course, to be some optimum level of diversity, but given the difficulties involved in measuring diversity, it would seem to be impossible to determine what it is.

Second: "Many organizations will adopt no major innovation unless there is a 'crisis'—an extreme change in conditions for which there is no adequate, programmed response."[19] Crises call the overall goals of the organization into question, and therefore emphasize for a time the incentives controlled by the leaders of the organization and minimize the importance of other incentives. In noncrisis situations, on the contrary, members may oppose innovations without subjecting everyone to the costs involved in threats to the integrity of the organization itself. This hypothesis suggests (although Wilson does not say this) that crises may compensate for a diverse organization's inability to adopt many of the proposals that its structure serves to encourage.

Third: "Decentralization can be regarded as a method for increasing the probability of ratification of new proposals by confining (in advance) their effect to certain subunits."[20] By decentralization Wilson here means that subunits have "a high degree of autonomy in the control of their own incentive and task structures." By decentralizing, an organization "reduces the number of wills that must be concerted before a proposal generated within a subunit can be adopted."[21] "Decentralization" and "diversity" are related but distinct notions. Because it is easy to confuse them, it will be helpful to dwell for a moment on the difference between them.

The difficulty with the word "decentralization" is that what is being decentralized is not often specified. If one is speaking of incentives, for example, then an increase in the number of each member's group affiliations might be taken as a form of decentralization, for it implies that control over some incentives has been dispersed. Nonetheless, it might still be true that the agreement of the management was necessary before important changes were made. Decentralization in Wilson's sense refers to instances in which that is no longer true: parts of an organization are, for some decisions, independent of the rest.

Organizations, then, can be diverse without being decentralized in this sense. One could probably characterize the two main political parties in Great Britain as diverse but centralized organizations. By contrast, political parties in the United States are, like other institutions in American politics, decentralized: parts of the organization may act independently of the leadership.

Decentralization increases an organization's diversity for all decisions that still must be made by the parent organization.[22] At the same time, it may increase the probability that any particular innovation will be adopted by in effect substituting a smaller, less diverse organization for the parent organization as the arena within which the decision must be made. It seems a fair inference that this further complicates the problem of estimating how innovative a particular organization will be, because the degree of innovation will depend partly on whether a decision can be made by part of the organization or must be made at the highest level (in which case the concerting of a larger number of individual decisions is required). One would suspect that by finding a receptive, semi-autonomous subsystem (e.g., a particular executive department with its attendant legislative committees and clientele groups, supported by an ad hoc legislative majority) the President can sometimes turn decentralization to his advantage. But where the co-operation of more than one semiautonomous subsystem is required, he will find that decentralization complicates his task.

For someone who thinks of a government as an individual agent intent upon finding the optimum solution to a given problem, what has to be explained is decisions that fall short of the optimum. For someone who thinks of a government as an organization that routinizes the behavior of large numbers of people in order to perform certain complex tasks, what has to be explained is the government's ability to respond to novel problems with novel solutions. Wilson's article provides some plausible clues to this second question. The United States government is an exceptionally diverse and also decentralized organization. It therefore generates an exceptionally large number of innovative proposals. On occasion decentralization facilitates their adoption. On other occasions it hinders their adoption. The result is a considerable amount of frustration, some of which is caused by exaggerating the expected benefits of proposed innovations and minimizing their costs, as defined in organizational terms. As Wilson points out, "proponents of a particular innovation are not likely to perceive fully the difficulties that stand in the way of successful innovation."[23]

Wilson deliberately avoids discussing the effect of an organization's environment on innovation. He does, however, mention one important way in which the environment impinges on an organization, and that is through the development of crises. (What counts as a crisis, of course, is defined by the organization itself.) But the frequency with which such events occur is at least partially determined by forces that the organization does not control. If a crisis threatens the very existence of the organization, it may be too late to respond. If the organization does not have available some conception of how to respond, the action it takes may be limited and inappropriate. But an organization with a stock of innovative proposals may, when faced with a limited crisis, respond with innovations that not only deal with the crisis adequately but serve to fend off other dangers.

It does not seem to me to be naïve to suggest that the United States government has been, since World War II, in just such a position. It is a decentralized organization whose decision making has been facilitated because the international environment has confronted it with a number of limited crises. Most of them have been related to the constant pressure of competition from the Soviet Union; most have arisen in circumstances such that the United States government could not hope for much of a response from any government other than itself. They have been limited crises because the same factors that have produced a bipolar world have also rendered the United States government seriously vulnerable only to large, cumulative changes in international politics.[24] To these pressures from the outside world must be added the internal crisis that occurs at least every eight years, when a new administration must be organized. Thus since World War II there have been many opportunities for the United States government to review its policies in Latin America and to choose new ones from the stock of suggestions turned up by an inventive political process.

One must not exaggerate, though, the similarity of organizational behavior to the norm of individual behavior even under conditions of crisis.[25] The momentum of existing organizational commitments, and the necessity for bargaining among independent groups whose cooperation is necessary for a decision, will both have their effects even then. Moreover, an inventive political process is not without its own peculiar costs. It probably encourages exaggerated expectations of how much other policies might differ from the ones actually chosen. And it complicates the task of communicating the government's intentions to other governments. Sometimes this is a liability, as when the government seems to be the servant of businessmen. At other times it is an asset, as when the government appears to be controlled by groups sympathetic to the problems of Latin America. But there are undoubtedly occasions when careful political management, guided by a viewpoint different from either of these, would accomplish better results than either.

It happens that the policies I have investigated affect the interests of domestic groups as well as those of foreign governments and groups within foreign countries. The nature of the political process in the United States guarantees that most domestic groups having the qualities and resources necessary to support an organization will be represented in the policy-making process. Where compromises can be reached between these groups and the makers of foreign policy, and there is not much conflict among the groups concerned, decentralization will facilitate the enactment of a stable program. The Export-Import Bank and P. L. 480 (providing for the disposal of agricultural surpluses abroad) are examples of this. Where compromise is not possible, however, and groups with conflicting interests are concerned, decentralization will additionally complicate the enactment of programs because of the number of points of view that must be concerted. Two political problems of the foreign aid program proper have been the impossibility of insulating it from a wide range of controversies about the goals of United States foreign policy and the extreme difficulty of finding a salient domestic group as a base of support. It therefore required a long time to commit the government to it as a long-range program, and routinization has been difficult.

Innovations in United States policies toward Latin America have involved incremental changes in institutions whose chief political concerns were originally domestic ones, and whose decentralized nature, together with the moderation of domestic conflicts, had meant that these domestic concerns were primarily those promoted by various private groups. The chief cause of change has come from the international environment. The threats of first Germany and then the Soviet Union to the United States government's interests in Latin America were largely responsible for its ability and willingness to compromise its goals to accommodate those of the Latin Americans. Each major reaction to these threats altered both the procedures for negotiating many of the economic issues that divide the United States from the countries of Latin America, and the role that private interests in the United States play in this process. This may be clearly seen by comparing the dollar diplomacy of the early part of this century, the Export-Import Bank, and the Alliance for Progress.

But these same innovations were also made possible by domestic transformations in the United States. The increased importance of the public as compared to the private sector of the domestic economy, and accompanying changes in standards of propriety, have increased the probability of finding compromises between the interests of United States citizens and those of the Latin Americans. Thus each innovation has been introduced into a domestic context more receptive than it had been before.

Experience with the Alliance for Progress

The proponents of the Alliance for Progress entertained exaggerated notions of what it might accomplish, as might be expected on the basis of what I have said about the political process in the United States. And, not surprisingly, they have been disillusioned. As one early reviewer of its work reported: "It does not seem possible to discuss the Alliance for Progress without being concerned about the success or failure of this experiment and today the tendency is to think in terms of failure."[26] Some of the exaggerated expectations resulted from the process of persuasion within the government that was needed to get the controversial program adopted. The Kennedy administration had to persuade Congress that longer-term aid commitments were vital to the effort to remove obstacles to planning in underdeveloped countries, while trying at the same time to persuade Latin Americans that domestic reforms were more important than outside assistance. Each already believed the opposite, and tended to hear the part of the administration's argument that coincided with its beliefs. Thus many

Latin Americans have been disappointed with the quantity of aid funds, and many people in the United States have been disappointed with the failure of the Latin Americans to live up to their commitments.[27]

Other expectations were based on policy makers' faulty perceptions of the problems. First, some of them believed that the failure to commit greater quantities of economic assistance to Latin America in the past was a major reason why governments in that area had failed to undertake reforms. They held too high hopes for the effectiveness of spending more dollars.

Second, they misjudged the extent to which the rapid economic development of Latin America would serve immediate interests of the United States government. Although Latin America's dependence on foreign capital and foreign trade had provided the government with difficult problems, these conditions had not in themselves threatened its security. Political instability in Latin America had, however. Clearly economic conditions in Latin America were relevant to the achievement of political stability; and rising birthrates, declining export markets, and low rates of growth in Latin America were matters of some concern. On the other hand, the American interest in these problems could not be satisfied just by a high rate of economic growth in Latin America. Poor economic performance helped force these questions to the intergovernmental level. But the problems could not be solved simply by allocating aid funds in a way that would maximize their contribution to economic development in Latin America.

Third, policy makers overestimated the number of interests shared by the government of the United States and the governments of Latin America. As Joseph Grunwald has pointed out, it was not even certain that the United States government and the Latin Americans meant the same thing by economic development.[28] Related to this inflated sense of common interest was an overemphasis on the importance of Latin American discontent with United States economic policies. It was widely assumed that such discontent was a threat to vital interests of the United States, and that it could be eliminated by major concessions.

Finally, policy makers exaggerated the ability of the United States government to promote desirable political developments in Latin America. Political changes in Latin America quickly demonstrated how dependent the innovations of both the Eisenhower and Kennedy administrations were on the existence of a favorable political environment in Latin America, and what the limits were on the ability of the United States government to preserve such an environment.[29] Several of the governments to whose initiatives the United States had to a certain extent been responding fell. Although this was widely attributed to the political ambitions of the military, the real problem was the political weakness of the civilian governments they replaced—a weakness that the United States government was powerless to overcome. For example, it could do nothing in the face of President Quadros's decision (one day after Lincoln Gordon, one of the authors of the Alliance for Progress, was appointed ambassador) simply to resign as President of Brazil.[30] Yet this decision helped precipitate the prolonged political crisis in Brazil that ended with the assumption of political power by the military.

All of this is not to deny the usefulness of the Alliance for Progress, and the rhetoric that heralded it, in coping with the immediate political effects of the Cuban Revolution. Moreover, the commitments undertaken by the United States government at the time offered firmer guarantees of the stability of the United States' intentions toward Latin America than had ever been offered before. Finally, the innovations of both the Eisenhower and the Kennedy administrations altered the framework in which economic issues were negotiated. Both by extending the scope of issues to include some of the social and political goals of the Latin Americans, and by altering the procedures for resolving differences, these innovations offered some hope of moderating the conflicts over economic issues that had plagued inter-American politics.

Nonetheless, on many points, interests remain in conflict. What is wanted is not offered, or what is done proves to have unwanted effects. For example, the Kennedy administration, which altered the Export-Import Bank's rigid policy of refusing to give public loans to state-owned oil companies, and from its beginning empha-sized the role of public investment, soon discovered that it could not be indifferent regarding the flow of private investment to Latin America, and that the amount was possibly related to its own pub-lic assistance policies. Edward Mason reported that "the adverse effect on the Latin American balance of payments" caused by the decline in new foreign investment and the export of domestic capital, "may have exceeded the beneficial effect of the flow of U.S. public funds during the first year of the Alliance."[31] The reasons for this are of course complicated. But, as Joseph Grunwald has pointed out, talk of reform can damage economic growth by fright-ening off private investors.[32] If reform is not achieved, then one may be worse off than before, by any standard of measurement. This, of course, is a point that any previous administration since the end of World War II would have appreciated. Although ex-actly what forces determine the level of private investment in Latin America are not well known, and thus the efficacy of any particular means of encouraging it may be criticized and the means abandoned, it will remain true that the United States gov-ernment will seek to avoid having private capital replaced by limited public funds, and the Latin Americans will tend to prefer the opposite.

Another unsolved problem concerns Latin American exports. The number of commodities amenable to international commodity agreements is apparently limited. The production and marketing of oil and minerals, for example, are instead controlled to a con-siderable degree by the major companies. The main problem lies in securing a larger share of the proceeds to the governments of underdeveloped countries. This raises difficult questions concern-ing the relations between those governments and the major com-panies. Import restrictions imposed by the United States periodi-cally lead to disagreements. And there are still other conflicts of interest between producing and consuming countries. Negotiations concerning a cocoa agreement broke down in 1963, and the coffee agreement that the United States government signed in 1962 has not been immune to such problems.[33]

Always these conflicts lead to the central questions, What form should aid take?, and What conditions should accompany it? Commodity agreements that stabilize prices at a level higher than would otherwise exist represent a form of foreign assistance, which is financed by a tax on consumers. Much of its attractiveness for producing countries lies in the fact that aid furnished in such a way has no strings attached and wins the governments the favor of their producing interests. It may not always be in the interest of consuming countries however. For not only does it help shield high-cost producers from market pressures, but the allocation of quotas under the agreements also leads to delicate international problems, and the manipulation of these quotas is a much less sensitive method of influencing underdeveloped countries than an aid program.

Conflicts between governments over the scale and direction of all forms of financial assistance are necessarily connected with, and complicated by, conflicts over the local political objectives to be served, since the governments concerned have different incentives. The United States government, for example, has an interest in limiting its outlay of funds, and consequently has the greater interest in fostering developments that might lead to a reduction in the assistance required in the future. It may not be sensitive to the political costs involved in meeting the demands that it makes as the price of its assistance.

Conflicts between governments, of course, will also continue to be connected with domestic political conflicts in Latin America because the success of social and economic programs is affected by the conditions on which external support is offered. And the nature of Latin American politics will continue, in many countries, to foster an association between the United States government and parties to domestic political disputes to a much greater extent than the United States government probably intends. Relations between the United States and Brazil since the beginning of the Alliance for Progress provide examples of both these problems.

Finally, there remains the most difficult source of conflict of all: the relationship between political change in Latin America and the competition for influence between the United States and the Soviet Union. It is important to state carefully what that relationship is, but difficult to do so. For what is important is not the nature of domestic change in itself, but its international implications. Yet it is virtually impossible to make generalizations about the connection between domestic and international events with confidence.

One must begin by rejecting two seductive statements of the problem: first, that the acceptance of assistance from the Soviet Union by a Latin American country is grounds for serious concern by the United States government; second, that radical domestic change or reliance on a local Communist party for political support is grounds for serious concern by the United States government. Whether the United States will in fact be seriously concerned about such developments is another matter, which will be discussed below. Here I am speaking merely of the significance of such events for a goal that, for the moment, I am recommending, and tentatively ascribing, to the United States government.

What is this goal? It is that the Soviet Union not be given an opportunity to extend its influence over the conduct of political conflict, either domestic or international, in the Western Hemisphere. There are two reasons for this objective. The first is that such gains would be likely to provide the Soviet Union with an opportunity seriously to inconvenience the United States government and perhaps threaten what it considered a vital interest. The second is that it would probably lead to the commitment of the Soviet Union and the United States on opposite sides of yet another local conflict, and therefore seriously complicate any effort to settle other outstanding differences between them. These reasons may seem intolerably vague to some people. But the Cuban missile crisis should provide an instructive example of how difficult it is to anticipate in just what way a Soviet advantage might develop and be exploited. And both Cuba and Vietnam show how commitments in local conflicts can tie the hands of the two major powers.

It is not difficult to see that neither Soviet economic assistance nor the political assistance of Communist parties necessarily has such an effect. It is less easy to specify what does, though there are two kinds of developments that should probably be at least regarded with some concern: the appearance either of a regime which concludes that its domestic goals can only be pursued through complete dependence on the Soviet Union, or of one that desires to export a revolution to other countries and seeks the support of the Soviet Union for that purpose. The former situation might, by example, disrupt the economic programs of other countries and the relationships with the United States foreign aid program that supported them. The latter, more serious development would very likely have some success in the unstable environment of Central America and the Caribbean, and would surely lead to international conflicts that would be very difficult for the United States government to manage without losing more political support in Latin America. Either, of course, could lead to commitments by the Soviet Union that it might have difficulty extricating itself from.

The Cuban Revolution seems to have had all these effects. The example of the revolution, and the fact that the Soviet Union was persuaded to support it, further diminished the already waning support in Latin America for the set of rules that governed its economic relations with the United States. Cuba posed a threat to the other governments in the Caribbean area by offering a source of support and training for revolutionaries. The revolution and the international activities supported by the Cuban government precipitated conflicts in the inter-American system that could not be resolved by the peculiar combination of unilateral and multilateral methods which had sufficed up to that time. And they seemed to bring the Soviet Union into the inter-American system for the first time. Whereas some regimes felt threatened by these events, they also gained from them some hope of influencing the United States government and of reducing the extreme isolation from the main currents of international politics that all the countries of Latin America had experienced since the end of World War II.[34]

The Alliance for Progress helped the United States government retrieve some of its lost support. But it did not diminish the significance of the Cuban regime's ability to establish itself firmly in power and resist all opposition, an achievement that distinguished the Cuban Revolution from the brief period of influence of the Communist party in Guatemala. The failure of the Bay of Pigs invasion and the apparent readiness of the Soviet Union to compensate the Cuban government for the economic losses involved in breaking relations with the United States were both indispensable in making this clear. Furthermore, the Soviet Union was intent on leaving the impression that it was prepared to offer direct military aid to Communist governments throughout Latin America; the restraint exercised by the United States government helped make this possible.

In circumstances like these there are two courses of action open to the United States government. The first is to take no military action and hope that over the long run its own superior economic position and the strength of local opposition groups will suffice to limit the damage to its position. The second is to assert its local military superiority by intervening in the dissident country or in countries that seem likely to yield to Soviet influence.

The danger in the first course is that the Soviet Union and local revolutionaries will be emboldened by the United States' restraint, that the Soviet Union will become implicated in further conflicts, and the position of the United States will become worse rather than better. The United States government may give extra weight to the danger of this course if it fears that signals given to the Soviet Union in the Western Hemisphere may be taken by the government of that country to apply elsewhere as well. The advantages of this course of action are two: first, no further action may prove necessary; second, if intervention does eventually prove necessary, there will be greater support for it in Latin America after the involvement of the Soviet Union than there would have been before. The intervention in the Dominican Republic was costly. But surely such a move would have been much more costly if it had been made before rather than after the Cuban Revolution and the missile crisis.

The dangers of the second course of action (military intervention) are that it may merely emphasize the disadvantages of dependence on the United States, without effectively emphasizing the disadvantages of association with the Soviet Union; and that the legitimacy of those groups in Latin America willing to cooperate with the United States may, in consequence, be damaged. This was probably the result of the limited intervention in Guatemala. Either course has its risks. Choosing between them requires cool judgment; prosecuting either one, and dealing with its repercussions, requires considerable diplomatic skill.

It is with regard to the making of choices such as these that the most serious questions about the efficacy of the political process in the United States arise. One cannot be perfectly confident that the arguments just made will govern the government's choices in the future, or even that they explain those made in the past, in Guatemala, Cuba, and the Dominican Republic. This lack of confidence derives from two effects of the decentralized structure of the political system. The first is that the momentum of semiautonomous parts of the executive branch may be difficult to overcome; consequently, plans made for remote contingencies will, because a semiautonomous agency has committed itself to them, be put into effect, regardless of the overall aims of the whole government. The second follows from the needs of the man who must attempt to manage the system, the President. He can accomplish some of his objectives by virtue of the authority of his office; others he can attain through the opportunities that decentralization makes available to him. But some of his goals can only be accomplished by overcoming decentralization in an ad hoc way, by utilizing such resources as his personality, his prestige, his popularity with the voters, his centrality in a process of bargaining and communication, and so forth.[35] Successes are cumulative. They provide resources that can be used to produce further successes. Failures can be cumulative as well. Decentralization usually guarantees that there is a limit to how much the President can lose, but losses are costly nonetheless. A foreign policy problem may threaten cumulative political losses at home, even if there is no immediate danger of serious losses abroad.

The President may suffer domestic political losses whatever choice he makes, as the Johnson administration has shown in Vietnam. One might suggest that he will then do what is "right." But there is no compellingly right choice. A President who, because of domestic political problems, is especially sensitive to the advantages of being firm, and who at the same time is confronted with a program of great momentum, may choose differently from one whose political resources are more nearly guaranteed by his office, whose activities are more nearly routinized and therefore capable of being learned through apprenticeship, and whose control over his subordinates is exercised routinely as well.

But if there is no compellingly right choice, some choices are not compellingly wrong either. For that reason it is always difficult to prove that a given decision is to be explained by the influences I have mentioned, or simply as a reasonable choice made under conditions of uncertainty.

The history of the Alliance for Progress thus far is replete with examples of the sources of conflict described in this chapter. Among them are the Kennedy administration's difficulties in dealing with the series of military coups in Latin America that shortly followed the inauguration of the Alliance, the Johnson administration's intervention in the Dominican Republic, and the conflict with Peru over the expropriation of an oil company. A more subtle development has been a spreading disillusionment with the use of public assistance as a bargaining tool in negotiations about conflicts of economic interest. In the United States, this disillusionment grows out of doubts about the effectiveness of these negotiations in promoting changes in the domestic policies of Latin American governments, and out of a keener appreciation of the costs of involvement in Latin American domestic politics which such negotiations entail. In Latin America, this disillusionment accompanies disappointment with the quantity of resources made available through these channels, and frustration at the fact that the United States domestic policies of interest to them (for example, trade restrictions) are not part of these negotiations.

Consequently, a movement has begun in Latin America toward

cooperation with other underdeveloped countries in attempts to alter the commercial policies of the United States. The next stage in the development of United States policies is, at the moment, in doubt. But the end of the Alliance for Progress decade seems to resemble the closing years of the Truman administration more than the exhilarating months of the beginning of the decade. The desire of the Soviet government to become embroiled again in Latin America is uncertain, and there is disillusionment with past efforts by the United States government to promote desirable political change there. The war in Vietnam has diverted the resources of the United States in much the same way the Korean War did. And there are strong pressures to liberate resources from the demands of foreign policy so that they might be used domestically.

Whatever the future of United States economic policies proves to be, it seems likely to me that the policies will be arrived at by a process similar to the one I have already described, and that many of the features of the domestic and international environments will be recognizable from this account as well.

8. Domestic and International Politics

Many participants in the policy-making process in the United States regard the economic policies of the United States government toward Latin America as instruments by which Latin America can be influenced in accordance with the interests of the United States. It is to the credit of most of them that they hope (and believe) that ways can be found to accommodate Latin American interests at the same time. A failure to satisfy either set of interests is taken to be evidence that something is wrong with the way policies are made.

This is the perspective of what Charles Lindblom calls "partisan analysis."[1] Analysis made by partisan participants in the policy-making process is often of a very high quality, especially in the United States, where scholars play an important political role. But the task of explanation can be joined with that of advocacy without tension only when it is possible to be fully rational. A theory of rational decisions can then be said to explain behavior that conforms to the theory and to indict behavior that does not. Of course, one might still want to explain how a collective decision could be a rational one. It migh prove to be the case that a rational collective decision was necessarily the result of much individual partisan activity, and that the rationality of the collective decision was not apparent to any of the participants. In such circumstances also, advocacy would interfere with explanation.

But it is not at all clear what the notion of rationality would imply for United States economic policies toward Latin America.

There are four different reasons for this. First, decisions are made in the context of bargaining with other governments. It is never obvious that there is a single optimum strategy to be pursued in those circumstances. Second, the effects of any decisions, even assuming Latin American cooperation, cannot be predicted with any accuracy. Third, the sheer number of decisions that have regularly to be made is so large (most partisan analysts greatly simplify the number of decisions that must be made) and the participants are so numerous that it may be impossible to determine how best to make each decision. Finally, among the goals of the government is the welfare of United States and Latin American citizens; but there is no way to demonstrate conclusively that everyone's welfare would be increased by any one decision, and no generally compelling argument for taking some people's welfare more seriously than others.

In the previous chapters I have tried to explain the decisions made by the United States government, first by showing that they were reasonable attempts to balance the claims of military security and other claims on public policies, and second by showing how these justifiable (if not impeccable) decisions were the result of the nature of the problems, the political process in the United States, and the recent structure of international politics.

Implicitly I have been engaged in a dialogue with partisan analysts. But I have done this because I was interested in their analyses, and not because I wanted to be a partisan. It is possible to accept the account of United States policy making that I have given and deplore the policies. But to deplore them one must engage in a form of argument that politics and not scholarship must resolve. Scholars may (and do) participate in politics. But they have an obligation to try to describe accurately and explain adequately whatever they may also want to praise or condemn. That has been my main concern. Unlike many partisan analysts I have emphasized the unavoidable conflicts of interest between the United States government, the governments of Latin America, and other interested parties. An implication of this emphasis is that the policies of the United States, the countries of Latin America, and the Soviet Union are interdependent. I have therefore tried to place the foreign policy of the United States in the context of international politics. As a rule, domestic groups that will be affected by foreign policy decisions insist (successfully) on participating in making the decisions. But in my opinion the effects of their influence on United States policies have not been quite what many partisan analysts have implied.

The preceding chapters were primarily devoted to a detailed examination of United States foreign policy decisions. In this chapter I shall turn to the task of analyzing United States economic policies toward Latin America as one component of a subsystem of international politics, estimating as nearly as possible the effects of domestic politics within the participating countries on the political process that takes place among them. This is different from the partisan analyst's question of whether the domestic political process worked well or poorly.

A good working definition of "politics" seems to me to be this: whenever two or more individuals or groups are affected by each other's decisions, disagree in their evaluation of the consequences, find it advantageous (or find it necessary) to submit to the consequences rather than to avoid them, and attempt to influence the outcome, then they may be said to constitute a political system, and their interaction may be said to be politics, or a political process. One thus wants to describe and explain the consequences of possible decisions, the values assigned to them by all concerned, the strategies used to affect the final outcome, and the final decision itself. I have already done much of this for decisions about United States economic policies toward Latin America. Here I will merely remind the reader briefly of what has been said earlier, and examine in somewhat greater detail the importance of domestic politics, in both the United States and Latin America, for this subsystem of international politics.

Inter-American Politics

To describe all the relevant consequences of all the decisions of all the participants in the Inter-American system would probably be impossible, and would certainly be unnecessarily tedious. My discussion is limited, therefore, to those considered to be most important by most participants. The occurrence of some of these consequences, of course, is doubted by some of the participants. To take the most obvious example, some people argue that increasing economic assistance has not led to desirable political developments in Latin America. This lack of agreement in itself has an effect on the outcome of a conflict.

The potential consequences of its policies that have mainly concerned the United States government are intervention by its principal international competitors in hemispheric conflicts, expenditure of too great a portion of its financial resources, and deleterious effects on the interests of United States citizens. It has accepted for a very long time the view that the rate of economic growth in Latin America directly affects the likelihood that the first and last of these things will happen. Since the beginning of World War II it has also accepted the view that its own economic policies make a necessary if not a sufficient contribution to the maintenance of any desired rate of economic growth in Latin America over the long run. But it has been difficult to get everyone to agree on what rate is desirable. (From the point of view of the United States government, it is whatever rate is necessary to isolate the Western Hemisphere from the cold war, at the least cost to its own budget and the expressed interests of its citizens. But it is not at all clear what that rate is.) And of course the difficulty has been compounded by having to take into account the effects of decisions made by Latin American governments. Often, because their evaluations of potential consequences are different, Latin Americans have had no incentive to cooperate with the United States government at all.

The values of many Latin American governments (which naturally differ among governments, and fluctuate for any given government over time) have led them to be sensitive to conditions that often are not even perceptible to the United States government, such as an increase or diminution of dependence on economic decisions made abroad, whether private or governmental ones. When the United States government has perceived these as relevant outcomes, its evaluation has often differed from that of the Latin Americans, at least in the short run. The desire for independence led Latin Americans to seek firm, long-term commitments of aid from the United States government and greater flexibility in their treatment of private foreign capital (in order to be less dependent on both), whereas the United States government desired just the opposite. Latin American governments have also been more sensitive to the effects of economic policies on their own domestic political positions and to the effects of changes in the price of or the demand for commodities such as coffee, lead, zinc, copper, and tin on their economies.

Naturally there have also been some events of significance to the United States government that have hardly entered into Latin American calculations at all—for example, the impact of its decisions on its own budget and on producers and consumers in the United States. The effect of economic decisions on the spreading of Soviet influence in the Western Hemisphere is also not nearly so close to the center of the Latin American view of things as to the center of the United States government's view.

Because of the great divergence among Latin American governments' evaluations of United States policies, these countries have been unable to put forward any unified opposition. At the same time, this lack of unanimity prevented the United States government from securing its main objective in Latin America because it made a stable commitment from all Latin American governments to any set of economic objectives impossible to secure.

The strength of the United States government's bargaining position was that it could afford to allow the level of economic performance in Latin America to fall quite low and to allow the Soviet Union's position there to improve significantly before these developments became unacceptable. Furthermore, at the point where they became unacceptable to the United States, they began to be unacceptable to the Soviet Union and the Latin Americans too. The strength of the Latin Americans' position lay in what from other points of view might be considered their weakness: their inability to gather support for the public policies that were required if they were to attain their ambitious economic objectives. This has meant that at least some of them have been prepared to allow economic performance to deteriorate to the point where the United States government has had to step in, and that they have made the United States government believe it must help manage political support for the necessary policies if its long-range objectives were to be achieved. In consequence, aid has been increased, and the United States government has taken an interest in counter-insurgency, social reform, and political democracy. But the Latin Americans have not accomplished this just as a matter of policy. They have been assisted by the lagging demand for their exports, the unwillingness of private foreign investors to cooperate in providing sufficient and relevant capital assistance, and the willingness of the Soviet Union to expend resources for purposes that it might just as easily have thought not worth the price.

To the extent that the Alliance for Progress represented a genuine replacement of conflict by cooperation, it is to be explained in part by these developments and in part by two others, of which one was a convergence of the various definitions of inter-American problems accepted by the participants in the system. This occurred partly as a result of some experience with each other's bargaining behavior and partly as a result of the devising of theories concerning economic development by scholars who had the political resources that enabled them to inject their ideas into the policy-making processes of their own governments, both in the United States and in Latin America. These theories, like the men who adhered to them, combined some of the qualities of both scientific theory and political ideology. The other development was the Cuban Revolution, which taught a number of different lessons about the nature of Latin America's problems and their urgency, and which compelled some response. Its effects on the decisions and actions of the United States government have been discussed. It is harder to document the effects in Latin America. The United States government hoped that the revolution would galvanize Latin American governments into taking decisions they would otherwise have been reluctant to take, thereby enabling them to cooperate more fully with the United States. This might have been true, but not necessarily in the way the United States government expected. Its demands for reforms that required unorthodox kinds of support in Latin America, together with a general fear of Communist subversion, may have encouraged military coups as much as it encouraged the democratic left. At any rate, the belief that the Cuban Revolution had a salutary effect on the Latin Americans seems to have played a role in the decisions of United States policy-makers.

The Relation Between Domestic and International Politics

In general, one can distinguish four different ways in which domestic politics affects international politics. First, because a government's international goals are related to the domestic goals pursued by itself and by groups and individuals in the society, the domestic political process will affect—perhaps modify—international goals. Second, domestic political experience may provide the basis for a government's understanding of international politics and of the political processes of other systems. Third, the domestic political process may affect the way a government communicates its intentions to the others. Fourth, the domestic political process will affect the capabilities of a government for mobilizing resources and devising and effectively pursuing a coherent strategy.

The importance of domestic politics for international politics will vary with the types of domestic and international political systems involved. It is therefore sometimes extremely difficult to tell whether the domestic attributes of nations are the primary determinants of the nature of international conflict, or whether the structure of international conflict emphasizes the domestic political processes of the countries involved.

What attributes of domestic political systems lead to the above-mentioned effects on international politics? First, to find out how domestic politics modifies international goals, we must ask what international goals a government would have if there were no domestic constraints on its behavior; what means it would employ in pursuing them; and what strategies it would follow. Much theory in political science is based on the supposition that whatever else governments might want they desire security from military attack. Whether there are definitive solutions to the problem of military security is at least debatable, and therefore the adequacy of explanatory theories (as well as normative theories) based on the notion that there are such solutions may be questioned. I will return to this point later. For the moment, I want to look more closely at military security as a goal, and to ask what domestic conditions are necessary for that to be the dominant objective of any country's foreign policy.

A government's interest in avoiding attack and defeat is not the same as an individual's desire to save his life (a goal that for many people would be better served by the government's surrendering in advance). It is rather an interest in avoiding being overthrown and replaced by another government. There are many other goals that governments might have (and have had), but the preservation of their independent existence is a necessary condition for pursuing them. Thus solving the problem of military security takes precedence over the solving of all other problems. When insecurity is great, or when the achievement of security is inconsistent with other objectives, military security will, by this argument, become the sole objective of a government's foreign policy.

To achieve security the government requires resources—at a minimum, manpower and weapons sufficient to maintain a military organization. It depends on its citizens to supply these resources. Among its citizens, however, there may be dissatisfied individuals and groups who, if their demands are not met, will seek to overthrow the government. They may even invite military attack as an aid in achieving their objectives.

Where the objectives of potential sources of domestic discontent extend beyond national boundaries, governments can relieve domestic discontent and acquire support for their goal of military security at the same time, by incorporating these objectives into their foreign policy. This only works when the objectives (for example, the export of an ideology, or assistance to foreign members of an ethnic group) are consistent with the government's military security, and when their proponents have some support to offer the government. In some instances, of course, the pursuit of such objectives is itself a form of support. By adopting these other goals (e.g., Communism or pan-Arab ideals) as its own, a government may acquire a means of pursuing its own military objectives that it would not otherwise have had.

Another possibility is to try to get support and resources by influencing the domestic environment alone. Through social welfare programs, for example, the government might secure the loyalty of citizen groups that would then support a government budget sufficient to finance the government's foreign policy at the same time. Where support for foreign policy was provided consciously rather than inadvertently, it would be from motives similar to those that prompt support for the suppression of domestic disorder: the desire to protect a source of benefits (i.e. the national government) when threatened by what seems a worse alternative.

Of course, support for military security may be provided even by revolutionaries, if they believe the source of the external threat inferior to their own hoped-for regime and decide to protect their opportunity to make a revolution entirely out of indigenous materials. And groups whose goals transcend national boundaries may provide support for military security, even if that is inconsistent with their own goals, if they hope for future benefits from the government they help make secure. But in such cases a government may risk its own security in order to compensate for domestic discontent and rally its latent support, and dissident groups will always have an incentive to try to shape defense policies to promote their own objectives, possibly at the expense of the government's security, and will demand satisfaction of non-defense goals when the requirements of security allow it. These domestic conditions will not lead a government to seek military security only, unless the government is faced with a clear threat to its security, unless it must choose between that objective and all others, and unless its domestic supporters feel the means of achieving their own objectives are also threatened, and perceive the same need to sacrifice all other goals for the moment to securing the means by which these goals may be achieved in the future. Thus they are not in themselves sufficient to restrict the government's objectives to the primary one.

By contrast, where a government's support comes entirely from groups anxious to preserve a source of domestic satisfactions (i.e., satisfactions that do not require the influencing of groups or governments outside the geographical boundaries of the political system), it seems more reasonable to expect that military security would become the sole foreign policy objective, and that when there was no apparent threat to security there would be opposition to using resources for foreign policy purposes at all. Yet is it plausible to expect to find such a condition? No politically revelant goals of any domestic groups seem to be restricted by the boundaries of any political system. Business interests, class interests, religious interests, ideological interests, ethnic interests, all may be focused entirely on the government of some particular geographical area, but need not be. And even a devotion to the state itself may lead to efforts to enlarge its boundaries or to demonstrate its greatness through magnifying its role in international politics. Any government that is completely dependent on any of these interests may, therefore, find itself faced with demands that its foreign policy concern itself with more than just military security.

Where a government is dependent on several such interests, united by a common adherence to the government as an arbitrator of conflicts among them, there seems to be more reason to expect a narrowing of foreign policy objectives. Any one group's demand that foreign policy serve its own interests would be countered by another group's objection to spending scarce resources for that purpose. Since all groups regard domestic objectives as more important than transnational ones, they would be more willing to compromise on foreign policy than on domestic policy. The result would very likely be agreement on military security as a foreign policy objective that could be shared by all and that would free the most resources for the resolution of domestic conflict. Where the achievement of military security and the pursuit of some domestic interest could be combined, of course, there would still be an incentive to combine them; but there would be opposition to any extension of foreign policy goals beyond the minimal goal of security.

These domestic conditions would seem to be the only ones, then, that would be in themselves sufficient to lead the government to restrict its foreign policy objectives to the single goal of military security. There are two main ways domestic conditions might differ from these and thereby lead to an emphasis on other foreign policy goals besides military security. First, the domestic environment might not be sufficiently diverse, and consequently the government might be completely dependent on one or two groups for support for its foreign policy. It would then have to cater to their international goals as well as their domestic ones. Second, the domestic environment might be disrupted by political conflicts that the government could not reconcile, in which case it could not become the focus of all groups' loyalty and might therefore be compelled to rely on one party to the conflict. Other parties would then have an incentive to invoke the assistance of other governments; or, if they did not, the government would have an incentive to risk its own security to mobilize their latent support. These, then, seem to be the two attributes of domestic political systems that will lead to significant modifications of foreign policy goals to make them compatible with domestic ones.

There were three other kinds of effect that domestic politics might have on international politics: the interpretation of international politics in the light of domestic politics; the intrusion of domestic groups into the process of intergovernmental communication; and the inhibition of a government's capability to mobilize resources and make decisions effectively. These all seem to me to be symptoms of a lack of institutionalization of foreign policy, that is, a failure to assign the making of foreign policy to a special agency that has its own internal routine and an adequate supply of resources from its domestic environment.[2] The extent of differentiation and institutionalization of foreign policy making is thus the third main domestic condition that effects the behavior of participants in international politics.

There will be tension, of course, between the institutionalization of the policy-making function and the desire of the parties to
domestic conflict to restrict that function to the pursuit of military
security. The regular provision of diverse resources gives considerable autonomy to the institution that makes foreign policy, and
therefore there is always some danger that it will pursue its own
goals rather than the goals of those who provide its support. But
the routinization of policy making offsets the institution's autonomy by limiting its alternatives. Apart from this tension, there are
good theoretical reasons for believing that the existence of a system of mild, overlapping political conflicts facilitates both the institutionalization of policy making and its restriction to the pursuit of security.[3]

If one accepts what I have said thus far, then domestic and international politics are alternative arenas for conflict among groups.
In a world where social and political conflicts are diverse and occur
within particular countries, whose governments are provided by
the conflicting parties with resources for both domestic needs and
military security, international politics is apt to be restricted to
conflicts resulting from military insecurity. In a world where these
conditions do not exist, however, conflicts among independent
governments (and their military organizations) will be complicated by conflicts among nongovernmental groups with other interests. Governments will need to bid for the support of groups
at home, in order to acquire resources, and abroad, in order to
ensure that the pledge of another government is not undermined
by its own domestic opposition, and to undermine the support
any of their citizens might give for whatever objectionable policies
the other government was pursuing. Where domestic political ex-
periences are diverse, conceptions of international politics will be
diverse as well, communications among governments will be harder
to interpret, and governments will be less capable of pursuing a
consistent (and hence predictable) policy.

I do not want to beg the question whether one of these types
of international system is more peaceful than the other. I merely
want to suggest that in the first type, international politics will be

monopolized by independent governments (since they will control all the relevant resources) whose objective will be restricted to the minimal goal of military security; whereas in the second type there will be many other sorts of participants and many other conflicts of interest. If one were to determine which system was more likely to be nonviolent, one would have to know more about the nature of the conflicts and how the capacity of the participants to manage them was affected by all the characteristics I have mentioned. The second system could lead to political integration at a higher level, or to the cumulative spread of violence. The first could lead to a stable balance of power, or to mutual annihilation as a result of incompatible requirements for military security.

International Systems and Domestic Politics

I said earlier that the extent to which domestic politics affected international politics could be expected to vary not only with the nature of the domestic political systems concerned, but also with the nature of the international political system. The significance of the nature of the international system can be seen by examining once again the notion of military security. Two assumptions were made about it in the discussion above: first, that there are noncontroversial, optimum ways of attaining it, which are distinguishable from the means of achieving domestic goals; second, that it can be pursued in a routinized manner by a stable, autonomous institution. Whenever these conditions are not met, it is impossible to insulate international politics from domestic politics. They may never be fully met; but some characteristics of international politics seem more conducive to them than others.

When there is no single, obvious solution to the problem of military insecurity, there is likely to be conflict among the proponents of different solutions. The conflict may be joined by groups whose goals would be served by one of the solutions (such as the desire of the military to expand or the desire of an ideologically motivated organization to pursue its own goals abroad), and proposed solutions will then appear to be mere disguises for the wants of special interests.

Once it is accepted that there may be more than one way of solving the problem, then the cost of each proposal becomes a relevant consideration in choosing among them. But costs typically fall on different groups, depending upon the solution chosen. And solutions will differ in the extent to which they may be combined with other goals, about which there may be conflict. Either appeasement or resistance, for example, might secure a country from an external military threat, but their costs differ and are allocated differently among domestic groups. Or to take a more specific example, once it was clear that the German army had defeated the French at the beginning of World War II, French security might have been achieved by surrendering and seeking as good terms as possible from the victor, or by carrying on the conflict from abroad. The two solutions had different implications for other interests within France, and thus they were each supported by different groups of Frenchmen.

Conflict over the means of achieving security inhibits the institutionalization of foreign policy and therefore leads to a tendency to interpret international politics in the light of domestic experience; to the intrusion of domestic groups into the process of policy making and therefore into the process by which governments communicate their intentions to each other; and to the inability of a government to mobilize resources or pursue a coherent strategy. But these same effects can also be produced by any major change in the nature of international conflict, for such changes will require alterations in foreign policy routines and perhaps an increase in the quantity of resources devoted to international conflict. And new relationships will have to be worked out between the government and its sources of foreign policy support. The result will be the intrusion of domestic political conflict into international politics, at least until a new institutional pattern can be devised.

These considerations provide some clues as to what characteristics of international political systems affect the extent to which domestic politics is a determinant of foreign policy. They are, first, whatever characteristics affect the obviousness of requirements for military security and their distinctiveness from other governmental goals; and, second, the rate of change in the intensity and content of international conflict.

There are probably *no* conditions that make the requirements of military security so obvious and distinctive as to bar rational dispute about them, and therefore no conditions that enable one to explain a government's foreign policy without examining the way it was arrived at. The decision to resist direct, conventional military attack rather than to surrender in advance is itself a decision which might be the subject of a controversy that could produce no compelling solution. It is this that helps explain the prominent role of traditional doctrines or objectives, such as the Monroe Doctrine or the notion that one should always resist aggression, in the foreign policies of all states. They help provide the focus for agreement that could not be achieved entirely through rational argument.[4]

Nonetheless, there are different degrees to which a government's foreign policy may become embroiled in domestic political conflict. So one must ask what international conditions, *given* certain domestic conditions within the constituents of the system, lead to an increase or decrease in the insulation of international from domestic politics. That is the question being asked here.

It seems plausible to me that the salience of solutions to the problem of military security will vary with the number of participants in an international political system, the intensity of conflict, the scope of conflict, the quantity of resources devoted to conflict, and the degree of similarity in the participants' domestic political systems.

The notion that it varies with the number of participants derives chiefly from the writings of Kenneth Waltz.[5] Waltz suggests that as the number of governments capable of affecting the outcome of military conflict declines, the importance of the problem of military security for those governments will increase, because they cannot hope that other governments will relieve them of the burden of their defense. The governments of the United States and the Soviet Union, therefore, have felt the problem of military security even more intensely than did the major European governments during the period between World War I and World War II. For Waltz, this proposition forms part of an argument that a bipolar system lends itself more to the limitation of violence than does a multipolar system; but one does not have to pursue the argument to that (controversial) conclusion to find this single proposition plausible. A corollary to it would seem to be that as the number of major powers declines, every other government's security problem is lessened.

It seems plausible that the more intense the conflict among governments, the more pressing will the problem of military insecurity be. This is, of course, just another way of saying that the more insecure governments are, the more salient is the problem of insecurity. But that is not an empty proposition, for international systems vary in the degree to which perceived security requirements of governments are compatible.

The scope of international conflict can vary functionally (from military conflict to conflict over economic issues or even athletic contests) as well as geographically. It seems reasonable that the further governments get from military conflict in the area that is militarily most vital to them, the less obvious is the connection between their policies and their military security, and the harder it is to distinguish their objectives from those of other groups. For instance, indirect military conflict between the United States and the Soviet Union in Southeast Asia is much less obviously connected with the military security of either than conflict between them in Europe would be. Nonmilitary competition, as in the giving of economic assistance, has an even less apparent bearing on security.

The significance of the quantity of resources devoted to international conflict should be obvious. The more resources governments require for their foreign policies, the more likely it is that their objectives will affect, by contradicting or reinforcing, the political objectives of other groups within the nation, and the harder it will be to separate the choice of strategies for achieving security from other issues.

Finally, when an international political system consists of di-

verse types of member states, it is likely that the domestic characteristics of the states will become an issue in whatever is the
dominant conflict within the system.[6] For then each government
will have an incentive to portray its opponents' policies as the
products of partial interests (the ruling class, the Communist
party) rather than the expressions of their national interests in
military security. Each can hope by this means to undermine support in the opposing country for the policies of the government
of that country and appeal to groups at home (such as liberal democrats and anti-Communists of all sorts) that are opposed to the
allegedly dominant group abroad. But by interpreting intergovernmental conflict in this way, a government may create a relationship between its own objectives and its domestic politics that
it is not able to control, for it will have obscured the fact that its
objective is military security, and thus narrowed the appeal of
its actions to groups at home, while at the same time it will have
intensified its conflict with its opponents.

These seem to be the chief characteristics of international politics that affect the importance of the objective of military security
and the salience of means of achieving it, and hence the extent to
which conflicts among governments can be insulated from the domestic conflicts in any country. To them must be added the rate of
change in the nature of international conflict. Rapid changes inhibit the institutionalization of foreign policies; stability increases
the likelihood that foreign policies will become institutionalized.

These are the conditions, then, that affect the extent to which
domestic politics is a determinant of any government's foreign
policy. They can now be used to help us understand the relations
between domestic and international politics in the Western Hemisphere. It will be convenient to discuss the attributes of the inter-
American system first, and then the domestic attributes of its
members.

Domestic and International Politics in the Western Hemisphere

Insofar as the United States government and the Soviet government participate together in inter-American politics, their behavior will be affected by other aspects of the relationship between

them. It is therefore necessary to say something about this relationship. These governments are the two poles of a bipolar world
(in Waltz's sense of that ambiguous term; see p. 209 n. 1). Each of
them has therefore been especially sensitive to the threat that the
other has posed to its military security since there has been no
nation in between that might absorb some of the burden of defense. The conflict between them over military security has been,
until recently, intense, first because it was difficult to devise a settlement of World War II that would leave both governments secure against both each other and any military force that might
be organized in the future by Germany, Japan, or China, and, second, because neither government felt secure against the military
forces of the other, especially the new weapons that were being
developed.

These conditions made each government's security problem
more compelling. But other attributes of the international system
have had the opposite effect. As a result of the intensity of this
central conflict over security, the United States and the Soviet
Union have become involved in many subordinate conflicts in
other parts of the world, and have utilized many instruments in
addition to military force. The further the conflict has spread from
the central arena, the more each government has had to face domestic controversy over the connection between its military security and foreign policy, and the harder it has been to distinguish
efforts to promote security from efforts to promote other ends,
such as Communism or American business interests. Furthermore,
the quantity of resources devoted to these conflicts has been enormous, and therefore the problem of obtaining them from the domestic environment has been great.

In addition, because the United States and the Soviet Union
have such very different political systems, with different political
formulas to justify them to their members, each of them has had
an incentive to justify its policies as opposition to the kind of political system of the other. Both have played up their differences in
seeking support among the citizens of other countries.

Finally, the rate of change in all these dimensions has been
great. In 1935 the Soviet Union and the United States stood on

the fringes of international politics, which was then dominated by European countries. Ten years later they were the main participants in a greatly changed international system, with little experience and little certain knowledge to guide them in their efforts to reorganize that system to their own advantage. It is little wonder that they have each relied so heavily on their own domestic political experience, or that participation in international politics has required continuous institutional innovation.

In Latin America these two governments confront each other far from the main arena of their conflicting interests in military security. And the relationship between the instruments of policy they manipulate there (economic agreements, ideology, and local alliances with political parties or military organizations) and whatever interests they have felt they had there has been far from obvious. Moreover, by using these instruments each government has obscured the relationship between its own goals and the goals of domestic groups (such as businessmen or political parties) that are indirectly affected by them. Each government has been dependent to some extent on those who control the instruments it has wanted to use and has therefore been subject to their influence. And the fact that the security interests of the governments are very similar to the interests of these other parties has made them even more vulnerable to such influence.

The international position of the Latin American governments and their domestic characteristics obscure even further the significance of military security for United States policies toward Latin America. The same characteristics of international politics that made security goals more pressing for the Soviet Union and the United States (bipolarity and incompatibility of security requirements) made them less pressing for Latin American governments. Whatever security problems they might have, it is obvious that the solution will be determined primarily by the two superpowers. Furthermore, all the attributes of international politics that make the selection of strategies controversial for the superpowers also make them controversial for the Latin Americans. Far from the main arenas of international conflict, they have focused their attention almost entirely on economic issues. The manner in which these issues are resolved does not affect immediate and obvious military security requirements, but rather the manner of resolving domestic political conflict and the nature of the position that Latin American governments will occupy in international politics decades from now. Thus the only thing that will prevent foreign policy issues from becoming the focus of intense domestic conflict in Latin American countries is the desire of all groups to protect themselves from the superpowers, chiefly the United States. Since this goal implies no obviously optimum strategies that will serve the interests of all groups equally, it remains merely an aspiration to be used as a weapon in domestic conflict rather than as a reason for avoiding it.

These characteristics of the inter-American political system would have led to domestic conflict over foreign policy in all the participating states, even if their domestic political systems had not encouraged it. But inter-American politics has also been powerfully affected by the peculiar domestic characteristics of each of the participating systems. It is therefore necessary to examine them; and by so doing we shall be able to view what was said earlier about United States politics and United States foreign policy in proper perspective.

The Soviet Union has lacked the domestic characteristics listed earlier as requisites for the limiting of a government's goals to military security. Far from having a multiplicity of overlapping political conflicts structured around a government supported by a general consensus, the Soviet government has appeared to be dependent on one base of domestic support, the Communist party, which incorporates transnational objectives and which is not in conflict with other domestic interests only because they are suppressed. As a result, the highest levels of decision making with regard to foreign policy have not been fully institutionalized, and Soviet foreign policy has thus been unpredictable, and has seemed to be subject to the influence of the transnational goals of at least some Communist party members as well as to the temptation to use foreign policy as a means of suppressing domestic political conflict.

This analysis of the Soviet system, which is widely accepted by United States government officials, has served to heighten the United States government's expectation of conflict with the Soviet Union even in areas not immediately important to Soviet security. It has also served, of course, to elicit support in the United States for carrying conflict far from these primary arenas—what might have been controversial efforts to achieve military security became widely supported efforts to prevent the spread of Communism. And partly as a result of this analysis, the United States government sought for some time to increase the pressure of military insecurity on Soviet foreign policy, rather than to minimize the degree of conflict between United States and Soviet security requirements. It hoped thereby to force a choice between military security and other goals, and to restrict conflict to the former area.

The political systems of Latin America are still further than the Soviet Union from meeting the domestic requirements for insulating international from domestic politics. They vary from traditional systems in which governmental decisions are dependent on the support of a very small group of relatively homogeneous interests, to systems that are torn by intense domestic conflicts and lack sufficient domestic resources to resolve them. In both cases there is a tendency for governments to be bypassed, so that the United States government seems to be dealing directly with individual parties to political conflict in Latin America. The responses of the United States government to this problem (when it has not simply taken advantage of these conditions) has ranged from attempts to insulate its relations with Latin American governments from Latin American domestic politics, to efforts to assist directly the process of political institutionalization in Latin America. Neither strategy can be expected to be fully successful in the near future. Meanwhile, the nature of Latin American politics will cause further controversy within the United States about the propriety of the United States government's relations with the governments of Latin America.

Thus both the international system and the nature of domestic politics in the Soviet Union and in Latin America have helped produce political conflict within the United States over policies toward Latin America. Although the obviousness of military security requirements has been increased in some areas, it has been diminished in others. The extent of the government's dependence on domestic sources of support has been increased, and at a rate that has made this new dependence difficult to institutionalize. And the government has been led to take an interest in functional areas (including the one under discussion here, economic policies), where its interests and the interests of private groups are difficult to disentangle.

But it is significant that whereas in both the Soviet Union and the United States the nature of the international system probably heightened the importance of ideology for foreign policy, in the United States it has also served to heighten the relevance of a diverse range of group interests, from businessmen's to Negroes'. The result, for the United States, is conflict, in which it is commonly alleged on all sides that foreign policy has been warped to serve the interests of one group or another, and that different political arrangements (e.g., a stronger Secretary of State, or stronger political parties) would make the foreign policy decisions of the government more coherent and less subject to the influence of special interests.

But the analysis of the international political system offered above suggests that this is not the correct way of phrasing one's criticism, for it assumes the possibility, where there is none, of compelling agreement by rational argument. What one must ask is not whether a political system permits its leaders to see the optimum strategies, but whether it structures conflicts over strategies in such a way as to represent all the relevant considerations and weight them properly.

Can one say that the political system of the United States structures controversies over foreign policy in such a way as to emphasize the pursuit of military security? There are two responses to that question, which together summarize the argument of the previous chapters. First, the system fosters the involvement of diverse interested groups in the making of foreign policy. Though not all these groups have military security as their dominant concern, nonetheless security does serve as the common focus when compromise is required; and any group with other interests in mind must at least attempt to show that military security will be served by them. The decentralization of the system sometimes enables a group to capture some segment of foreign policy, but it also often works to force conflict among groups whose cooperation is required for a decision. These facts help explain why, for all the domestic controversy about United States foreign policy, efforts to explain it as the result of the pursuit of military security are as successful as they are. But to say that the political process focuses on the *goal* of security, is not to imply that the process encompasses all the relevant means of achieving the goal or weights properly the conflicting interests of all those on whom the costs must fall. I doubt that it is possible to state unambiguously what either of these statements means, or to establish whether they are true. Hence this question is itself a major focus of political controversy about foreign policy in the United States. And such controversy is encouraged by the nature of the political process.

Second, the characteristics mentioned above make the tension between political conflict over foreign policy and institutionalization of it especially great in the United States. As a result, the political system of the United States probably reinforces the tendencies, resulting from the nature of the international system, for domestic experience to become the basis of governments' understanding of international politics, for domestic groups to become involved in intergovernmental communications, and for governments to experience difficulty in mobilizing resources and pursuing coherent strategies. Whether this helps or inhibits the limitation of violence between the Soviet Union and the United States would be difficult to determine. I have already pointed out that its effects on the resolution of inter-American conflict are ambiguous.[7]

The routinization of the making of foreign policy would be made difficult by the international system whatever the nature of United

States politics. Given that fact, it is possible to argue that greater routinization would be undesirable as well—that it is better to foster general controversy over the relation between means and ends than to foster the routinization of the means. This is especially true if one is not convinced that the single-minded pursuit of military security by the two superpowers is the best form of political organization for mankind.

Notes

Notes

The abbreviations GPO (United States Government Printing Office)
and ECLA (United Nations Economic Commission for Latin America)
are used in the Notes.

Introduction

1. "Bipolarity" has no fixed meaning in writings on international
politics. Throughout this book it refers to the distribution of military
force among states, rather than to any particular pattern of behavior
they might exhibit.

2. Max Beloff, *The Great Powers* (London: Allen and Unwin, 1958),
p. 107.

3. See, for example, J. David Singer, "The Level-of-Analysis Problem in International Relations," in Klaus Knorr and Sidney Verba, eds.,
The International System (Princeton: Princeton University Press, 1961),
pp. 77–92; and James Rosenau, "Pre-Theories and Theories of Foreign
Policy," in R. Barry Farrell, ed., *Approaches to Comparative and International Politics* (Evanston: Northwestern University Press, 1966), pp.
27–92.

Chapter 1

1. Bryan is quoted in Samuel Flagg Bemis, *The Latin American Policy of the United States* (New York: Harcourt, Brace, and World, 1943),
p. 186.

2. Bryce Wood, *The Making of the Good Neighbor Policy* (New
York: Columbia University Press, 1961); Dana Munro, *Intervention
and Dollar Diplomacy in the Caribbean, 1900–1921* (Princeton: Princeton University Press, 1964).

3. Wood, *Good Neighbor Policy*, pp. 136–55.

4. *Ibid.*, pp. 349–51. The recalcitrance of the government of Panama
nearly provided a test case. See *ibid.*, pp. 354–55.

5. These hopes were concentrated mainly in the Office of the Coordinator of Inter-American Affairs (CIAA), then headed by Nelson Rockefeller. See *History of the Office of the Coordinator of Inter-American Affairs* (Washington, D.C.: GPO, 1947).

6. Quoted, *ibid.*, p. 21.

7. *Ibid.*, pp. 169–73, 191–92, and 271.

8. Laurence Duggan, *The Americas* (New York: Henry Holt, 1949), p. 161; Philip Glick, *The Administration of Technical Assistance: Growth in the Americas* (Chicago: The University of Chicago Press, 1957).

9. See, for example, the interesting article entitled "Is the Good Neighbor Policy Sound?" in *New York Times Magazine*, March 28, 1948, p. 11. The article was written shortly before the Bogotá conference and was signed by "Americus," a pseudonym "of a United States Government official who for several decades has specialized in Latin American affairs." It pointed out that the United States would be under considerable pressure to provide financial assistance to Latin America, and that the government should be careful not to lose the gains which had been made during the war in relations with the countries of that area. But it noted that the United States obviously could not "continue indefinitely a program of official subsidization of that area merely on the basis of being 'good neighbors.' "

The article argued that the Latin American ruling class was more interested in its own welfare than in the good of the national economies of Latin America and that the governments of the area would have to be persuaded to eliminate their excessive tariff barriers and official controls. "If the Latin Americans demand further official American aid at Bogotá in order to perpetuate the anachronistic systems that exist in virtually all of their countries, we shall have no obligation to give them any financial assistance. But if they show a tendency to meet us half way and create a genuinely favorable climate for foreign enterprise and investment, it would be good business to work out a deal. That is the real job to be done at Bogotá." (*Ibid.*, p. 25.)

The United States government should make clear, the author said, that past loans had been made largely for reasons of national security, and that in the future, aid must have other and more tangible peacetime justifications. "We should not close the door in advance to possible further official aid provided we can be reasonably sure of obtaining a *quid pro quo* in the way of really opening up Latin America to mutually advantageous foreign private initiative and investments and of bringing about an observance of sound fiscal and administrative methods." *Ibid.* But it is not clear whether the author felt that this was what the national security of the United States now required (in order to foster sound development in Latin America) or whether national security was no longer at stake, and therefore private interests should once again provide the main standard for judging United States policies.

10. Dexter Perkins, *The United States and the Caribbean* (Cambridge, Mass.: Harvard University Press, 1947), p. 160.

11. One of the most impressive arguments to this effect may be found in S. N. Eisenstadt's *The Political Systems of Empires* (New York: The Free Press, 1963).

12. See the discussion of this problem by Assistant Secretary of State William Miller, U.S. Dept. of State, *Bulletin*, XXII (Nov. 15, 1950), 768–70.

13. See Secretary of State Acheson's speech reprinted in the *New York Times*, Sept. 20, 1949, p. 18; see also Assistant Secretary of State Miller's speech in U.S. Dept. of State, *Bulletin*, XXII (April 3, 1950), 521–22.

14. *New York Times*, Sept. 20, 1949, p. 18.

15. Robert J. Alexander, *Communism in Latin America* (New Brunswick, N.J.: Rutgers University Press, 1957), pp. 404–5.

16. James M. Daniel, "Latin America," in Cyril E. Black and Thomas P. Thornton, eds., *Communism and Revolution: The Strategic Uses of Political Violence* (Princeton: Princeton University Press, 1964), pp. 334–41.

17. *Ibid.*

18. For a general discussion of the role this view played in United States economic policies as a whole, see David Baldwin, *Economic Development and American Foreign Policy, 1943–1962* (Chicago: University of Chicago Press, 1966). See also Eugene R. Black, *The Diplomacy of Economic Development* (New York: Atheneum, 1963), p. 116; and UN, ECLA, *International Cooperation in a Latin American Development Policy* (E/CN.12/359; Sept. 1954) (New York, 1954), pp. 24–26 and 84–85.

By extending financial aid to Guatemala after the fall of Jacobo Arbenz Guzmán's regime, the United States government did attempt to compensate for some of the political deprivations that accompanied the overthrow of that government. But its efforts were limited by the capacities of Castillo Armas, the insurgent military leader who replaced Arbenz, and finally disrupted by his assassination. See H. Bradford Westerfield, *The Instruments of America's Foreign Policy* (New York: Thomas Y. Crowell, 1963), pp. 438–42.

19. For the relation between the lessons of Guatemala and the course Castro followed in Cuba, see Daniel, "Latin America," pp. 340–41 and 349–52.

20. Henry Holland, speech to Pan American Society, Oct. 27, 1954,

U.S. Dept. of State, *Bulletin*, XXXI (Nov. 8, 1954), 688–89; Secretary of the Treasury George Humphrey, speech at Rio de Janeiro, U.S. Dept. of State, *Bulletin*, XXXI (Dec. 6, 1954), 863–69.

21. F. Benham, "The Economics of Underdevelopment," in Geoffrey Barraclough, ed., *Survey of International Affairs 1956–1958* (London: Oxford University Press for the Royal Institute of International Affairs, 1962), pp. 242–45; UN, ECLA, *Economic Survey of Latin America: 1958* (E/CN.12/498/Rev. 1, Sept. 1959) (Mexico City, 1959), pp. 3–8.

22. UN, ECLA, *Economic Survey . . . 1958*, p. 5.

23. *Ibid.*, p. 43. See also *ibid.*, *Economic Survey . . . 1957* (E/CN. 12/485/Rev. 1), New York, 1959), pp. 51–64.

24. *Ibid.*, *Economic Survey . . . 1958*, pp. 55–60.

25. *Ibid.*, p. 71.

26. *Ibid.*, p. 72.

27. *Ibid.*, p. 75.

28. Barraclough, *Survey . . . 1956–1958*, pp. 458–64.

29. Welles Hangen, *New York Times*, Jan. 17, 1956, p. 1; UN, ECLA, *Economic Survey . . . 1958*, pp. 62–67; Robert L. Allen, *Soviet Influence in Latin America: The Role of Economic Relations* (Washington, D.C.: The Public Affairs Press, 1959); Corporation for Economic and Industrial Research, "Soviet Bloc Latin American Activities and Their Implications for United States Foreign Policy," Study No. 7, U.S., Congress, Senate, Committee on Foreign Relations, *United States–Latin American Relations*, 86th Cong., 2d Sess., Doc. No. 125, 1960; Barraclough, *Survey . . . 1956–1958*, pp. 465–68; Albert Hirschman, "Soviet Bloc–Latin American Economic Relations and U.S. Policy," (Santa Monica, California: RAND Corporation, RM 2457, Sept. 28, 1959).

30. Richard B. Bilder, "The International Coffee Agreement: A Case History in Negotiation," *Law and Contemporary Problems*, XXVIII (Spring 1963), 337; James Reston, *New York Times*, April 15, 1958; U.S., Congress, Senate, Committee on Foreign Relations, *Hearings, Review of Foreign Policy: 1958*, 85th Cong., 2d Sess., 1958, p. 341; U.S., Congress, House, Committee on Foreign Affairs, *Hearings, Review of the Relations of the United States and Other American Republics*, 85th Cong., 2d Sess., 1958, p. 243.

31. J. W. F. Rowe, *The World's Coffee* (London: Her Majesty's Stationery Office, 1963), p. 182; Bilder, "The International Coffee Agreement," pp. 337–38.

32. Bemis, *Latin American Policy of the United States*, pp. 353–54; Adolf Berle, "To the South: A Continent of Problems," *New York Times Magazine*, July 15, 1956, p. 39.

33. U.S., Congress, Senate, Committee on Foreign Relations, *Hearings, Inter-American Development Bank*, 86th Cong., 1st Sess., 1959, p. 31; U.S., Congress, House, Committee on Banking and Currency, *Hearings, Inter-American Development Bank Act*, 86th Cong., 1st Sess., 1959, p. 31. See also the remarks by Dean Acheson, in House Banking and Currency Committee, *Hearings* . . . , p. 55.

34. Milton Eisenhower, *The Wine Is Bitter* (Garden City, New York: Doubleday and Company, 1963), pp. 152–54. This subject had been discussed at the meetings of United States and Latin American presidential representatives in 1957, who had recommended that an inter-American technical committee be created to assist Latin American governments, on request, in the development of projects for which foreign assistance would be requested. White House press release, May 26, 1957, reprinted in U.S. Dept. of State, *Bulletin*, XXXVI (June 24, 1957), 678.

35. Eisenhower, *The Wine Is Bitter*, pp. 154–56.

36. See Chester Bowles, "A New Approach to Foreign Aid," *Bulletin of the Atomic Scientists*, XIII (Feb. 1957), 42–47.

37. U.S., Congress, House, Committee on Foreign Affairs, *Hearings, Mutual Security Act of 1958*, 85th Cong., 2d Sess., 1958, pp. 1507, 1517–18, and 1521–22. Interest in such projects could obviously be reinforced by the argument that events such as the Nixon riots of 1958 represented protests against the maldistribution of wealth as much as against the United States, as Milton Eisenhower was shortly to argue in connection with the riots in Panama. For an example of such an argument, see U.S., Congress, House, Committee on Appropriations, *Hearings, Mutual Security Appropriations for 1959*, 85th Cong., 2d Sess., 1958, p. 1134.

38. Raymond Mikesell, "Problems and Policies in Public Lending for Economic Development," in Raymond Mikesell, ed., *United States Private and Government Investment Abroad* (Eugene, Ore.: University of Oregon Press, 1962), p. 343. See also National Planning Association, "United States and Latin American Policies Affecting Their Economic Relations," in Senate Foreign Relations Committee, *United States–Latin American Relations*, Doc. No. 125, 1960, p. 421.

39. For some early interest in using such a bank for these purposes see Eisenhower, *The Wine Is Bitter*, pp. 205–7.

40. John Dreier, *The Organization of American States and the Hemisphere Crisis* (New York: Harper and Row, for the Council on Foreign Relations, 1962) p. 83.

41. Under Secretary of State Dillon, remarks to the Committee of Twenty-One, Washington, D.C., Nov. 18, 1958, in U.S. Dept. of State, *Bulletin*, XXXIX (Dec. 8, 1958), 920; Senate Foreign Relations Com-

mittee, *Hearings, Inter-American Development Bank*, 86th Cong., 1st Sess., 1959, pp. 31 and 38–39; House Banking and Currency Committee, *Hearings, Inter-American Development Bank Act*, 86th Cong., 1st Sess., 1959, pp. 31 and 55.

42. House Banking and Currency Committee, *Hearings, Inter-American Development Bank Act*, pp. 31 and 55.

43. *New York Times*, Jan. 11, 1959, p. 1; *ibid.*, March 11, 1959, p. 38; G. Warner, "Latin America," in Geoffrey Barraclough, ed., *Survey of International Affairs: 1959–1960* (London: Oxford University Press for the Royal Institute of International Affairs, 1964), p. 464.

44. *New York Times*, Nov. 19, 1958, p. 1; remarks of Secretary of the Treasury Anderson at the first meeting of the Board of Governors of the Inter-American Development Bank, San Salvador, Feb. 8, 1960, U.S. Dept. of State, *Bulletin*, XLII (March 14, 1960), 428.

45. Remarks of Secretary Anderson, Feb. 8, 1960, U.S. Dept. of State, *Bulletin*, XLII, 428; Mikesell, "Problems and Policies in Public Lending for Economic Development," pp. 358–59.

46. Senate Foreign Relations Committee, *Hearings, Inter-American Development Bank*, 86th Cong., 1st Sess., 1959, pp. 10 and 34; remarks of Secretary Anderson, U.S. Dept. of State, *Bulletin*, XLII (March 14, 1960), 428.

47. For the controversy within the administration about social development at this time, see Milton Eisenhower, *The Wine Is Bitter*, pp. 202, 207, 209, 216, 221–25, and 229; and Milton Eisenhower, "United States–Latin American Relations, 1953–1958," U.S. Dept. of State, *Bulletin*, LX (Jan. 19, 1959), 91.

48. Richard Nixon, *Six Crises* (New York: Doubleday, 1962), pp. 183–86; *New York Times*, April 27, 1958, p. 26; May 1, 1958, p. 6; and May 11, 1958, IV, p. 3.

49. See, for example, Tad Szulc, *The Winds of Revolution* (New York: Praeger, 1963), pp. 106–17; cf. House Foreign Affairs Committee, *Hearings, Review of the Relations of the United States and Other American Republics*, 85th Cong., 2d Sess., 1958, p. 65; see also Eisenhower, *The Wine Is Bitter*, p. 211; *New York Times*, May 19, 1958, p. 1; and Nixon, *Six Crises*, pp. 183–234.

50. See the memorandum presented by the Brazilian delegation at the meeting of foreign ministers, Washington, D.C., Sept. 24, 1958, reprinted in Gillian King, ed., *Documents on International Affairs: 1958* (London: Oxford University Press, for the Royal Institute of International Affairs, 1962), pp. 433–42. The quotation is from p. 437. According to Dr. Milton Eisenhower, the notion of Operation Pan America was first mentioned by Kubitschek shortly after his inauguration, when he visited President Eisenhower in Key West, Florida. Milton Eisenhower, *The Wine Is Bitter*, p. 202.

51. For accounts of these negotiations, see the *New York Times* for 1958, June 4, p. 15; June 7, p. 1; June 8, p. 5; June 11, p. 14; June 12, p. 18; June 19, p. 8; June 22, p. 26; July 6, p. 1; Aug. 3, p. 1; Aug. 6, p. 2; Aug. 7, p. 1; Aug. 17, p. 1; and for 1959, March 27, p. 7, and April 9, p. 1. See also U.S. Dept. of State, *Bulletin*, XXXVIII (June 30, 1958), 1090–91; *ibid.*, XXXIX (Aug. 25, 1958), 301–9; *ibid.*, XXXIX (Oct. 20, 1958), 597–604; *ibid.*, XL (Jan. 12, 1959), 48–50; *ibid.*, XL (April 6, 1959), 479–83; Barraclough, ed., *Survey . . . 1959–1960*, p. 464; and Richard Stebbins, *The United States in World Affairs: 1959* (New York, Vintage Books, 1960), p. 366.

52. G. Warner, "Latin America," in Barraclough, ed., *Survey . . . 1959–1960*, p. 489.

53. *Ibid.*, pp. 489–90.

54. *Ibid.*, p. 491.

55. David Wise and Thomas B. Ross, *The Invisible Government* (New York: Bantam Books, 1964), p. 24.

56. Dreier, *Organization of American States*, pp. 68–73; Warner, "Latin America," in Barraclough, ed., *Survey . . . 1959–1960*, pp. 470–72, 476–78, 492–93, 495, 498–99.

57. See Juan de Onis, *New York Times*, Nov. 29, 1959, IV, p. 8.

58. Daniel, "Latin America," in Black and Thornton, *Communism and Revolution*, pp. 331–52; Theodore Draper, *Castroism: Theory and Practice* (New York: Praeger, 1965); George Blanksten, "Fidel Castro and Latin America," in Morton Kaplan, ed., *International Politics in a Revolutionary World* (New York: John Wiley, 1962), pp. 113–36; Ernst Halperin, "Castro and Latin American Communism," (Cambridge, Mass.: Center for International Studies, MIT, May 2, 1963); Andres Suarez, *Cuba: Castroism and Communism, 1959–1966* (Cambridge, Mass.: The MIT Press, 1967).

59. Draper, *Castroism*, pp. 97–103.

60. Blanksten, "Fidel Castro and Latin America"; Draper, *Castroism*, pp. 103–16.

61. Draper, *Castroism*; Blanksten, "Fidel Castro and Latin America"; Halperin, "Castro and Latin American Communism."

62. Ernst Halperin, "Why Castro Can't Be Neutral," *New Republic*, Nov. 27, 1961, pp. 11–13; Herbert Dinerstein, "Soviet Policy in Latin America," *American Political Science Review*, LXI (March 1967), 80–90.

63. Blanksten, "Fidel Castro and Latin America"; Draper, *Castroism*, pp. 103–16. On political institutionalization, see Samuel Huntington, "Political Development and Political Decay," *World Politics*, XVII (April 1965), 386–430. See also Hugh Thomas, "The Origins of the Cuban Revolution," *World Today*, XIX (Oct. 1963), 448–60.

64. See, for example, Warner, "Latin America," in Barraclough, ed.,

Survey . . . 1959–1960, pp. 503–4; and Richard Stebbins, *The United States in World Affairs: 1960* (New York: Vintage Books, 1961), pp. 332–35; remarks of Representative Judd, *Congressional Record*, 86th Cong., 2d Sess., Aug. 31, 1960, CVI, part 14, p. 18724; remarks of Under Secretary Dillon, U.S., Congress, House, Committee on Foreign Affairs, *Hearings, American Republics Cooperation Act*, 86th Cong., 2d Sess., 1960, pp. 15–16.

65. House Foreign Affairs Committee, *Hearings . . .* , pp. 4–6, 13, 18–20, 32, 78–83.

66. For an outline of the approach of the Kennedy administration to foreign aid, see U.S., President, Task Force on Foreign Economic Assistance, *An Act for International Development*, Summary Presentation, June, 1961. For one of the most important origins of these ideas, see Max Millikan and Walt Rostow, *A Proposal: Key to an Effective Foreign Policy* (New York: Harper and Brothers, 1957). See also Arthur Schlesinger, Jr., *A Thousand Days* (Boston: Houghton Mifflin, 1965), pp. 585–94.

67. Hollis Chenery, "Objectives and Criteria for Foreign Assistance," in Robert A. Goldwin, ed., *Why Foreign Aid?* (Chicago: Rand McNally and Company, 1962), p. 44. See also Edward S. Mason, *Foreign Aid and Foreign Policy* (New York: Harper and Row for the Council on Foreign Relations, 1964), pp. 77–79.

68. Eugene Black, *Diplomacy of Economic Development*, p. 116.

69. U.S., Congress, Senate, Committee on Appropriations, *Hearings, Inter-American Social and Economic Cooperation Program and the Chilean Reconstruction and Rehabilitation Program*, 87th Cong., 1st Sess., 1961, p. 65.

70. U.S. Dept. of State, *Bulletin*, XLIV (May 1, 1961), 618.

Chapter 2

1. See, for example, John Powelson, *Latin America: Today's Economic and Social Revolution* (New York: McGraw-Hill, 1964), for a discussion of Latin American views of inter-American economic relations.

2. *Ibid.*

3. Edwin Lieuwin, *United States Policy in Latin America: A Short History* (New York: Praeger, 1965), pp. 58–60.

4. Richard F. Behrendt, *Inter-American Economic Relations: Problems and Prospects* (New York: Committee on International Economic Policy, 1948), pp. 21–42; George Soule, David Efron, and Norman T. Ness, *Latin America in the Future World* (New York: Farrar and Rinehart, Inc., 1945), pp. 149–61; Donald M. Dozer, *Are We Good Neighbors?* (Gainesville, Florida: University of Florida Press, 1961), pp. 188–273.

5. See Sumner Welles, *Where Are We Heading?* (New York: Harper and Brothers, 1946), pp. 237–41.

6. For suggested measures to deal with the transition, and their relation to longer-range objectives, see Soule, Efron, and Ness, *Latin America in the Future World*, pp. 297–333.

7. Laurence Duggan, *The Americas* (New York: Henry Holt, 1949), p. 123; E. F. Penrose, *Economic Planning for the Peace* (Princeton: Princeton University Press, 1953), pp. 340–43.

8. See, for example, Penrose, *Economic Planning*, pp. 340–42 and 355–56; and Arthur Whitaker, ed., *Inter-American Affairs: 1944* (New York: Columbia University Press, 1945), p. 212.

9. *New York Times*, April 2, 1948, p. 12.

10. For reports of conflicts with the State Department over Latin America, see U.S., Congress, House, Select Committee on Foreign Aid, "Latin America and the European Recovery Program," in *Final Report on Foreign Aid*, 80th Cong., 2d Sess., Report No. 1845, 1948, pp. 446–47; and the *New York Times*, 1948, June 20, p. 41; June 24, p. 17; June 25, p. 10; July 29, p. 10; and, in 1949, Jan. 4, p. 75.

11. House Select Committee on Foreign Aid, "Latin America and the European Recovery Program," p. 449.

12. *Ibid.*, pp. 447–48. The Herter Committee devoted considerable attention to the problems of Latin America. See *ibid.*, pp. 446–63.

13. Hawthorne Arey, "History of the Operations and Policies of the Export-Import Bank of Washington," in U.S., Congress, Senate, Committee on Banking and Currency, *Hearings, Study of the Export-Import Bank and the World Bank*, 83d Cong., 2d Sess., 1954, p. 110; Message of President Truman to Congress, April 8, 1948, reprinted in U.S. Dept. of State, *Bulletin*, XVIII (April 15, 1948), 548.

14. See, for example, U.S., Council of Economic Advisers, "The Annual Economic Review: A Report to the President," Jan. 1950, in *The Economic Report of the President: 1950* (Washington, D.C.: GPO, 1950), p. 125.

15. Gardner Patterson and Jack N. Behrman, *Survey of United States International Finance: 1951* (Princeton: Princeton University Press, 1952), pp. 102–4.

16. U.S., President, *Report to the President on Foreign Economic Policies* (Gordon Gray Report) (Washington, D.C.: GPO, 1950), pp. 51–52. On March 31, 1950, President Truman had asked Gordon Gray, as his special assistant, to study the whole complex of United States foreign economic relations and to develop recommendations for him.

17. U.S. Dept. of State, *Bulletin*, XXIII (Dec. 25, 1950), 1014. For the allocation principles followed, see U.S., Congress, House, Committee on Foreign Affairs, *Hearings, Mutual Security Program*, 82d Cong., 1st Sess., 1951, p. 220. See also the statement by Mike Mansfield at the

United Nations, in U.S. Dept. of State, *Bulletin,* XXV (Dec. 17, 1951), 993. For other statements of the problem and the commitments of the American government, see the remarks by Assistant Secretary of State for Economic Affairs Willard Thorp, U.S. Dept. of State, *Bulletin,* XXIV (April 30, 1951), 696; and the summary of the issues by John Dreier, *ibid.,* p. 692.

18. See Assistant Secretary of State Miller's speech on this subject, U.S. Dept. of State, *Bulletin,* XXVII (Nov. 3, 1952), 706.

19. Statement of Assistant Secretary of State Miller at Inter-American Economic and Social Council, U.S. Dept. of State, *Bulletin,* XXV (Sept. 17, 1951), 476.

20. U.S. Dept. of State, *Bulletin,* XXIV (April 9, 1951), 569–73; *ibid.* (April 16, 1951), pp. 606–13; *ibid.* (April 30, 1951), pp. 688–98. See also J. Lloyd Mecham, *The United States and Inter-American Security 1889–1960* (Austin: University of Texas Press, 1961), pp. 429–36.

21. See Milton Bracker, "Waging Peace in the Americas," *New York Times Magazine,* March 25, 1951, p. 16. See also the reports of Latin American discussions of the problem at the fourth ECLA conference in the *New York Times,* 1951: May 29, p. 8; May 30, p. 7; June 1, p. 12.

22. See the statement of Assistant Secretary of State Miller, U.S. Dept. of State, *Bulletin,* XXIII (July 24, 1950), 140–44.

23. John Powelson, *Latin America: Today's Economic and Social Revolution* (New York: McGraw-Hill, 1964), pp. 156–57.

24. *Ibid.,* p. 157.

25. *Ibid. New York Times,* Feb. 12, 1954, p. 1.

26. Powelson, *Latin America,* pp. 128–38; Assistant Secretary of State Edward Miller, speech to 3d Kentucky World Trade Conference, U.S. Dept. of State, *Bulletin,* XXVII (Nov. 3, 1952), 705; press release, U.S. Dept. of State, *Bulletin,* XXIV (May 21, 1951), 819; Thomas J. Hamilton, *New York Times,* March 6, 1951, p. 10; *New York Times,* Jan. 6, 1954, p. 57; Percy Bidwell, *Raw Materials: A Study of American Policy* (New York: Harper and Brothers for the Council on Foreign Relations, 1958), pp. 102–29.

27. John M. Cabot, speech to Pan American Society of New England, Oct. 9, 1953, U.S. Dept. of State, *Bulletin,* XXIV (Oct. 19, 1953), 518.

28. *New York Times,* Feb. 12, 1954, p. 8.

29. Joe Wilkinson, *Politics and Trade Policy* (Washington, D.C.: Public Affairs Press, 1960), p. 60.

30. For a discussion of the organization and methods of the Randall Commission, see Raymond Bauer, Ithiel de Sola Pool, and Anthony Dexter, *American Business and Public Policy* (New York: Atherton Press, 1963), pp. 23–49.

31. UN, ECLA, *International Cooperation in a Latin American Development Policy* (E/CN.12/359, Sept. 1954) (New York: 1954), p. 5.

32. U.S., President, Commission on Foreign Economic Policy (Randall Commission), *Report to the President and the Congress* (Washington, D.C.: GPO, 1954), p. 35.

33. See Wilkinson, *Politics and Trade Policy*; Bauer, Pool, and Dexter, *American Business*.

34. Richard B. Bilder, "The International Coffee Agreement: A Case History in Negotiation," *Law and Contemporary Problems*, XXVIII (Spring 1963), 333–35.

35. *Ibid.*, p. 333.

36. Edward Cale, speech at Pebble Beach, California, U.S. Dept. of State, *Bulletin*, XXXII (July 6, 1955), 943.

37. Assistant Secretary of State for Latin American Affairs Henry Holland, speech to National Coffee Association, U.S. Dept. of State, *Bulletin*, XXXIII (Oct. 24, 1955), 658.

38. Geoffrey Barraclough, ed., *Survey of International Affairs: 1956–1958* (London: Oxford University Press for the Royal Institute of International Affairs, 1962), p. 309; Bilder, "International Coffee Agreement," p. 337.

39. J. W. F. Rowe, *The World's Coffee* (London: Her Majesty's Stationery Office, 1963), pp. 27–63 and 182–83.

40. For surveys of American policies on commodity agreements, see Gardner Patterson and Jack Behrman, *Survey of United States International Finance: 1950* (Princeton: Princeton University Press, 1951), pp. 221–22 and 230–31; Gardner Patterson and John Gunn, Jr., *Survey of United States International Finance: 1952* (Princeton: Princeton University Press, 1953), pp. 231–32; and Gardner Patterson, John Gunn, Jr., and Dorothy Swerdlove, *Survey of United States International Finance: 1953* (Princeton: Princeton University Press, 1954), pp. 265–67.

41. Raymond Mikesell, *United States Economic Policy and International Relations* (New York: McGraw-Hill, 1952, pp. 199–206.

42. *History of the Office of the Coordinator of Inter-American Affairs* (Washington, D.C.: GPO, 1947), p. 23.

43. Thomas F. Conroy, *New York Times*, Aug. 29, 1948, III, p. 5.

44. *New York Times*, Feb. 6, 1949, p. 62; *ibid.*, Feb. 10, 1949, p. 14.

45. Philip Glick, *The Administration of Technical Assistance: Growth in the Americas* (Chicago: University of Chicago Press, 1957), p. 124.

46. *Ibid.*, pp. 124–25. See also *The Development of Brazil: Report of the Joint Brazil–United States Economic Development Commission* (Washington, D.C.: GPO, 1953); *New York Times*, 1952, Jan. 4, p. 41; Feb. 23, p. 25; Feb. 15, p. 1; Feb. 22, p. 5; May 30, III, p. 1; May 5,

p. 8; May 17, p. 17; and 1953, March 20, p. 9, and July 19, p. 15. For the results of the commission's work, see Stefan Robock, *Brazil's Developing Northeast* (Washington, D.C.: The Brookings Institution, 1963), p. 126. See also the report by Pat M. Holt, the staff director of the Senate Subcommittee on Technical Assistance Programs, in U.S., Congress, Senate, Committee on Foreign Relations, *Technical Assistance: Final Report*, Report No. 139, 85th Cong., 1st Sess., 1957, pp. 595–614.

47. For some remarks on the relation between the technical assistance program and applications for Export-Import Bank loans, see the testimony of Glen Edgerton, President of the Export-Import Bank, in U.S., Congress, Senate, Committee on Foreign Relations, *Hearings, Technical Assistance Programs*, 84th Cong., 1st Sess., 1955, pp. 66–70.

48. See especially the discussion in Milton Eisenhower, *The Wine Is Bitter* (Garden City, N.Y.: Doubleday and Co., 1963), pp. 148–57. Dr. Eisenhower wrote that some technical assistance was given to governments by the International Bank, and studies made by the Export-Import Bank indirectly had the effect of giving technical assistance. "But in general I found that the lending institutions had misgivings about providing help in planning for fear that, as in Brazil, the host governments would consider the technical assistance to constitute firm commitments for loans." *Ibid.*, p. 153.

49. On Guatemala, see U.S., Congress, Senate, Committee on Foreign Relations, *Hearings, Mutual Security Act of 1955*, 84th Cong., 1st Sess., 1955, p. 312; *ibid., Act of 1956*, 84th Cong., 2d Sess., 1956, p. 272; *ibid., Act of 1957*, 85th Cong., 1st Sess., 1957, p. 612. See also Richard N. Adams, "Social Change in Guatemala and United States Policy," in Lyman Bryson, *et al., Social Change in Latin America Today* (New York: Vintage Books, 1960), pp. 236–37; and Thomas Palmer, *Search for a Latin American Policy* (Gainesville, Florida: University of Florida Press, 1957), pp. 134–73.

On Bolivia, see Milton Eisenhower, *The Wine Is Bitter*, pp. 194–95; U.S., Congress, House, Committee on Appropriations, *Hearings, Mutual Security Appropriations for 1955*, 83d Cong., 2d Sess., 1954, p. 389; Palmer, *Latin American Policy*, pp. 163–64; Richard W. Patch, "United States Assistance in a Revolutionary Setting," in Bryson *et al., Social Change*, pp. 151–76; and U.S., Congress, Senate, Committee on Government Operation, *Administration of U.S. Foreign Aid Programs in Bolivia*, 86th Cong., 2d Sess., Report No. 1030, 1960.

On Haiti, see U.S., Congress, House, Committee on Appropriations, *Hearings, Mutual Security Appropriations for 1958*, 85th Cong., 1st Sess., 1957, pp. 655–56.

50. See, for example, U.S., Congress, House, Committee on Foreign Affairs, *Hearings, Institute of Inter-American Affairs*, 81st Cong., 1st

Sess., 1949, pp. 5–6. The technical assistance program was one of the last contacts between the United States and Cuba to be broken. *Ibid.*, *Mutual Security Act of 1960*, 86th Cong., 2d Sess., 1960, pp. 863–65.

51. Senate Foreign Relations Committee, *Technical Assistance: Final Report*, pp. 4–5. For some statistics on the number of transfers of *servicios* that had been made by 1954, see U.S., Congress, House, Committee on Foreign Affairs, *Hearings, Mutual Security Act of 1954*, 83d Cong., 2d Sess., 1954, pp. 398–99. See also John Powelson, *Latin America: Today's Economic and Social Revolution* (New York: McGraw-Hill, 1954), pp. 228–29.

52. U.S., President, Commission on Foreign Economic Policy, *Staff Papers* (Washington, D.C.: GPO, 1954), pp. 57, 71–73, and 176; and Senate Foreign Relations Committee, *Technical Assistance: Final Report*, esp. p. 6. It can be argued to the contrary that the *servicio* was the only possible way of seducing an underdeveloped country into genuine institutional change. See Glick, *Technical Assistance*, p. 350.

53. For the origins of these policies in the 1930's, see Simon G. Hanson, *Economic Development in Latin America* (Washington, D.C.: Inter-American Affairs Press, 1951), pp. 392–99.

54. Testimony of Deputy Secretary of the Treasury Randolph Burgess, U.S., Congress, Senate, Committee on Banking and Currency, *Hearings, Export-Import Bank Amendments, 1954*, 83d Cong., 2d Sess., 1954, pp. 17–18. Senate Foreign Relations Committee, *Mutual Security Act of 1956*, pp. 293–94; U.S. Dept. of State, *Bulletin*, XXXIV (June 18, 1956), 1010.

55. U.S. Dept. of State, *Bulletin*, XXXI (Sept. 20, 1954), 413–14.

56. Cf. James Reston, *New York Times*, June 20, 1954, IV, p. 8.

57. Cf. John Dreier, *The Organization of American States and the Hemisphere Crisis* (New York: Harper and Row for the Council on Foreign Relations, 1962), pp. 77–78.

58. G. Warner, "Latin America," in Geoffrey Barraclough, ed., *Survey of International Affairs: 1959–1960* (London: Oxford University Press for the Royal Institute of International Affairs, 1964), pp. 498–99.

59. U.S. Dept. of State, *Bulletin*, XLV (July 24, 1961), 143.

60. *Ibid.*, p. 144.

61. For the Brazilian claims, see E. W. Kenworthy, *New York Times*, May 10, 1959, IV, p. 6. See also Raymond Mikesell, "Problems and Policies in Public Lending for Economic Development," in Mikesell, ed., *Private and Government Investment*, pp. 356–57.

62. *New York Times*, April 22, 1958, p. 22, and, in 1959: June 21, p. 23; Feb. 22, p. 20; April 12, p. 1; May 10, IV, p. 6; June 11, p. 15; June 12, p. 8; June 15, p. 10; June 21, p. 27; June 24, p. 12; Aug. 10, p. 24; Oct. 11, p. 33; Nov. 15, p. 13.

63. For a general discussion of lending by the Export-Import Bank during this period, see Raymond Mikesell, "The Export-Import Bank of Washington," in Mikesell, ed., *United States Private and Government Investment Abroad* (Eugene, Ore.: University of Oregon Press, 1962), pp. 459–82. See also the article by Juan de Onis in *New York Times*, Sept. 12, 1959, p. 9.

64. U.S., Congress, Senate, Committee on Foreign Relations, *Some Observations on the Alliance for Progress: The First Six Months*, prepared by Raymond Mikesell, 87th Cong., 2d Sess., Committee Print, Aug. 3, 1962, p. 12.

65. Robert Allen, *Soviet Influence in Latin America: The Role of Economic Relations* (Washington, D.C.: Public Affairs Press, 1959); UN, ECLA, *Economic Survey of Latin America: 1958* (E/CN.12/498/Rev. 1, Sept. 1959) (Mexico City, 1959), pp. 62–67; Corporation for Economic and Industrial Research, "Soviet Bloc–Latin American Activities and Their Implications for United States Foreign Policy," Study No. 7, U.S., Congress, Senate, Committee on Foreign Relations, *United States–Latin American Relations*, 86th Cong., 2d Sess., Doc. No. 125, 1960.

66. Allen, *Soviet Influence*, p. 65.

Chapter 3

1. Quoted in William Langer and Everett Gleason, *The Challenge to Isolation* (New York: Harper Torchbooks, 1964), p. 279.

2. *History of the Office of the Coordinator of Inter-American Affairs* (Washington, D.C.: GPO, 1947), p. 8.

3. Cf. Laurence Duggan, *The Americas* (New York: Henry Holt, 1949), pp. 74–82.

4. See, for example, Adolf Berle's articles in the *New York Times Magazine*, July 4, 1954, p. 8; and July 15, 1956, p. 7. See also *New York Times*, June 6, 1958, p. 8; and Nelson Rockefeller's report on United States Latin American policies, summarized in the *New York Times*, June 16, 1958, p. 1.

5. *New York Times*, April 23, 1952, p. 11. U.S., Congress, Senate, Committee on Foreign Relations, *Hearings, Nomination of John Foster Dulles, Secretary of State Designate*, 83d Cong., 1st Sess., 1953, p. 31; *New York Times*, Jan. 28, 1953, p. 8.

6. *New York Times*, April 24, 1952, p. 30.

7. U.S., Congress, Senate, Committee on Foreign Relations, *American Republics Cooperation Act*, 86th Cong., 2d Sess., 1960, pp. 81–82.

8. Speech by Senator Mansfield, *Congressional Record*, 86th Cong., 2d Sess., Aug. 8, 1960, XCVI, part 12, 15948.

9. See Adolf A. Berle, Jr., "The Cuban Crisis: Failure of American Foreign Policy," *Foreign Affairs*, XXXIX (Oct. 1960), 40–55.

10. For a discussion of these attributes of United States politics, see Samuel Huntington, "Political Modernization: America versus Europe," *World Politics*, XVIII (April 1966), 378–414; and Morton Grodzins, *The American System* (Chicago: Rand McNally, 1966). For a discussion of the differentiation of political systems from the rest of society, see S. N. Eisenstadt, *The Political Systems of Empires* (New York: The Free Press, 1963).

11. Warner R. Schilling, "The Politics of National Defense: Fiscal 1950," in Warner Schilling, Paul Hammond, and Glenn Snyder, *Strategy, Politics, and Defense Budgets* (New York: Columbia University Press, 1962), p. 19.

12. *Ibid.*, pp. 24–27. See also Roger Hilsman, "Congressional-Executive Relations and the Foreign Policy Consensus," *American Political Science Review*, LII (Sept. 1958), 724–44; and Rogert Hilsman, "The Foreign Policy Consensus: An Interim Research Report," *Journal of Conflict Resolution*, IV (Dec. 1959), 361–82.

13. Richard Neustadt, *Presidential Power* (New York: John Wiley, 1960); Richard Fenno, *The President's Cabinet* (Cambridge, Mass.: Harvard University Press, 1954); Morton Grodzins, "Party and Government in the United States," in Robert A. Goldwin, ed., *Political Parties, USA* (Chicago: Rand McNally, 1964), pp. 102–36.

14. For a similar interpretation, see Theodore Lowi, "Making Democracy Safe for the World: National Politics and Foreign Policy," in James Rosenau, ed., *Domestic Sources of Foreign Policy* (New York: The Free Press, 1967), pp. 295–332.

15. See David Baldwin, *Economic Development and American Foreign Policy 1943–1962* (Chicago: University of Chicago Press, 1966).

16. See Samuel Huntington, *The Common Defense* (New York: Columbia University Press, 1961), pp. 384–404.

17. For the notion of allocation systems, see Charles Wolf, *Foreign Aid: Theory and Practice in Southern Asia* (Princeton: Princeton University Press, 1960).

18. Philip M. Glick, *The Administration of Technical Assistance: Growth in the Americas* (Chicago: University of Chicago Press, 1957), pp. 39 and 44–59; Wolf, *Foreign Aid*, pp. 186–87; U.S., Congress, Senate, Committee on Foreign Relations, *Technical Assistance: Final Report*, 85th Cong., 1st Sess., Report No. 139, 1957, pp. 61 and 220–26.

19. *The Political Economy of American Foreign Policy*, Report of a Study Group sponsored by the Woodrow Wilson Foundation and the National Planning Association (W. Y. Elliott, chairman) (New York: Henry Holt and Co., 1955), pp. 343 and 373.

20. For information on the Export-Import Bank, see especially U.S., Congress, Senate, Committee on Banking and Currency, *Hearings, Study of the Export-Import Bank and the World Bank*, 83d Cong., 2d

Sess., 1954; and Raymond Mikesell, "The Export-Import Bank of Washington," in Mikesell, ed., *United States Private and Government Investment Abroad* (Eugene, Ore.: University of Oregon Press, 1962), ch. 16, esp. pp. 459–82.

21. Joe Wilkinson, *Politics and Trade Policy* (Washington, D.C.: Public Affairs Press, 1960), chs. 1 and 2; Raymond Bauer, Ithiel de Sola Pool, and Lewis Dexter, *American Business and Public Policy: The Politics of Foreign Trade* (New York: Atherton Press, 1963), pp. 9–104.

22. Wilkinson, *Politics and Trade Policy*, p. 60.

23. For a discussion of some of the different sets of criteria that might be applied to commodity policies, see Percy Bidwell, *Raw Materials: A Study of American Policy* (New York: Harper and Brothers for the Council on Foreign Relations, 1958), chs. 1–3.

24. *Ibid.*, pp. 38–41.

25. *Political Economy of American Foreign Policy*, pp. 375–76. For some congressional views, see Bidwell, *Raw Materials*, pp. 41–43.

26. *Political Economy of American Foreign Policy*, p. 378.

27. Samuel Huntington, "Political Development and Political Decay," *World Politics*, XVII (April 1965), 386–430; S. N. Eisenstadt, *Essays on Comparative Institutions* (New York: John Wiley, 1965), pp. 3–68.

28. See Talcott Parsons, "On the Concept of Political Power," in Parsons, *Sociological Theory and Modern Society* (New York: The Free Press, 1967), pp. 297–354.

Chapter 4

1. Quoted in Charles Wolf, *Foreign Aid: Theory and Practice in Southern Asia* (Princeton: Princeton University Press, 1960), p. 242.

2. U.S., President, *Report to the President on Foreign Economic Policies* (Gordon Gray Report) (Washington, D.C.: GPO, 1950), pp. 49–56. For a systematic discussion of the distinction between value judgments and estimates of productivity, see Wolf, *Foreign Aid*.

3. Wolf, *Foreign Aid*, p. 126.

4. Gordon Gray Report, p. 13.

5. Wolf, *Foreign Aid*, pp. 81, 112–13, 128, 136–37, 180–81.

6. U.S., Congress, House, Committee on Foreign Affairs, *Hearings, Mutual Security Program*, 82d Cong., 1st Sess., 1951, p. 236.

7. *Ibid.*, p. 244. See the testimony of Adolf Berle during the same hearings, *ibid.*, esp. pp. 622 and 626.

8. U.S., President, Commission on Foreign Economic Policy (Randall Commission), *Staff Papers* (Washington, D.C.: GPO, 1954), p. 38.

9. For a discussion of these expectations, see John D. Montgomery,

The Politics of Foreign Aid (New York: Praeger, for the Council on Foreign Relations, 1962), Appendix II, pp. 295–304.

10. U.S., Congress, Senate, Committee on Foreign Relations, *Hearings, Nomination of John Foster Dulles, Secretary of State Designate,* 83d Cong., 1st Sess., 1953, p. 31; *New York Times,* Jan. 28, 1953, p. 8.

11. Raymond Bauer, Ithiel de Sola Pool, and Lewis Dexter, *American Business and Public Policy: The Politics of Foreign Trade* (New York: Atherton Press, 1963), pp. 23–49.

12. See Klaus Knorr and Gardner Patterson, *A Critique of the Randall Commission Report* (Princeton: International Finance Section, Princeton University, 1954), p. 65.

13. In order to solve the problem in this way, it was necessary to make a number of rather optimistic assumptions. For a clear statement of these, see Randall Commission, *Staff Papers,* pp. 49–50.

14. Milton Eisenhower, *The Wine Is Bitter* (Garden City, N.Y.: Doubleday and Company, 1963), p. 188.

15. *Ibid.,* p. 189.

16. Milton Eisenhower, "United States–Latin American Relations: A Report to the President," U.S. Dept. of State, *Bulletin,* XXIX (Nov. 23, 1953), 716; U.S., President, Commission on Foreign Economic Policy (Randall Commission), *Report to the President and the Congress* (Washington, D.C.: GPO, 1954), pp. 9–10 and 23–26.

17. *Ibid.,* pp. 35–36.

18. Eisenhower, *The Wine Is Bitter,* p. 199.

19. *Ibid.,* pp. 697 and 701; *New York Times,* Feb. 12, 1954, p. 8; letter from Secretary of the Treasury Humphrey to Senator Potter, *Congressional Record,* 83d Cong., 1st Sess., June 30, 1953, XCIX, part 6, pp. 7619–20.

20. Eisenhower, "United States–Latin American Relations," p. 716.

21. *Ibid.,* pp. 695–717.

22. Assistant Secretary of State Henry Holland, speech to Pan American Society, U.S. Dept. of State, *Bulletin,* XXI (Nov. 8, 1954), 685.

23. See the speech by Edward Cale, U.S. Dept. of State, *Bulletin,* XXI (July 19, 1954), 80–81.

24. *Ibid.,* p. 81. See also U.S. Dept. of State, *Bulletin,* XXX (April 19, 1954), 605.

25. Edward Cale, U.S. Dept. of State, *Bulletin,* XXI (July 19, 1954), 80–81.

26. Randall Commission, *Report,* pp. 54–61.

27. Henry Holland, speech to Pan American Society, p. 688.

28. *Ibid.,* p. 689; speech of Secretary of Treasury Humphrey at Rio de Janeiro Conference, U.S. Dept. of State, *Bulletin,* XXI (Dec. 6, 1954), 863–69. See also Bronislaw Matecki, *Establishment of the Inter-*

national Finance Corporation and United States Policy (New York: Praeger, 1957), pp. 148–50.

29. *New York Times*, Feb. 12, 1954, p. 8.

30. Henry Holland, speech to Pan American Society, p. 688.

31. U.S., Foreign Operations Administration, Office of Research, Statistics, and Reports, *Report on the Economic Situation in Latin America*, prepared for the International Development Advisory Board, Aug. 1954, p. 2.

32. *Ibid.*

33. *Ibid.*, p. 84.

34. *Ibid.*, pp. 78–81.

35. *Ibid.*, p. 4.

36. *Ibid.*, p. 3.

37. *Ibid.*, p. 1.

38. *Ibid.*, p. 15.

39. The report's exact words were as follows: "On balance, it seems that many of the very things that the Latin Americans want from us, we cannot readily grant for the same kind of reasons that inhibit the Latin Americans from doing the things we suggest and consider necessary for accelerating their economic development. For example, the same kinds of domestic economic and political pressures that operate in the U.S. to oppose greater trade liberalization—such pressures also inhibit many of the Latin American governments from taking necessary actions to control inflation, stimulate balanced industrialization, etc." *Ibid.*, p. 86.

40. The Brookings Institution, "The Formulation and Administration of United States Foreign Policy," U.S., Congress, Senate, Committee on Foreign Relations, *United States Foreign Policy: Compilation of Studies*, 87th Cong., 1st Sess., Doc. No. 24, 1961, pp. 862–63; on the Council on Foreign Economic Policy, see also President Eisenhower's letter to Joseph M. Dodge, White House press release, Dec. 11, 1954, reprinted in U.S. Dept. of State, *Bulletin*, XXXI (Dec. 27, 1954), 987–88; and the report of Clarence Randall, U.S. Dept. of State, *Bulletin*, LXIV (Jan. 30, 1961), 157–59. See also the Brookings Institution, "Administrative Aspects of United States Foreign Assistance Programs," Study No. 6, U.S., Congress, Senate, Committee on Foreign Relations, *Foreign Aid Program: Compilation of Studies and Surveys*, 85th Cong., 1st Sess., Doc. No. 52, 1957, pp. 519–22.

41. The Brookings Institution, "Administrative Aspects of U.S. Foreign Assistance Programs," p. 519; *The Political Economy of American Foreign Policy*, Report of a Study Group sponsored by the Woodrow Wilson Foundation and the National Planning Association (W. Y. El-

liott, Chairman) (New York: Henry Holt and Co., 1955), pp. 375–76.

42. Percy Bidwell, *Raw Materials: A Study of American Policy* (New York: Harper and Brothers for the Council on Foreign Relations, 1958), pp. 41–43; U.S., Congress, Senate Committee on Interior and Insular Affairs, Subcommittee on Minerals, Materials, and Fuels, *Hearings, Stockpile and Accessibility of Strategic and Critical Materials to the United States in Time of War*, 83d Cong., 1st and 2d Sess., 1953 and 1954; *Idem, Accessibility of Strategic and Critical Materials to the United States in Time of War and for Our Expanding Economy*, 83d Cong., 2d Sess., Report No. 1627, 1954.

43. P.L. 480 (83:2), Title I, Section 104 (b), and Title III, Section 303.

44. Bidwell, *Raw Materials*, pp. 45–46, 89; testimony of Gordon Gray, U.S., Congress, House, Committee on Ways and Means, *Hearings, Lead and Zinc*, 85th Cong., 1st Sess., 1957, p. 42.

45. Testimony of Gordon Gray, *ibid.*, p. 53; exchange of letters between President Eisenhower and Representative Cooper, U.S. Dept. of State, *Bulletin*, XXXVII (Sept. 23, 1957), 490–92; Bidwell, *Raw Materials*, pp. 98–101; U.S., Congress, House, Committee on Interior and Insular Affairs, Subcommittee on Mines and Mining, *Hearings, Domestic Mineral Act of 1958*, 85th Cong., 2d Sess., 1959, pp. 18–19.

46. Edwin L. Dale, Jr., "Captain of Our Economic Campaign," *New York Times Magazine*, Aug. 31, 1958, p. 8.

47. White House press release, Sept. 22, 1958, reprinted in U.S. Dept. of State, *Bulletin*, XXXIX (Oct. 13, 1958), 579–83.

48. Bidwell, *Raw Materials*, pp. 317–22; John Powelson, *Latin America: Today's Economic and Social Revolution* (New York: McGraw-Hill, 1964), p. 153.

49. U.S., Congress, Senate, Committee on Banking and Currency, *Hearings, Export-Import Bank Amendments, 1954*, 83d Cong., 2d Sess., 1954, pp. 17–18.

50. U.S., Congress, Senate, Committee on Foreign Relations, *Hearings, Mutual Security Act of 1956*, 84th Cong., 2d Sess., 1956, pp. 293–94.

51. David K. E. Bruce, "South America," Survey No. 3, U.S., Congress, Senate, Committee on Foreign Relations, *Foreign Aid Program: Compilation of Studies and Surveys*, 85th Cong., 1st Sess., Doc. No. 52, 1957, pp. 1263–64. See also The Research Center in Economic Development and Cultural Change of the University of Chicago, "The Role of Foreign Aid in the Development of Other Countries," Study No. 3, *ibid.*, p. 206; and Thomas C. Schelling, "American Aid and Economic Development: Some Critical Issues," in The American Assembly, *Inter-*

national Stability and Progress: United States Interests and Instruments (New York: The American Assembly, Columbia Univesity, 1957), p. 125.

52. James Minotto, "Central America and the Caribbean Area," Survey No. 9, Senate Foreign Relations Committee, *Foreign Aid Program*, pp. 1511–12.

53. See also U.S., International Development Advisory Board, *A New Emphasis on Economic Development Abroad*, 1957, pp. 12–13.

54. Center for International Studies, MIT, "The Objectives of United States Economic Assistance Programs," Study No. 1, Senate Foreign Relations Committee, *Foreign Aid Program*, p. 60.

55. Brookings Institution, "Administrative Aspects of United States Foreign Assistance Programs," Study No. 6, *ibid.*, pp. 407–538.

56. U.S., Congress, Senate, Special Committee to Study the Foreign Aid Program, *Foreign Aid*, 85th Cong., 1st Sess., Report No. 300, 1957, pp. 19 and 28–29; U.S., Congress, Senate, Committee on Foreign Relations, *The Mutual Security Act of 1957*, 85th Cong., 1st Sess., Report No. 417, 1957, p. 24.

57. Dale, "Captain of Our Economic Campaign," p. 8; Sydney Hyman, "Mr. Dillon and the Fight for Foreign Aid," *The Reporter*, March 20, 1958, pp. 10–15.

58. Eisenhower, *The Wine Is Bitter*, pp. 205–7.

59. *Ibid.*; U.S., Congress, House, Committee on Foreign Affairs, *Hearings, Mutual Security Act of 1958*, 85th Cong., 2d Sess., 1958, pp. 1507, 1517–22.

60. James Reston, *New York Times*, April 15, 1958; U.S., Congress, Senate, Committee on Foreign Relations, *Hearings, Review of Foreign Policy: 1958*, 85th Cong., 2d Sess., 1958, p. 341; U.S., Congress, House, Committee on Foreign Affairs, *Hearings, Review of the Relations of the United States and Other American Republics*, 85th Cong., 2d Sess., 1958, p. 243.

61. Milton Eisenhower, *The Wine Is Bitter*, p. 209.

62. *Ibid.*, pp. 222–23, 229.

63. Eisenhower, "United States–Latin American Relations," pp. 97 and 99.

64. Eisenhower, *The Wine Is Bitter*, p. 239.

65. See below, pp. 113–15.

66. See, for example, U.S., Congress, Senate, Committee on Foreign Relations, *Hearings, Mutual Security Act of 1954*, 83d Cong., 2d Sess., 1954, pp. 365–67; U.S., Congress, Senate, Committee on Foreign Relations, *Hearings, Mutual Security Act of 1955*, 84th Cong., 1st Sess., 1955, pp. 315–16.

67. J. Fred Rippy, "United States Aid to Latin America: 1956 and 1957," *Inter-American Economic Affairs*, XI (Spring 1958), 52; see

also the remarks by Senator Smathers in *Congressional Record*, 85th Cong., 1st Sess., May 2, 1957, CIII, part 5, pp. 6272–73.

68. Remarks of Senator Smathers, *Congressional Record*, CIII, part 5, pp. 6272–73; testimony of Rollin Atwood, U.S., Congress, House, Committee on Appropriations, *Hearings, Mutual Security Appropriations for 1958*, 85th Cong., 1st Sess., 1957, pp. 656–57.

69. House Appropriations Committee, *Hearings, Mutual Security Appropriations for 1958*, p. 686; U.S., Congress, Senate, Committee on Appropriations, *Hearings, Mutual Security Appropriations for 1958*, 85th Cong., 1st Sess., 1957, pp. 161 and 162; letter from Senator Smathers to Senate Appropriations Committee in U.S., Congress, Senate, Committee on Appropriations, *Hearings, Mutual Security Appropriations for 1959*, 85th Cong., 2d Sess., 1958, p. 68. See also the Senate Hearings for 1958, p. 375.

70. U.S., Congress, Senate, Committee on Foreign Relations, *The Mutual Security Act of 1957*, 85th Cong., 1st Sess., Report No. 417, 1957, p. 11.

71. U.S., Congress, Senate, Committee on Foreign Relations, *Hearings, Mutual Security Act of 1957*, 85th Cong., 1st Sess., 1957, pp. 334–36.

72. See especially the *Congressional Record*, 85th Cong., 1st Sess., July 8, 1957, CIII, 10946, and Aug. 26, 1957, CIII, 15948–50; and U.S., Congress, Senate, Committee on Foreign Relations, *Hearings, The Nomination of Roy Rubottom*, 85th Cong., 1st Sess., 1957, pp. 16, 22–23, 45–53, 60–64, and 97–98.

73. *Congressional Record*, 86th Cong., 1st Sess., July 6, 1959, Vol. CV, part 10, p. 12688.

74. U.S., Congress, Senate, Committee on Foreign Relations, *Report of Senator Aiken on a Study Mission*, 86th Cong., 2d Sess., Committee Print, Feb. 2, 1960. For Senator Mansfield's statement, see U.S., Congress, Senate, Committee on Foreign Relations, *Hearings, Mutual Security Act of 1960*, 86th Cong., 2d Sess., 1960, p. 381.

75. *Congressional Record*, 86th Cong., 2d Sess., March 24, 1960, Vol. CVI, part 5, p. 650.

76. *Ibid.*

77. Remarks of Senator Smathers, *ibid.*, Aug. 17, 1960, p. 16570. For President Eisenhower's statement, see *U.S. Department of State Bulletin*, XLII (Aug. 29, 1960), pp. 346–47.

78. *Congressional Record*, 86th Cong., 2d Sess., Aug. 19, 1960, Vol. CVI, part 13, p. 16795.

Chapter 5

1. For a history of the Export-Import Bank, see Hawthorne Arey, "History of the Operations and Policies of the Export-Import Bank of

Washington," in U.S., Congress, Senate, Committee on Banking and Currency, *Hearings, Study of the Export-Import Bank and the World Bank*, 83d Cong., 2d Sess., 1954, pp. 86–132.

2. Laurence Duggan, *The Americas* (New York: Henry Holt, 1949), pp. 78–79.

3. Raymond Alexis Clark, "The Export-Import Bank of Washington —Legislative History," in Senate Banking and Currency Committee, *Study of the Export-Import Bank*, p. 17.

4. Duggan, *Americas*, pp. 79–80; Donald M. Dozer, *Are We Good Neighbors?* (Gainesville, Florida: University of Florida Press, 1961), p. 200.

5. Arey, "Export-Import Bank," pp. 98–101.

6. Raymond Mikesell, "The Export-Import Bank of Washington," in Raymond Mikesell, ed., *United States Private and Government Investment Abroad* (Eugene, Ore.: The University of Oregon Press, 1962), p. 463.

7. See, for example, U.S., President, Commission on Foreign Economic Policy (Randall Commission), *Staff Papers* (Washington, D.C.: GPO, 1954), p. 137; Senate Banking and Currency Committee, *Study of the Export-Import Bank*, pp. 65–67; U.S., Congress, House, Committee on Appropriations, *Hearings, Mutual Security Appropriations for 1960 (and Related Agencies)*, 86th Cong., 1st Sess., 1959, pp. 87 and 118; U.S., Congress, Senate, Committee on Appropriations, *Hearings, Mutual Security Appropriations for 1960 (and Related Agencies)*, 86th Cong., 1st Sess., 1959, pp. 64 and 66.

8. See also the opinions on this expressed by businessmen, as reported in Randall Commission, *Staff Papers*, pp. 134–36.

9. Simon G. Hanson, *Economic Development in Latin America* (Washington, D.C.: Inter-American Affairs Press, 1951), pp. 392–99.

10. Arey, "Export-Import Bank," pp. 107 and 118–21; Mikesell, "Export-Import Bank," p. 463.

11. Marjorie Hald, "The Export-Import Bank and Development Lending" (Santa Monica, Calif.: RAND Corporation, P-1668, April 15, 1959), pp. 3–7. See also Arey, "Export-Import Bank."

12. Hald, "Development Lending."

13. Arey, "Export-Import Bank," p. 110; Message of President Truman to Congress, April 8, 1948, in U.S. Dept. of State, *Bulletin*, XVIII (April 25, 1948), 548.

14. See the text of Reorganization Plan No. 5 and the President's message in Senate Banking and Currency Committee, *Study of the Export-Import Bank*, pp. 11–13.

15. The head of the Export-Import Bank at the time denied that the reorganization plan increased the power of the NAC over the bank.

See U.S., Congress, House, Committee on Appropriations, *Hearings, The Supplemental Appropriation Bill, 1954,* part 1, 83d Cong., 1st Sess., 1953, p. 205. This denial does not seem credible in view of the controversy that ensued.

16. For the role of the Treasury on the NAC, see U.S., Congress, House, Select Committee on Foreign Aid, *Final Report on Foreign Aid,* 80th Cong., 2d Sess., Report No. 1845, 1948, pp. 724–26, and 763–76. See also U.S., Congress, House, Special Committee on Postwar Economic Policy and Planning (Colmer Committee), *Economic Reconstruction in Europe,* 79th Cong., 1st Sess., Nov. 12, 1945, House Report No. 1205, pp. 49–51. See also *The Political Economy of American Foreign Policy,* Report of a Study Group Sponsored by the Woodrow Wilson Foundation and the National Planning Association (W. Y. Elliott, Chairman) (New York: Henry Holt and Co., 1955), pp. 373 and 375.

For the relation between the Treasury and the Export-Import Bank, see staff memorandum, Senate Committee on Government Operations, reprinted in *Congressional Record,* 83d Cong., 1st Sess., June 30, 1953, Vol. XCIX, part 6, p. 7618.

17. Staff memorandum, Senate Government Operations Committee, p. 7618.

18. U.S., Commission on the Organization of the Executive Branch of the Government (Hoover Commission), *Treasury Department, Report to Congress* (Washington, D.C.: GPO, March 1949), pp. 12 and 30; see also Mikesell, "Export-Import Bank," p. 466.

19. Letter from Secretary of the Treasury Humphrey to Senator Charles Potter, reprinted in *Congressional Record,* 83d Cong., 1st Sess., June 30, 1953, Vol. XCIX, part 6, pp. 7619–20. See also U.S., Congress, Senate, Committee on Banking and Currency, *Hearings, Nomination of Samuel C. Waugh,* 84th Cong., 2d Sess., 1956, pp. 13–15.

20. Mikesell, "Export-Import Bank," p. 461.

21. Senate Banking and Currency Committee, *Study of the Export-Import Bank.* U.S., Congress, Senate, Committee on Banking and Currency, *Study of Latin American Countries; Interim Report,* 83d Cong., 2d Sess., Report No. 1082, 1954, pp. 647–48.

22. Paul Kennedy, *New York Times,* Nov. 26, 1954, p. 1.

23. U.S., Congress, House, Committee on Appropriations, *Hearings, Supplemental Appropriation Bill, 1956,* 84th Cong., 1st Sess., 1955, p. 3.

24. *Congressional Record,* 83d Cong., 2d Sess., May 10, 1954, Vol. C, part 5, p. 6271.

25. *Ibid.,* June 22, 1954, p. 8567.

26. U.S., Congress, House, Committee on Foreign Affairs, *Hearings, Mutual Security Act of 1955*, 84th Cong., 1st Sess., 1955, p. 321.

27. On the attitude of the Export-Import Bank, see staff memorandum, Senate Government Operations Committee, p. 7619.

28. U.S., President, Commission on Foreign Economic Policies (Randall Commission), *Report to the President and the Congress* (Washington, D.C.: GPO, 1954), pp. 24–26; *Minority Report*, p. 20.

29. United Nations, Economic Commission for Latin America, *Economic Survey of Latin America 1954* (E/CN.12/362/Rev. 1, July, 1955) (New York, 1955), pp. 50–51 and 72–73; Assistant Secretary of State Holland, speech to Washington Board of Trade, U.S. Dept. of State, *Bulletin*, XXXII (April 11, 1955), 603.

30. White House press release, reprinted in *Congressional Record*, 83d Cong., 2d Sess., June 11, 1954, C, 8024.

31. U.S., Congress, Senate, Committee on Banking and Currency, *Hearings, Export-Import Bank Amendments, 1954*, 83d Cong., 2d Sess., 1954, p. 13.

32. *Ibid.*, p. 15.

33. Senate Banking and Currency Committee, *Nomination of Samuel C. Waugh*, p. 15.

34. U.S., Congress, House, Committee on Foreign Affairs, *Hearings, Act for International Development, part 2*, 81st Cong., 2d Sess., 1950, pp. 455–75; David S. McClellan and Charles E. Woodhouse, "The Business Elite and Foreign Policy," *Western Political Quarterly*, XIII (March 1960), 172–90; testimony of Representative Herter, U.S., Congress, House, Committee on Foreign Affairs, *Hearings, International Technical Cooperation Act of 1949*, 81st Cong., 1st Sess., 1949, pp. 185–86.

35. House Committee on Foreign Affairs, *International Technical Cooperation Act of 1949*, pp. 23–26.

36. U.S., Congress, Senate, Committee on Foreign Relations, *Technical Assistance: Final Report*, 85th Cong., 1st Sess., Report No. 139, 1957, p. 3; *Idem, Technical Assistance and Related Programs*, 84th Cong., 2d Sess., Report No. 1956, May 7, 1956, reprinted in *ibid.*, p. 31.

37. The peril point and escape clause provisions of the trade agreements legislation created procedures by which industries threatened with foreign competition could ask the Tariff Commission to recommend import restrictions to the President.

38. Letter from President Eisenhower to Representative Joseph Martin, reprinted in U.S. Dept. of State, *Bulletin*, XXXII (March 7, 1955), 388.

39. Joe Wilkinson, *Politics and Trade Policy* (Washington, D.C.: Public Affairs Press, 1960), pp. 99–100.

40. *Ibid.*, p. 102. See also the remarks by Senator Douglas, *Con-*

gressional Record, 84th Cong., 1st Sess., May 4, 1955, Vol. CI, part 4, p. 5584.

41. Percy Bidwell, *Raw Materials: A Study of American Policy* (New York: Harper and Brothers for the Council on Foreign Relations, 1958), p. 359; also pp. 95–101.

42. Quoted in Bidwell, *Raw Materials*, pp. 43–44.

43. *Ibid.*; U.S., President, "Recommendations Concerning United States Foreign Economic Policy," Message to Congress, March 30, 1954, U.S. Dept of State, *Bulletin*, XXX (April 19, 1954), 605; White House press release, Dec. 1, 1954, in U.S. Dept. of State, *Bulletin*, XXXI (Dec. 27, 1954), 988–90.

44. Statement by Director of Office of Defense Mobilization, quoted in Bidwell, *Raw Materials*, p. 88.

45. P.L. 480 (83:2), Title I, Section 104(b).

46. *Ibid.*, Title III, Section 303.

47. White House press release, Aug. 20, 1954, in U.S. Dept. of State, *Bulletin*, XXXI (Sept. 6, 1954), 339–40.

48. White House press release, Sept. 22, 1958, in U.S. Dept. of State, *Bulletin*, XXXIX (Oct. 13, 1958), 579–83. For the effects on Latin American exports, see National Planning Association, "United States and Latin American Policies Affecting Their Economic Relations," in U.S., Congress, Senate, Committee on Foreign Relations, *United States–Latin American Relations: Compilation of Studies*, Doc. No. 125, 86th Cong., 2d Sess., 1960, p. 440.

49. The Brookings Institution, "The Formulation and Administration of United States Foreign Policy," U.S., Congress, Senate, Committee on Foreign Relations, *United States Foreign Policy: Compilation of Studies*, 87th Cong., 1st Sess., Doc. No. 24, 1961, pp. 862–63; on the Council on Foreign Economic Policy, see also President Eisenhower's letter to Joseph M. Dodge, White House press release, Dec. 11, 1954, in U.S. Dept. of State, *Bulletin*, XXXI (Dec. 27, 1954), 987–88; and the report of Clarence Randall, *ibid.*, LXIV (Jan. 30, 1961), 157–59. See also the Brookings Institution, "Administrative Aspects of United States Foreign Assistance Programs," Study No. 6, U.S., Congress, Senate, Committee on Foreign Relations, *Foreign Aid Program: Compilation of Studies and Surveys*, 85th Cong., 1st Sess., Doc. No. 52, 1957, pp. 519–22.

50. Edwin L. Dale, Jr., "Captain of Our Economic Campaign," *New York Times Magazine*, Aug. 31, 1958, p. 8.

Chapter 6

1. Milton Eisenhower, *The Wine Is Bitter* (Garden City, N.Y.: Doubleday and Company, 1963), p. 216.

2. *Ibid.*, p. 221.

3. *Ibid.*, pp. 222–23.
4. *Ibid.*, p. 224.
5. *Ibid.*, pp. 224–25.
6. Louis Halle, "On Teaching International Relations," *Virginia Quarterly Review*, XL (1964), 11–25.
7. The analysis that follows is drawn from Bronislaw Matecki, *Establishment of the International Finance Corporation and United States Policy* (New York: Praeger, 1957).
8. *Ibid.*, p. 79.
9. *Ibid.*
10. *Ibid.*, pp. 80–81.
11. *Ibid.*, pp. 82–83.
12. *Ibid.*, p. 83.
13. *Ibid.*, pp. 122–44.
14. *Ibid.*, p. 148.
15. *Ibid.*, p. 149.
16. *Ibid.*, p. 150.
17. U.S., Advisory Committee on Underdeveloped Areas, *Economic Strength for the Free World*, A Report to the Director of Mutual Security, May 1953, p. 32. See also *The Political Economy of American Foreign Policy*, Report of a Study Group Sponsored by the Woodrow Wilson Foundation and the National Planning Association (W. Y. Elliott, chairman) (New York: Henry Holt and Co., 1955), pp. 344–45.
18. U.S., International Development Advisory Board, *A New Emphasis on Economic Development Abroad*, 1957, p. 18.
19. Eisenhower, *The Wine Is Bitter*, pp. 201–3.
20. See Tad Szulc, *New York Times*, July 25, 1956, p. 9.
21. Eisenhower, *The Wine Is Bitter*, p. 205.
22. *Ibid.*, p. 206.
23. *Ibid.*
24. White House press release, May 26, 1957, in U.S. Dept. of State, *Bulletin*, XXXVI (June 24, 1957), 678.
25. Assistant Secretary of State Roy Rubottom, speech to Council on Foreign Relations, in U.S. Dept. of State, *Bulletin*, XXXVII (Oct. 28, 1957), 678.
26. See, for example, Tad Szulc, *The Winds of Revolution* (New York: Praeger, 1963), pp. 106–17.
27. *New York Times*, Aug. 13, 1958, p. 1; *ibid.*, Aug. 14, 1958, p. 1; John Dreier, *The Organization of American States and the Hemisphere Crisis* (New York: Harper and Row for the Council on Foreign Relations, 1962), p. 83.
28. James Reston, *New York Times*, April 15, 1958.
29. See above, pp. 96–97 and 121–22.

30. U.S., Congress, Senate, Committee on Foreign Relations, *Hearings, Review of Foreign Policy: 1958*, 85th Cong., 2d Sess., 1958, p. 341.

31. U.S., Congress, House, Committee on Foreign Affairs, *Hearings, Review of the Relations of the United States and Other American Republics*, 85th Cong., 2d Sess., 1958, p. 243.

32. *New York Times*, May 13, 1958, p. 13.

33. National Planning Association, "United States and Latin American Policies Affecting Their Economic Relations," in U.S., Congress, Senate, Committee on Foreign Relations, *United States–Latin American Relations*, 86th Cong., 2d Sess., Doc. No. 125, 1960, p. 534; International Economic Consultants, Inc., "Commodity Problems in Latin America," *ibid.*, pp. 149–53.

34. See also Secretary of State Dulles's remarks in April 1958, U.S. Dept. of State, *Bulletin*, XXXVIII (May 5, 1958), 722–23.

35. Assistant Secretary of State Rubottom, speech at Santa Barbara, California, U.S. Dept. of State, *Bulletin*, XXXIX (Oct. 27, 1958), 657.

36. Milton Eisenhower, "United States–Latin American Relations, 1953–1958," U.S. Dept. of State, *Bulletin*, LX (Jan. 19, 1959), 99.

37. *New York Times*, 1958, Aug. 3, p. 1; Aug. 6, p. 2; Aug. 7, p. 1; Aug. 17, p. 1.

38. Geoffrey Barraclough, ed., *Survey of International Affairs: 1956–1958* (London: Oxford University Press for the Royal Institute of International Affairs, 1962), p. 469; Secretary of State Dulles's news conference, Sept. 30, 1958, in U.S. Dept. of State, *Bulletin*, XXXIX (Oct. 20, 1958), 597–604.

39. Barraclough, ed., *Survey ... 1956–1958*, pp. 470–71.

40. Remarks by Under Secretary of State Dillon, U.S. Dept. of State, *Bulletin*, XL (Jan. 12, 1959), 48–50.

41. For the U.S. government's position, see U.S. Dept. of State, *Bulletin*, XL (April 6, 1959), 479–83; for the various Latin American positions, see the *New York Times*, May 3, 1959, p. 13, and May 4, 1959, p. 1; Geoffrey Barraclough, ed., *Survey of International Affairs: 1959–1960* (London: Oxford University Press for the Royal Institute of International Affairs, 1964), p. 465.

42. U.S., Congress, Senate, Committee on Foreign Relations, *Hearings, American Republics Cooperation Act*, 86th Cong., 2d Sess., 1960, p. 11.

43. For an early general statement of such interests, see Chester Bowles, "A New Approach to Foreign Aid," *Bulletin of the Atomic Scientists*, XIII (Feb. 1957), 42–47.

44. U.S., Congress, House, Committee on Foreign Affairs, *Hearings, Mutual Security Act of 1958*, 85th Cong., 2d Sess., 1958, p. 1507.

45. *Ibid.*, pp. 1521–22.

46. *Ibid.*, pp. 1517–18.

47. John Montgomery, *The Politics of Foreign Aid* (New York: Praeger for the Council on Foreign Relations, 1962), p. 154; testimony of Samuel Waugh, president of the Export-Import Bank, U.S., Congress, House, Committee on Appropriations, *Hearings, Mutual Security Appropriations for 1960 (and Related Agencies)*, 86th Cong., 1st Sess., 1959, p. 73.

48. Eisenhower, *The Wine Is Bitter*, p. 154.

49. *Ibid.*, p. 209.

50. *Ibid.*, pp. 222–23.

51. *Ibid.*, p. 223.

52. Dr. Eisenhower has written that this committee had been planned as early as February 1959. *Ibid.*, p. 231.

53. U.S., Congress, House, Committee on Foreign Affairs, *Hearings, Mutual Security Act of 1960*, 86th Cong., 2d Sess., 1960, p. 842.

54. Eisenhower, *The Wine Is Bitter*, p. 239.

55. Cf. Tad Szulc, *New York Times*, Dec. 20, 1959, p. 1; Juan de Onis, *ibid.*, Nov. 29, 1959, IV, 8.

56. G. Warner, "Latin America," in Barraclough, ed., *Survey . . . 1959–1960*, p. 489.

57. See, for example, Douglas Dillon, speech in Philadelphia, Feb. 12, 1960, U.S. Dept. of State, *Bulletin*, XLII (Feb. 29, 1960), 318.

58. Warner, "Latin America," in Barraclough, ed., *Survey . . . 1959–1960*, pp. 484–87.

59. President Eisenhower's address to the Brazilian Congress, Feb. 24, 1960, U.S. Dept. of State, *Bulletin*, XLII (March 28, 1960), 476.

60. Warner, "Latin America," in Barraclough, ed., *Survey . . . 1959–1960*, p. 487.

61. U.S., Congress, House, Committee on Apppropriations, *Hearings, Inter-American Programs for 1961*, 87th Cong., 1st Sess., 1961, pp. 211–12. For a list of these illustrative projects, see U.S., Congress, Senate, Committee on Appropriations, *Hearings, Inter-American Social and Economic Cooperation Program and the Chilean Reconstruction and Rehabilitation Program*, 87th Cong., 1st Sess., 1961, pp. 13–18.

62. U.S., Congress, Senate, Committee on Foreign Relations, *Hearings, American Republics Cooperation Act*, 86th Cong., 2d Sess., 1960, p. 10.

63. White House press release, July 11, 1960, in U.S. Dept. of State, *Bulletin*, XLIII (Aug. 1, 1960), 168.

64. David Wise and Thomas B. Ross, *The Invisible Government* (New York: Bantam Books, 1964), p. 24.

65. Warner, "Latin America," in Barraclough, ed., *Survey . . . 1959–1960*, p. 491.

66. *New York Times*, 1961, May 21, p. 12; June 23, p. 8; July 24, p. 1. See also Arthur Schlesinger, Jr., *A Thousand Days* (Boston: Houghton Mifflin, 1965), pp. 186–205.

67. See, for example, Dreier, *Organization of American States*, pp. 77–78.

Chapter 7

1. The most explicit statement of such an analogy is in Gunnar Myrdal, *Beyond the Welfare State* (New Haven, Conn.: Yale University Press, 1960), pp. 221–25.

2. Sumner Welles, *Where Are We Heading?* (New York: Harper and Brothers, 1946), pp. 239–40.

3. *Ibid.*, p. 241.

4. Dexter Perkins, *The United States and the Caribbean* (Cambridge, Mass.: Harvard University Press, 1947), pp. 160–61.

5. *Ibid.*, p. 162.

6. Laurence Duggan, *The Americas* (New York: Henry Holt, 1949), esp. pp. 1–5 and 123–217.

7. Ernst Halperin, "The Chilean Presidential Election of 1964" (Cambridge, Mass.: Center for International Studies, MIT, Nov. 1964), pp. 15–17.

8. U.S., *Congressional Record*, 86th Cong., 2d Sess., Aug. 31, 1960, CVI, part 14, 18724.

9. U.S., Congress, House, Committee on Foreign Affairs, *Hearings, American Republics Cooperation Act*, 86th Cong., 2d Sess., 1960, pp. 15–16.

10. *Ibid.*, pp. 78–79.

11. *Ibid.*

12. Albert O. Hirschman, *Journeys Toward Progress* (New York: Twentieth Century Fund, 1963), p. 260.

13. Wilson's article is in James D. Thompson, ed., *Approaches to Organizational Design* (Pittsburgh: University of Pittsburgh Press, 1966), pp. 193–218.

14. *Ibid.*, p. 196.

15. *Ibid.*, p. 198.

16. *Ibid.*; emphasis in original.

17. *Ibid.*, pp. 200–202.

18. *Ibid.*, pp. 204–5 (in italics in original).

19. *Ibid.*, p. 208 (first 12 words in italics in original).

20. *Ibid.*, pp. 211–12 (in italics in original).

21. *Ibid.*, p. 212.

22. *Ibid.*, p. 204.

23. *Ibid.*, p. 208.

24. Kenneth Waltz, "The Stability of a Bipolar World," *Daedalus*,

XCIII (Summer 1964), 881–909; Kenneth Waltz, "The Relations of States to Their World," paper presented to the Annual Meeting of the American Political Science Association, Chicago, 1967.

25. See especially Graham Allison, "Policy, Process, and Politics: Conceptual Models and the Cuban Missile Crisis," unpublished Ph.D. thesis, Harvard University, 1968.

26. Joseph Grunwald, "The Alliance for Progress," *Proceedings of the American Academy of Political Science*, XXIV (May 5, 1964), 386.

27. See, for example, Secretary of the Treasury Dillon's remarks at his news conference, Aug. 22, 1961, in U.S. Dept. of State, *Bulletin*, XLV (Sept. 11, 1961), 442; and Adlai Stevenson's remarks at the National Press Club, June 26, 1961, *ibid.* (July 24, 1961), p. 143.

28. Grunwald, "Alliance for Progress," pp. 397–98.

29. For an account of these changes and the reactions to them in the United States, see Edwin Lieuwin, *Generals versus Presidents: Neo-militarism in Latin America* (New York: Praeger, 1964); and Arthur Schlesinger, Jr., *A Thousand Days* (Boston: Houghton Mifflin, 1965), pp. 759–93.

30. *New York Times*, Aug. 26, 1961, p. 1.

31. Edward S. Mason, *Foreign Aid and Foreign Policy* (New York: Harper and Row for the Council on Foreign Relations, 1964), p. 89.

32. Grunwald, "Alliance for Progress," p. 395; see also Emilio Collado, "Economic Development Through Private Enterprise," *Foreign Affairs*, XLI (July 1963), 708–20.

33. Mason, *Foreign Aid*, pp. 86–87.

34. Cf. the discussion in Raymond Aron, *Paix et guerre entre les nations* (Paris: Calmann-Levy, 1962), pp. 388–91. See also *New York Times*, 1961, Jan. 1, p. 14; Jan. 9, p. 8; Feb. 27, p. 11; April 26, p. 2.

35. See Richard Neustadt, *Presidential Power* (New York: John Wiley, 1960).

Chapter 8

1. Charles Lindblom, *The Policy-Making Process* (Englewood Cliffs, N.J.: Prentice-Hall, 1968), pp. 32–34.

2. See the discussion in Chapter 3 and the references cited there, pp. 83–84.

3. See especially S. N. Eisenstadt, *The Political Systems of Empires* (New York: The Free Press, 1963).

4. See Ernest May, "The Nature of Foreign Policy: The Calculated and the Axiomatic," *Daedalus*, 91 (Fall 1962), 653–67.

5. See Kenneth Waltz, "The Stability of a Bipolar World," *Daedalus*, XCIII (Summer 1964), 881–909; "The Relations of States to Their World," paper presented to the Annual Meeting of American Political

Science Association, Chicago, 1967; and "International Structure, National Force, and the Balance of Power," *Journal of International Affairs,* XXI (1967), 215–31.

6. See Raymond Aron, *Paix et guerre entre les nations* (Paris: Calmann-Levy, 1962), pp. 108–13.

7. See above, pp. 170–71.

Index